The Canon Law of Marriage and the Family

This work has three parts: the first deals with the substantive law on marriage; the second deals with procedures, such as nullity procedures and procedures for the dissolution of marriage; the final part deals with issues of family law.

Part One expounds the theory that underpins the canon law on marriage, questions such as the nature of Christian marriage, the sacramentality of marriage, the essential properties of marriage and the formation of the bond of marriage. It explains the impediments to marriage, the grounds of nullity, preparation for marriage and the formalities that precede the celebration of marriage. It also outlines the law regarding mixed marriages and validation of marriage.

Part Two explains procedures in Church law that relate to marriage and highlights the rights of the persons involved in them.

Part Three presents elements of Church law that concern the family: the place of the family in the Church, the role of parents in preparation for and celebration of the sacraments, the role of parents in handing on the faith, the role of the Church in promoting the welfare of children, and finally the situation of the divorced and remarried *vis-à-vis* the sacraments.

The book concludes with a number of appendices which deal with the application of church law in areas such as the Pre-Nuptial Enquiry, marriage in Rome and mixed marriages.

John McAreavey is a priest of the diocese of Dromore, Ireland. Since 1988 he has taught Canon Law at St Patrick's College, Maynooth.

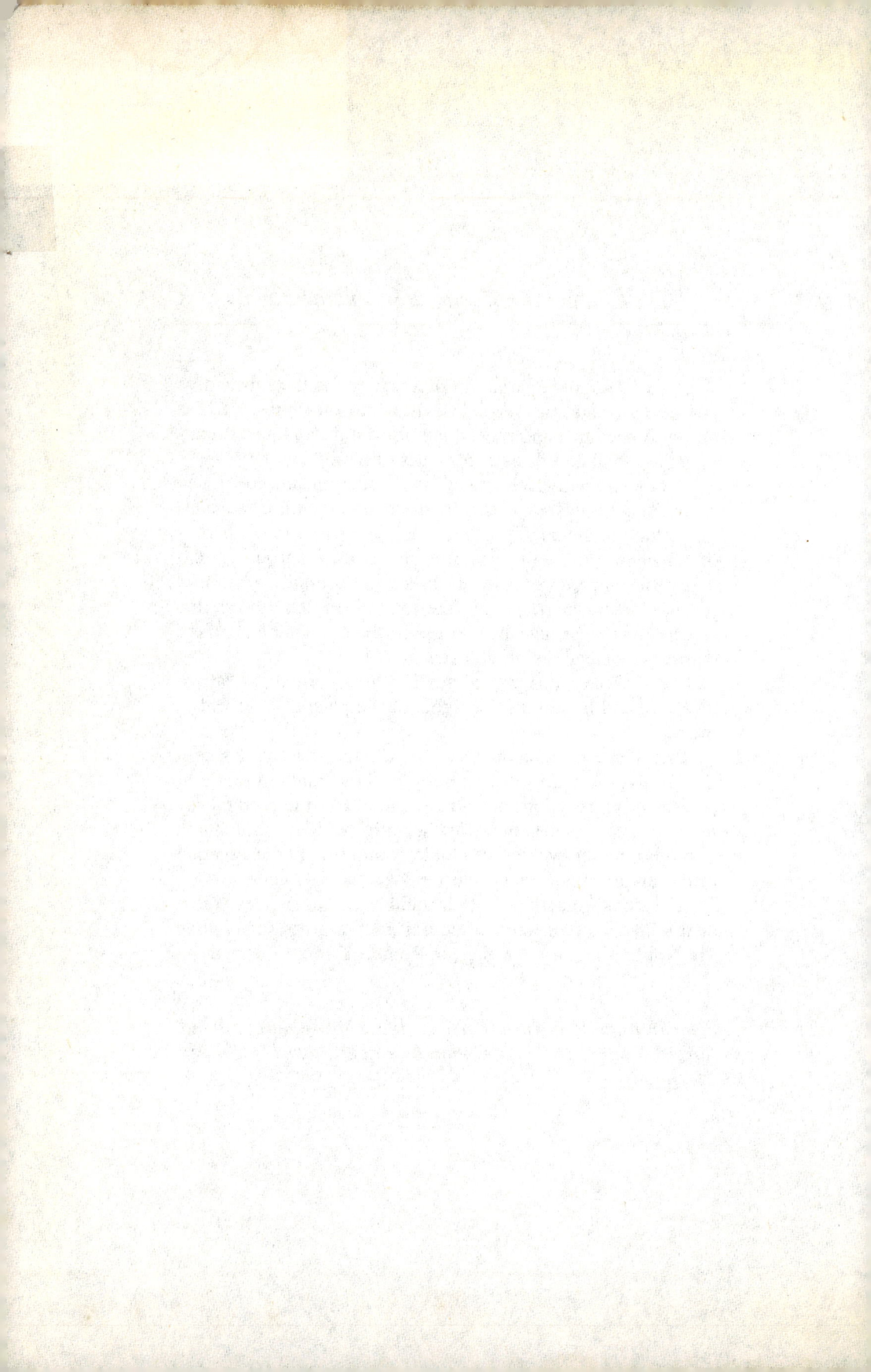

The Canon Law of Marriage and the Family

JOHN McAREAVEY

Professor of Canon Law
St Patrick's College, Maynooth

FOUR COURTS PRESS

Set in 10.5 on 12 Times New Roman by
Gough Typesetting Services for
FOUR COURTS PRESS
Fumbally Lane, Dublin 8, Ireland
and in North America for
FOUR COURTS PRESS
c/o ISBS, 5804 N.E. Hassalo Street, Portland, OR 97213.

A catalogue record for this title
is available from the British Library.

ISBN 1-85182-342-5 hbk
1-85182-356-5 pbk

Printed in Ireland
by Colour Books Ltd, Dublin

Contents

CONTENTS IN DETAIL

Appendices

11

Abbreviations

AAS	*Acta Apostolicae Sedis*
ASS	*Acta Sanctae Sedis*
c. [no]	canon of the 1917 Code of Canon Law
Can.	canon of the 1983 Code of Canon Law
CLD	*Canon Law Digest*
CLSA	Canon Law Society of America
CLSGBI	Canon Law Society of Great Britain and Ireland
Comm	*Communicationes*
Decision c.	decision of a court in which the named judge was *ponens* (decisions cited are rotal decisions unless otherwise stated)
DOL	*Documents on the Liturgy 1963-79,* Collegeville, Minn., 1982
DS	*Enchiridion Symbolorum definitionum et declarationum de rebus fidei et morum,* Denzinger-Schönmetzer, editio XXXIV emendata, Herder 1967
DSM IV	*Diagnostic and Statistical Manual of Mental Disorders* (fourth edition), Washington, D.C.: APA, 1994
FC	*Familiaris consortio*: Apostolic Exhortation of Pope John Paul II on The Christian Family in the Modern World.
Fl	*Vatican Council II: The Conciliar and post-Conciliar Documents,* general editor Austin Flannery (2 vols), Dominican publications, Dublin 1975/1982
GS	*Gaudium et spes,* Pastoral Constitution on the Church in the Modern World of Vatican II
OBP	*Ordo baptismi puerorum* (Rite of Infant Baptism)
OCM	*Ordo celebrandi matrimonium* (Rite of Marriage)
OT	*Optatam totius,* decree on the training of priests of Vatican II
PG	*Patrologia Graeca*
PL	*Patrologia Latina*
SC	*Sacrosanctum concilium,* Constitution on the Sacred Liturgy of Vatican II

Preface

Since 1988 I have taught a course on the Canon Law of Marriage in the Pastoral Studies Programme at St Patrick's College, Maynooth. The course caters both for deacons who are preparing for ordination to the priesthood and for lay students who are training for various forms of ministry. This book developed from course-notes which I prepared for these students and it has taken shape in response to their needs and interests.

This work is divided into three parts: Part I deals with the substantive law on marriage and consists in a commentary on the issues covered in the canons of Book IV, title VII of the Code of Canon Law. Part II deals with the procedural law that touches on marriage. This is outlined in Book VII of the Code. The commentary on this section is less detailed; I have set out an outline of the structure of matrimonial procedures and their principal elements. Part III deals with various canonical issues relating to marriage and the family which are scattered throughout the Code of Canon Law; I have gathered them together under the heading of "family law".

Since most of my students in Maynooth were Irish and were preparing to minister in Ireland, the examples I used originally were drawn from the experience of the Irish Church. I have included those areas which are of direct relevance to Ireland in a number of Appendices.

This book is primarily a textbook for students of canon law. The material it covers will, I hope, be of interest to a wider readership. Marriage and the family have taken their place at the centre of pastoral developments in the Church; courses on family ministry abound, and yet, many people are unaware of developments in the canon law of marriage. As far as clergy are concerned, many who were trained in the 1917 Code have lost confidence in their grasp of the canon law of marriage, thinking – often wrongly – that the law had changed entirely. Those who were trained in the post-Vatican II period – when the 1917 Code became outdated and before the new Code was promulgated – often feel ill-equipped to deal with the present law. The younger clergy have been formed in the thinking of the 1983 Code, but commentaries on this Code are still few.

Canon law is the law of the Church; it is not – or should not be – the preserve of the clergy. It is my hope that this book will make the matrimonial law of the Church accessible to lay people who, out of interest or need, are searching for a fuller understanding of the mind of the Church on matters such as the indissolubility of marriage, pre-marriage courses, nullity of marriage, mixed marriages, and the pastoral care of the divorced and remarried.

I am indebted to many people for help in writing this book. I am indebted to my colleagues on the staff of St Patrick's College, Maynooth for their help in areas that are outside my own competence. I am grateful to the College Library and the Computer Centre for their assistance. I wish also to record my thanks to the judicial Vicars of the Regional Marriage Tribunals in Ireland and the National Appeal Tribunal for their assistance in describing the procedures which are followed in their Tribunals. I owe a special debt of gratitude to the Reverend Donal Kelly of the Dublin Regional Marriage Tribunal who read earlier drafts of this book; his comments and advice were extremely helpful. In preparing a final text for the publisher I received invaluable help from Olan Rynn, a student for the diocese of Galway. Finally, I am indebted to the students whom I taught at Maynooth from 1988 'til 1997. Their interest and enthusiasm encouraged me to write this book.

Introduction

In the Apostolic Constitution with which he promulgated the Latin Code of **1**
Canon Law, *Sacrae disciplinae leges*, Pope John Paul II wrote:

> As the Church's fundamental legislative document, and because it is
> based on the juridical and legislative heritage of revelation and tradi-
> tion, the Code must be regarded as the essential instrument for the
> preservation of right order, both in the individual and social life and in
> the Church's zeal.[1]

If the Code is to become an effective guiding force in the life of the **2**
Church, it must be received in the spirit in which it was promulgated. In
order to receive the law, the Church must understand the values which it
intends to uphold.[2] This work is based on the conviction that "legal rules in
the Church were born from theology".[3] As such they reflect – and grow out
of – the faith and experience of the Church. The values that canon law promotes arise from and reflect the nature and mission of the Church. The
Code emphasises this point when it states that "the salvation of souls ...
must always be the supreme law" (Can. 1752).

Canonical norms and procedures are bearers of Gospel values. It is a **3**
characteristic of the Western canonical tradition that it seeks "to define the
binding value of doctrinal truth by the [practical] concreteness of the juridical norm".[4] In other words, it strives to translate its faith into practical legal
norms. While this approach is deeply rooted in the Western Catholic tradition, it is important to acknowledge that other Christian traditions choose
other means of expressing what are, for the most part, similar convictions.[5]

---

1 The Code of Canon Law, new revised translation, prepared by the Canon Law Society
of Great Britain and Ireland in association with the Canon Law Society of Australia and
New Zealand and the Canadian Canon Law Society, HarperCollins, London, 1997, xiv.
2 L. Örsy, *Theology and canon law*, Michael Glazier, Wilmington, Delaware, 1986.
3 Ibid., 103. **4** E. Corecco, *The theology of canon law: a methodological question*,
Duquesne University Press, Pittsburgh, 1992, 77. **5** A report on "Inter-Church Marriages" submitted to the General Assembly of the Presbyterian Church in 1976 stated:
"While our Church does not promulgate detailed regulations in the manner of the Roman Catholic Church this should not be taken as implying less regard for the issues

4   The purpose of the canon law of marriage is to express and promote theological and human values and to help the Christian community to appropriate those values.[6] The most significant values are the stability of marriage, its protection against human weakness and sinfulness, respect for the seriousness of human commitment in marriage, the freedom of the parties in entering marriage, respect for the intimacy of human sexuality and the sacramentality of the marriage bond.

5   Recent popes have stressed the pastoral character of canon law. Pope John Paul II has stated that "the juridical and pastoral dimensions are united inseparably in the Church, a pilgrim on this earth":

> Above all, they are in harmony because of their common goal: the salvation of souls. But there is more. In effect, juridical-canonical work is pastoral by its very nature. It constitutes a special participation in the mission of Christ the Shepherd (*pastore*) and consists in bringing into reality the structures of intra-ecclesial justice willed by Christ himself. Pastoral work, in its turn, while extending far beyond juridical aspects alone, always includes a dimension of justice. In fact, it would be impossible to lead souls towards the kingdom of heaven without that minimum of love and prudence which is found in the commitment to seeing to it that the law and the rights of all in the Church are observed faithfully.[7]

6 Pope John Paul II has stressed that the pastoral ministry must be based on justice; it must involve respect for the fundamental rights of Church members. The canons express the mind of the Church and provide reliable guidelines for sound pastoral practice.

7   Canon law must take account of the social and cultural context in which it is being applied. This context is defined by history, civil law, customs and by the faith-culture of a particular region or country. Canon law represents the inculturation of faith-values in a particular time and place. For this reason the canon law of marriage is not static; it is in continual dynamic dialogue with the culture in which it is being applied. Fundamental faith-values are not subject to change, but the ways in which they are expressed is subject to constant change. This is particularly true in areas such as mixed marriages, but it applies in all aspects of canon law.

8   The Code of Canon Law contains the general law of the Church. The present Code, unlike its predecessor, presupposes that the principles and

involved, but rather a reliance on the Christian understanding, responsibility and conscience of those most directly involved".   **6** L. Orsy, *Marriage and canon law*, 11. **7** *Papal allocutions to the Roman Rota 1939-1994* (ed. W.H. Woestman), Faculty of Canon Law, Saint Paul University, Ottawa 1994 (hereafter *Papal allocutions to the Roman Rota*), 210-1, n. 4.

procedures it contains will require further application in the historical and cultural context of each region or diocese, whether by Bishops' Conferences or by individual diocesan Bishops. Hence the importance of local or particular law. The current law acknowledges the importance of particular law in several ways: firstly, it requires Bishops' Conferences to make provision for certain institutions to which the Code of Canon Law refers in general terms. The obligation "to lay down norms for the questions to be asked of the parties, the publication of banns, and the other appropriate means of enquiry to be carried out before marriage" (Can. 1067) is an example of this. Secondly, the Church acknowledges the right of civil authorities to make laws and provisions "in respect of the merely civil effects of the marriage" (Can. 1059). The Church wishes to act in harmony with the civil authorities in areas that concern the common good, the stability of marriage and the welfare of its members. For example, special care must be taken in regard to marriages which, for whatever reason, "cannot be recognised by the civil law or celebrated in accordance with it" (Can. 1071 §1, 2°). Thirdly, the Church acknowledges that the general law of the Church must, when it is applied in pastoral practice, take account of local custom. For example, the Code of Canon Law asks pastors of souls to dissuade young people "from entering marriage before the age customarily accepted in the region" (Can. 1072). The effective application of the canon law of marriage presupposes a dialogue between the general law of the Church and the particular culture of the region or diocese in which it is being applied. This demands pastoral creativity and imagination, as well as fidelity to the tradition of the Church.

1

Canonical doctrine of marriage

9 Towards the end of his study of Christian marriage, Schillebeeckx writes:

> What has clearly emerged, however, is that any dogmatic study of marriage is bound to take two fundamental facts into account: first, that marriage is without qualification a secular reality, fully human and consequently subject to development and evolution; and secondly that this reality has not been somehow "added" to salvation, but has been included in its total and human dimension – and that this incorporation into God's salvation has not come about ... simply because the state of being a Christian has to be experienced within the purely worldly sphere, but also and above all because this secular reality, which has been taken up into salvation, has itself become sacramental in the technical sense.[1]

10   These two dimensions of marriage form the basis of the Vatican II teaching on marriage in *Gaudium et spes*. The opening section of n. 48 considers marriage as a state that has been "established by the creator and endowed by him with its own proper laws";[2] the second section states that "authentic married love is caught up into divine love and is directed and enriched by the redemptive power of Christ and the salvific action of the Church".[3] These two dimensions of marriage are reflected in the revised law of the Church. The Latin Code begins its exposition of marriage with a theological statement regarding the nature of marriage. Can. 1055 §1 states:

> The marriage covenant by which a man and a woman establish between themselves a partnership of their whole life, and which of its own very nature is ordered to the well-being of the spouses and to the procreation and upbringing of children, has, between the baptised, been raised by Christ the Lord to the dignity of a sacrament.

11   This formulation encapsulates both the nature of marriage as "established by the creator" and the specific sacramental dignity of marriage when it is celebrated between the baptised. The distinction is brought out more clearly

---

1 *Marriage: human reality and saving mystery*, Sheed and Ward, London, 1965, 396-7. **2** Fl I, 950. **3** Ibid., 951.

18

in the equivalent canon in the Code of Canons of the Eastern Churches. Can. 776 states:

> The matrimonial covenant, established by the Creator and ordered by His laws, by which a man and a woman by an irrevocable personal consent establish between themselves a partnership of the whole of life, is by its nature ordered toward the good of the spouses and the generation and education of children.
>
> From the institution of Christ, a valid marriage between baptised persons is by that very fact a sacrament, by which the spouses, in the image of an indefectible union of Christ with the Church, are united by God and, as it were, consecrated and strengthened by sacramental grace.

The distinction between these two dimensions of marriage is used here to structure this section on the canonical doctrine of marriage.   **12**

THE NATURE OF MARRIAGE

Can. 1055 §1 The marriage covenant, by which a man and a woman establish between themselves a partnership of their whole life, and which of its own very nature is ordered to the well-being of the spouses and to the procreation and upbringing of children, has, between the baptised, been raised by Christ the Lord to the dignity of a sacrament.
§2 Consequently, a valid marriage contract cannot exist between baptised persons without its being by that very fact a sacrament.

The tradition prior to Vatican II

Within the canonical tradition, various conceptual systems have been used   **13**
to express the Church's teaching on the nature of marriage. St Augustine identified three *goods* or values of marriage (*bona matrimonii*): fidelity, offspring and sacrament, that is, permanence.[4] Classical canon law distinguished between marriage at the moment of its celebration (*matrimonium in fieri*) and marriage as a state of life (*matrimonium in facto esse*). One author comments that "while the classical theologians acknowledged that *conjugal society* (i.e., *matrimonium in facto esse*) was the true object of marital consent, by the late nineteenth century, the Western canonical tendency to equate the

---

4 Fidelity means that one refrains from sexual contact outside the marriage bond; offspring, that (the child) is lovingly received, tenderly nurtured, religiously brought up; the sacrament, that the marriage is not broken and the abandoned spouse marry another, not even for the sake of having children. This can be considered the rule of marriage, by which natural fecundity is adorned and the baseness of sexual disorder is restrained (*De genesi ad litteram*, lib. 9, Can. 7, n. 12).

right to sexual intercourse with the essence of marriage had become firmly established".[5] The third schema used to define marriage focused on the *properties* of marriage. These are unity and indissolubility, and in christian marriage "they acquire a distinctive firmness by reason of the sacrament" (Can. 1056). Finally, the 1917 Code of Canon Law referred to the *ends* of marriage: "The primary end of marriage is the procreation and education of offspring; the secondary end of marriage is mutual assistance and the remedy of concupiscence".[6] This doctrine corresponded to the emphasis found already on the procreative aspect of marriage.

From Vatican II to the promulgation of the Code of Canon Law

14 The nature of marriage was considered at Vatican II during the debate on the Pastoral Constitution on the Church in the Modern World, *Gaudium et spes*. The teaching of the Council is outlined in the first paragraph of n. 48. It begins:

> The intimate partnership of life and the love which constitutes the married state has been established by the creator and endowed by him with its own proper laws: it is rooted in the covenant of its partners, that is, in their irrevocable consent. It is an institution confirmed by the divine law and receiving its stability, even in the eyes of society, from the human act by which the partners mutually surrender themselves to each other; for the good of the partners, of the children, and of society this sacred bond no longer depends on human decision alone. For God himself is the author of marriage and has endowed it with various benefits and with various ends in view: all of these have a very important bearing on the continuation of the human race, on the personal development and eternal destiny of every member of the family, on the dignity, stability, peace and prosperity of the family and of the whole human race. By its very nature the institution of marriage and married love is ordered to the procreation and education of the offspring and it is in them that it finds its crowning glory. Thus the man and woman, who "are no longer two but one" (Mt 19:6), help and serve each other by

5 P. Connolly, "The nature of marriage as proposed in the Codex Iuris Canonici and in the Codex Canonum Ecclesiarum Orientalium", dissertation submitted to the Faculty of Canon Law, St Paul's University, Ottawa, 1995, 22. The view of that period is reflected in Wernz's statement in *Ius matrimoniale* I, 23-4, as translated by Connolly: "If marriage is considered *in fieri*, it can be defined: the lawful and undivided contract of man and wife for the generation and education of offspring... If, on the other hand, marriage is taken as the bond or permanent society, as in common speech and even that proper to theologians and canonists, it is defined as the lawful and undivided union of man and wife for the generation and education of offspring, or more briefly: the undivided conjugal or marital society of man and wife." 6 C. 1013: "Matrimonii finis primarius est procreatio atque educatio prolis; secundarius mutuum adiutorium et remedium concupiscentiae."

their marriage partnership; they become conscious of their unity and experience it more deeply from day to day. The intimate union of marriage, as a mutual giving of two persons, and the good of the children demand total fidelity from the spouses and require an unbreakable unity between them.[7]

The first feature of the conciliar teaching is the use of "covenant" instead **15** of "contract" which was used more widely in the pre-conciliar period.[8] In Roman law *foedus* (covenant) was used "for agreements which transcended the ordinary categories of contract, e.g., treaties between nations or peoples, pacts with religious significance, promises among friends or the members of a family without creating strict right-and-duties situations".[9] Kasper has observed that it expresses the personal character of consent as well as connoting "a public and legal matter concerning the whole community of believers".[10] In the conciliar setting "covenant" refers to a personal commitment which cannot be revoked. Secondly, consent is defined as "the human act whereby spouses mutually bestow and accept each other". Thirdly, the essential properties of marriage were related to the wider purpose of marriage: "the intimate union of marriage, as a mutual giving of two persons, and the good of the children, demand total fidelity from the spouses and require an indissoluble unity between them". Finally, the Council avoided any reference to primary or secondary ends of marriage.[11]

The conciliar teaching on the nature of marriage as "established by the **16** creator" was developed further in the years following Vatican II. This can be seen in *Humanae vitae*[12] and in *Familiaris consortio*.[13] In the latter the

---

7 Fl I, p. 950. **8** The use of the term "covenant" has also important ecumenical implications. The Final Report of the Roman Catholic-Lutheran-Reformed study on marriage states: "We all agree that the biblical concept of "covenant" best describes the mystery of marriage. The catholic Church calls this covenant a sacrament. The Reformation Churches prefer not to use this term primarily because of their definition of the sacraments, because of marriage's special place in relationship to the sacraments of baptism and the Eucharist, and finally because of past arguments and misunderstandings. We believe that on the basis of the different mentalities and various historical situations we are able to achieve a deep, common view of marriage" ("The theology of marriage and the problem of mixed marriages" in *Information Service* 36 (1978), 21, n.18). **9** L. Örsy, *Marriage in canon law*, 50. For a study of the influence of Roman law on canon law, cf. A.-M. Gauthier, *Roman law and its contribution to the development of canon law*, second edition, Faculty of Canon Law, St Paul's University, Ottawa, 1996. **10** *Theology of Christian marriage*, 41. **11** For a study of the implications of conjugal love on matrimonial consent, cf. *L'amore coniugale* (ed. V. Fagiolo) (Annali di dottrina e giurisprudenza canonica I), Libreria Editrice Vaticana, Rome, 1971. **12** Cf. Fl II, 401, n. 9. Married love is described in highly personal terms. It is "fully human"; it is "total - that very special form of personal friendship in which husband and wife generously share everything, allowing no unreasonable exceptions or thinking just of their own interests"; it is "faithful and exclusive of all other until death"; it is "creative of new life, for it is not exhausted by the loving interchange of husband and wife, but also contrives to go beyond this to bring new life into being". **13** Fl II, 814-98.

perspective is somewhat different. The human person is made in the image of God, and God, who is love, has inscribed in the humanity of each person "the vocation, and thus the capacity and responsibility, of love and communion".[14] As an incarnate spirit, the human person is called to love "in his unified totality". Hence love expresses itself through the human body. Christian revelation recognises two specific ways of realising the vocation of the human person, in its entirety, to love: marriage and virginity or celibacy: "Either one is, in its own proper form, an actuation of the most profound truth of man, of his being created in the image of God".[15] Within this context, human sexuality "is by no means something purely biological, but concerns the innermost being of the human person as such". Pope John Paul II continues:

> [Human sexuality] is realised in a truly human way only if it is an integral part of the love by which a man and a woman commit themselves totally to one another until death. The total physical self-giving would be a lie if it were not the sign and fruit of a total personal self-giving, in which the whole person, including the temporal dimension, is present.[16]

17   The total commitment which conjugal love requires corresponds also to the demands of responsible fertility: "this fertility is directed to the generation of a human being, and so by its nature ... surpasses the purely biological order and involves a whole series of personal values".[17] Where does marriage come into the picture? Marriage is "the only place in which this self-giving in its whole truth is made possible".[18] The institution of marriage is not something imposed from without: "it is an interior requirement of the covenant of conjugal love which is publicly affirmed as unique and exclusive, in order to live in complete fidelity to the plan of God, the Creator".[19] Marriage then is the context within which personal relationships, sexual commitment and parenthood find expression in a way that most fully respects the nature of the human person and the sexuality that is inherent in human nature.

18   It was the task of the Revision Commission to translate the conciliar teaching of marriage into clear and workable norms. The secretary of the group charged with revising the marriage law reported in 1971 on decisions that had been made until that point in the revision process:

> On the question of how the personal relationship of the spouses and the ordering of marriage to procreation should be expressed in the [re-

---

14 Fl II, 822, n. 11b. **15** Ibid., 11d. **16** Ibid., n. 11e. **17** Ibid., 823., n. 11f. **18** Ibid., n. 11g. **19** Ibid.

vised] Can. 1013 §1[20] ... the majority of the committee members finally agreed to affirm the nature of marriage as an *intima totius vitae coniunctio* [an intimate union of the whole of life] between man and woman which, of its very nature, is ordered to the procreation and education of offspring. Following *Gaudium et spes*, the committee decided that in this paragraph [Canon 1013 §1] the idea of the primary end, that is, the procreation and education of offspring, and the secondary end, namely mutual aid and the remedy for concupiscence, should no longer be used ...[21]

With regard to the definition of the matrimonial consent, it reached the **19** following conclusion:

As in canon 1013 [of the 1917 Code], the teaching of Vatican Council II on marriage and on matrimonial consent requires that in this chapter too several changes in the canons regarding marriage consent be introduced, namely with respect to the object of consent by reason of the exclusion of an essential element of that object. By majority vote of the committee consent is described as an act of the will whereby a man and a woman mutually pledge to enter a *consortium vitae coniugalis* [partnership of married life], [which is] perpetual and exclusive, [and] which of its very nature is ordered to the generation and education of offspring. Whence it follows that among the essential elements of the object of consent, the exclusion of which renders the consent invalid, there should be listed the *ius ad vitae communionem* [right to a communion of life]. The result is that canon 1086 §2 [of the 1917 Code] would read thus: "But if either or both parties by a positive act of the will exclude marriage itself, or the *ius ad vitae communionem* [right to a communion of life], or the right to the conjugal act, or an essential property of marriage, they contract invalidly". As will be evident to those who are acquainted with the subject, the expression the *right* to a communion of life was deliberately used, so that consent would be invalid only if in the very act of contracting marriage the *communio vitae* [communion of life], in so far as it belongs to the essence of matrimony, should be excluded; that is, when "marriage" would be intended in such a way that that right [to a *communio vitae*] would not be given to one of the parties. Furthermore, the *communio vitae* [com-

---

20 This stated: "Matrimonii finis primarius est procreatio atque educatio prolis; secundarius mutuum ajiutorium et remedium concupiscentiae" (The primary end of marriage is the procreation and education of offspring; the secondary end is mutual assistance and the remedy of concupiscence). **21** *Comm* 3 (1971), 70. This translation is taken from D. E. Fellhauer, "The *consortium omnis vitae* as a juridical element of marriage" in *Studia Canonica* 13 (1979), 117.

munion of life] which is proper to marriage is not to be confused with cohabitation.[22]

20   The drafts approved in 1971 were circulated to the various consultative bodies. The responses were returned and the Commission met early in 1975. Can. 243 §1 (Can. 1055 in the final text) had been interpreted by some of the consultative groups as affirming that the end of marriage was procreation. The committee decided to amend it to stress the personal ends of marriage. The following formulation was approved: "Marriage is an intimate partnership of their whole life between a man and a woman which of its nature is ordered to the good of the spouses and the procreation and education of children".[23]

21   While it was clear that the committee wished to affirm the personal dimension of marriage, there was some concern regarding the precise meaning of some phrases in the draft canons. What, for example, did it mean to define marriage as a *communio* (communion) or a *consortium vitae* (sharing of life)? Navarrete wrote: "It seems that the essential object of this right and obligation cannot be other than an undefined and undefinable unity of attitudes, of behaviour and of activities – which vary in their expression in different cultures – without which it is impossible to establish or preserve the communion of life and love required for achieving the essential ends of marriage".[24]

22   Lesage attempted to circumscribe what Navarrete had described as "undefined and undefinable". He gave a list of examples of behaviour or attitudes which are essential to a partnership of conjugal life. The absence of these *to a vital degree* would deprive the partner to an essential right in marriage:

1.   Oblatory love, which is not simply egoistic satisfaction, but which provides for the welfare and happiness of the partner;

2.   Respect for conjugal morality and for the partner's conscience in sexual relations;

3.   Respect for the heterosexual personality or "sensitivity" of the marriage partner;

4.   Respective responsibility of both husband and wife in establishing conjugal friendship;

---

22 *Comm* 3 (1971), 75-6. Translation from Fellhauer, ibid. **23** *Comm* 9 (1977), 123: "Matrimonium est viri et mulieris intima totius vitae coniunctio quae indole sua naturali ad bonum coniugum atque ad prolis procreationem et educationem ordinatur."
24 "Problemi sull'autonomia dei capi di nullità del matrimonio per difetto di consenso causato da perturbazioni della personalità", in *Perturbazioni psichiche e consenso matrimoniale nel diritto canonico*, Catholic Book Agency, Rome, 1976, 135.

5. Respective responsibility of both husband and wife in providing for the material welfare of the home: stability in work, budgetary foresight, etc;

6. Moral and psychological responsibility in the generation of children;

7. Parental responsibility, proper to both father and mother, in the care for, love and education of children;

8. Maturity of personal conduct throughout the ordinary events of daily life;

9. Self-control or temperance which is necessary for any reasonable and human form of conduct;

10. Mastery over irrational passions, impulses or instincts which would endanger conjugal life and harmony;

11. Suitability of conduct and capability of adapting to circumstances;

12. Gentleness and kindness of character and manners in mutual relationships;

13. Mutual communication or consultation on important aspects of conjugal or family life;

14. Objectivity and realism in evaluating the events and happenings that are part of conjugal or family life;

15. Lucidity in the choice or determination of goals or means to be sought for jointly.[25]

Debate continued on the draft of Can. 1101 §2, that is, the object of **23** matrimonial consent. In 1977 the Commission removed the phrase *ius ad vitae communionem* (right to a communion of life) and replaced it with *ius ad ea quae vitae communionem essentialiter constituunt* (a right to those things that constitute a communion of life).[26] This formulation was deleted in 1980 on the grounds that it would undermine the stability of marriage.[27]

At a meeting of the Cardinals' Commission in 1977, it was agreed that **24** the concept of marriage as a *consortium vitae* be included in the description of marriage "as long as expressions are avoided which can furnish an opportunity for false interpretations in jurisprudence".[28] At this point the formulation found in Can. 1055 §1 was substantially agreed.

A final discussion of the marriage canons was held in 1980 and an at- **25**

---

25 "The *consortium vitae coniugalis*: nature and application" in *Studia Canonica* 6 (1972), 103-4. **26** *Comm* 9 (1977), 375. **27** *Comm* 15 (1983), 233. **28** *Comm* 10 (1978), 125.

tempt was made to have the phrase *bonum coniugum* (the good of the spouses) removed from Can. 1055 §1. The Commission refused to do this on the grounds that the ordering of marriage "towards the good of the spouses" is an essential element of the marriage covenant.[29]

26   The Revision Commission left it to ecclesiastical jurisprudence to determine what was meant by "the good of the spouses". Pompedda has written that "the essence of matrimony is a partnership (*consortium*) between a man and a woman ... of the whole of life, (which is) perpetual and exclusive, (which is) directed toward the good of the spouses and the generation and raising of children".[30] Burke, another Rotal judge, holds however that there is no such thing as a right to the *bonum coniugum* (good of the spouses): "what each party can claim, as a matter of right, is that the other does not exclude from his or her consent the natural ordering of marriage to the good of the spouses".[31]

Conclusion

27   The attempt to determine what constitutes the nature or essence of marriage has important juridical implications. Can. 1095 refers to those who are unable to contract marriage because they lack discretion of judgement concerning the *essential rights and obligations* to be mutually given and accepted (2°); it also refers to those who, due to causes of a psychological nature, are unable to assume *the essential obligations of marriage* (3°). Can. 1101 §2 refers to the exclusion of *any essential element of marriage or any essential property*. There is no doubt that the Church's canonical definition of marriage has been enriched by the teaching of Vatican II. It will take some time before there is a consensus as to the precise implications of this new definition for the interpretation of Cann. 1095 and 1101. It will be the task of those engaged in jurisprudence and canonical reflection to promote the achievement of this consensus.

THE SACRAMENTALITY OF MARRIAGE

Can. 1055 §1 The marriage covenant, by which a man and a woman establish between themselves a partnership of their whole life, and which of its own very nature is ordered to the well-being of the spouses and to

---

29 *Comm* 15 (1983), 221. It should be noted that those drafting the equivalent canon in the Code of Canons of the Eastern Churches also included this phrase because "the essential end of marriage and therefore the essential object of marriage is not only the procreation and education of children, but also the personal good of the couple" (*Nuntia* 8 (1979), 16). **30** *Incapacity for marriage* (ed. R. M. Sable) (hereafter referred to as *Incapacity for marriage*), 190. **31** "The *bonum coniugum* and the *bonum prolis*: ends or properties of marriage", in *The Jurist* 49 (1989), 709.

the procreation and upbringing of children, has, between the baptised, been raised by Christ the Lord to the dignity of a sacrament.

§2 Consequently, a valid marriage contract cannot exist between baptised persons without its being by that very fact a sacrament.

The marriage covenant

The use of the word "covenant" to describe marriage "as established by the **28** Creator" makes it easier to present the Church's teaching on the sacramentality of marriage. Few words carry a more profound religious connotation.[32] The image of marriage (and infidelity) is used by the prophets, especially Hosea (2:2) and Jeremiah (3:1) to convey the irrevocable nature of God's relationship to the Chosen People and the ingratitude of Israel's response.[33] As the covenant relationship breaks down due to the infidelity of Israel, the prophets begin to direct the hopes of the Jews to a new covenant (Jer 31:31-34).

In the Epistle to the Hebrews, Jesus is presented as the mediator of the **29** new covenant (9:15) and he is the surety of a covenant better than that made with the Jews. "By the blood of the eternal covenant" the Lord Jesus has become the great shepherd of the sheep" (13:20). By his death which has redeemed the transgressions of the first covenant, he has given the promised eternal inheritance to all who are called (9:15-16). For St Paul, the great instrument of the establishment of the new covenant was the Lord's Supper: "This cup is the new covenant in my blood. Do this as my memorial" (1 Cor 11:25).

The nuptial imagery which was used by the prophets is taken up again in **30** the New Testament in relation to Christ. He is the bridegroom (Mt 9:15: Mk 2:19-20; Lk 5:34-5) and his disciples "associated with Jesus by their faith in the gospel ... have therefore entered into the nuptial mystery of the kingdom, inaugurated here on earth at his coming".[34]

St Paul develops this marriage symbolism in Ephesians 5:21-32: **31**

> Give way to one another in obedience to Christ. Wives should regard their husbands as they regard the Lord, since as Christ is head of the Church and saves the whole body, so is a husband the head of his wife; and as the Church submits to Christ, so should wives to their husbands, in everything. Husbands should love their wives just as Christ loved the Church and sacrifices himself for her to make her holy. He made her clean by washing her in water with a form of words, so that when he took her to himself she would be glorious, with no speck or wrinkle

---

[32] H. Cazelles, "Covenant" in *Sacramentum mundi*, II, 18-23. [33] Cf. W. Kasper, *Theology of christian marriage*, Burns & Oates, London, 1980, 27: "Marriage, then, is the grammar God uses to express his love and faithfulness." [34] P. Grelot, *Man and wife in scripture*, Burns & Oates, London, 1964, 103.

or anything like that, but holy and faultless. In the same way, husbands must love their wives as they love their own bodies; for a man to love his wife is for him to love himself. A man never hates his own body, but he feeds it and looks after it; and that is the way Christ treats the Church, because it is his body – and we are its living parts. For this reason, a man must leave his father and mother and be joined to his wife, and the two will become one body. This mystery has many implications; but I am saying it applies to Christ and the Church.[35]

32   Grelot writes that in this passage St Paul "establishes a bridge between the doctrine of marriage on the one hand and the mystery of the Church on the other".[36] He adds:

> From the very beginning the importance of the couple extended far beyond the sphere assigned it by the psychology and metaphysics of love, both of which are restricted by a natural order obscured and corrupted by sin. It was even then a parallel of the mystery in which the relationship between God and men is realised in all its fullness ... The symbol is written into creation itself, although the archetype which underlies it is an event in time: the incarnation of the Son of God, in which human nature – and with it every creature – is involved by its Creator in an indissoluble union of love.[37]

33   In the scriptures – and in the tradition of the Church – "married love becomes the image and symbol of the covenant that unites God and his people".[38] Unlike most of the other sacraments, the sacramental nature of marriage cannot be established by pointing to individual words of institution. It is more important, as Kasper notes, "to show that marriage is sacramental because it is fundamentally related to the saving work of Jesus Christ".[39]

34   The Church did not immediately perceive that marriage of the baptised was one of the seven sacraments; this realisation is the culmination of a long development.[40] It was not until the twelfth century that marriage between the baptised was formally declared to be a sacrament. From then onwards, explicit statements were made by the Church's teaching office.[41]

---

35 The translation is from the Jerusalem Bible. 36 Ibid., 105. 37 Ibid., 107-8. 38 Fl II, 823, *FC* n. 12b. 39 *Theology of christian marriage*, 28. 40 Cf. P. J. Elliott, *What God has joined ...*, Alba House, New York, 1990. 41 Second Lateran Council (1139): DS 718; Council of Verona (1184): DS 761; Innocent III (1198-1216): DS 769, 793; Second Council of Lyons (1274): DS 860; John XXII (1318): DS 916; Council of Florence (1439): DS 1327; Council of Trent (1545-63): DS 1801; Pius IX, *Syllabus* (1864): DS 2965-74; Leo XIII, encyclical *Arcanum* (1880): DS 3142ff; decree *Lamentabili* (1907): DS 3451; Pius XI, encyclical *Casti connubii* (1930): DS 3700, 3710ff; Second Vatican Council, pastoral constitution *Gaudium et spes* n.48.

This is the firm teaching of the Church and it has been restated in all   **35**
modern teaching of the Magisterium on marriage. Vatican II stated: "Just as
of old God encountered his people with a covenant of love and fidelity, so
our Saviour, the spouse of the Church, now encounters Christian spouses
through the sacrament of marriage."[42]

The Church teaches that marriage between the baptised is a sacrament   **36**
both at the moment in which it is celebrated, that is, at the moment of consent, and in an on-going way. In *Casti connubii* Pope Pius XI wrote that
"(spouses should be) mindful that they have been consecrated and strengthened for the duties and the dignity of their state by a sacrament whose effi-
cacy, though it does not confer a character, remains nonetheless permanently".[43]

Requisites for sacramental marriage

Three things are essential for marriage to be a sacrament: firstly, the parties   **37**
must be baptised; secondly, they must give consent, and thirdly they must
have a sacramental intention.

Baptism   The *General Introduction to Christian Initiation* states: **38**

> Baptism is ... first of all the sacrament of that faith by which men and
> women, enlightened by the grace of the Holy Spirit, respond to the
> gospel of Christ. [It] ... is the sacrament by which men and women are
> incorporated into the Church, assembled together into the house of
> God in the Spirit, into a royal priesthood and a holy nation. It is the
> sacramental bond of unity between all those who have received it... [It]
> ... cleanses men and women of all stain of sin, original and personal,
> makes them sharers in God's life and his adopted children... [It] is wa-
> ter of heaven-sent regeneration of God's children and of their re-birth...
> Signed with this name[of the Trinity], they are consecrated to the blessed
> Trinity and enter into fellowship with the Father, the Son and the Holy
> Spirit. Baptism ... produces these effects by the power of the mystery
> of the Passion and Resurrection of the Lord. When people are bap-
> tised, they share sacramentally in Christ's death, they are buried with
> him and lie dead, they are brought back to life with him and rise with
> him.[44]

The baptised participate in the priestly, prophetic and kingly office of   **39**
Christ (Can. 204 §1). What this means is elaborated in Pope John Paul II's
post-synodal exhortation on the vocation and mission of the lay faithful in
the Church and the world, *Christifideles laici*.[45]

---

42 Fl I, 950, GS n. 48b. **43** *The Christian Faith*, n. 1833. **44** Fl II, 23-4, nn. 3-6. **45** *The
vocation and mission of the laity*, Veritas , Dublin, 1989.

40 *Priestly mission* The baptised are united to Christ and to his sacrifice "in the offering they make of themselves and their daily activities".[46] It mentions "their ordinary married and family life" as an area of life which, if carried out in the Spirit, can become a spiritual sacrifice acceptable to God through Jesus Christ. In the Eucharist married people offer this sacrifice of their lives along with the Lord's body.

41 *Prophetic mission* By virtue of their baptism, the lay faithful "are given the ability and responsibility to accept the gospel in faith and to proclaim it in word and deed".[47] They are called "to allow the newness and the power of the gospel to shine out everyday in their family and social life, as well as to express patiently and courageously in the contradictions of the present age their hope of future glory".[48]

42 *Kingly mission* The lay faithful exercise their kingship as Christians "above all in the spiritual combat in which they seek to overcome in themselves the kingdom of sin (cf. Rom 6:12), and then to make a gift of themselves so as to serve, in justice and in charity, Jesus who is himself present in all his brothers and sisters, above all in the very least (cf. Mt 25:40).[49]

43 *Familiaris consortio* affirms the significance of baptism in the sphere of marriage as follows:

> Indeed, by virtue of baptism, man and woman are definitively placed within the new and eternal covenant, in the spousal covenant of Christ with the Church. And it is because of this indestructible insertion that the intimate community of conjugal life and love, founded by the Creator, is elevated and assumed into the spousal charity of Christ, sustained and enriched by his redeeming power.[50]

44 **Consent** The nature of consent will be considered in more detail below. In the present context it will suffice to note that when a man and a woman consent to marry they give themselves to each other as husband/wife and undertake "to love each other truly for better, for worse, for richer, for poorer, in sickness and in health, till death do us part".[51] In conjugal consent a man

---

46 Ibid., n. 14e. **47** Ibid., n. 14f. **48** Ibid. **49** Ibid., n. 14g. Pope John Paul II emphasises the secular character of the lay vocation. It is in the sphere of family and social life, from which the very fabric of their existence is woven, that the lay faithful live out their vocation (ibid., n. 15g). **50** Fl II, 824, n. 13f. The status of a marriage in which only one party is baptised was raised by canonists in the manual tradition. The opinion of Bouscaren-Ellis reflects their view: "It is now morally certain that the baptism of only one party does not make the marriage a sacrament even for that party" (*Canon Law: a text and translation*, 398). Cf. also Vermeersch-Creusen, *Epitome iuris canonici*, II, n. 276, 191).
51 OCM, second editio typica, 1991, n. 96.

and a woman radically commit themselves to each other for life. Monden writes: "Other actions constitute peak moments, decisive instants – "kairos", the hour of man's life, as Scripture calls it – crossroads where freedom chooses a direction and determines its attitude for a whole stage, perhaps even for the whole remainder, of life".[52]

Such actions carry an element of risk, the risk of failure or unhappiness. **45** Nevertheless, as is clear from the parable of the talents, it is the servant who opted for security and refused the decisive commitment who is condemned and punished. In making such life-time commitments – such as marriage or ordination or religious profession – men and women respond to the words of Jesus: "For he who would save his life will lose it, but he who loses his life for my sake will save it" (Mk 8:35).[53]

Matrimonial consent is an act of total trust in one's partner; it is an act of **46** love for that partner; it involves an unconditional acceptance of that person, his or her strengths and weaknesses; it involves a willingness to allow oneself to be known and loved; it is "a commitment to a very special form of friendship in which husband and wife generously share everything, allowing no unreasonable exceptions or thinking just of their own interests".[54]

The sacramental sign The sacramental nature of consent between the bap- **47** tised is expressed in *Familiaris consortio*:

> The communion of love between God and his people ... finds a meaningful expression in the marriage covenant which is established between a man and a woman. For this reason the central word of Revelation, "God loves his people", is likewise proclaimed through the living and concrete word whereby a man and a woman express their conjugal love. Their bond of love becomes the image and the symbol of the covenant which unites God and his people.[55]

In other words, the matrimonial consent of the baptised is the sign which **48** points to and makes present the saving love of Christ for his Church. Kasper writes that marriage is a form by means of which God's eternal love and faithfulness are made historically present:

> The love and faithfulness existing between Christ and his Church is therefore not simply an image or example of marriage, nor is the self-

52 *Sin, liberty and law*, Geoffrey Chapman, London and Dublin, 1966, 35. **53** Harrington writes: "Marriage is a call to a life of total sacrifice and self-giving ... if one's spouse is unfaithful, a life dedicated to him or her may have to be totally thrown away, laid down in love (since there is no possibility of enjoying another similar partnership) ... Christian love must continue faithful, even if rejected, loyal even if deserted, and abiding even if unrequited ..." ("Jesus' attitude towards divorce" in *Irish Theological Quarterly* 37 (1970), 201). **54** *Humanae vitae*, Fl II, 401, n. 9c. **55** Fl II, 823, n. 12a-b.

giving of man and woman in marriage an image and likeness of Christ's giving of himself to the Church. The love that exists between man and wife is rather a sign that makes the reality present, in other words, an epiphany of the love and faithfulness of God that was given once and for all time in Jesus Christ and is made present in the Church.[56]

49   The sign is the irrevocable loving commitment of the parties to each other in a faithful, life-long partnership. The view that the mutual consent of the persons contracting a marriage is the external sign of the sacrament is the product of a long development.[57]

50   While the sign of Christ's love for the Church is "the human act by which the partners mutually surrender themselves to each other"[58] , the state of life that arises from that consent also has a sacramental character. As *Familiaris consortio* states, "the couple participate in and are called to live the very charity of Christ who gave himself on the Cross".[59]

51   What is the relationship of Christ to his Church which is sacramentally represented in the covenant love of baptised husband and wife? The love of Christ for his Church is a covenant love, a love that was sealed in the blood of Christ on Calvary; it is a love that is never withdrawn from us, no matter how faithless we are; it is a love that accompanies us at all times, especially when we are weak and discouraged; it is a love that forgives us; it is a love that rejoices in our welfare; it is a love that heals and builds us up; it is a love that gives us life and restores our strength. The personification of that love is the Good Shepherd "who lays down his life for his sheep" (Jn 10:11).

52   It is important not to draw too close a parallel between the relationship between Christ and the Church on the one hand, and that between a baptised husband and wife on the other. Pope John Paul II has stated that "whereas in the relationship between Christ and the Church the subjection is only on the part of the Church, in the relationship between husband and wife the subjection is not one-sided but mutual".[60]

53   *The ministers of the sacrament* In the Latin Church the bride and groom are considered to be the ministers of the sacrament of marriage.[61] This teaching is an affirmation of the baptismal dignity of the lay faithful and of their participation in the priestly ministry of Christ.

54   The Eastern tradition however holds that the blessing of a priest is necessary for marriage in Christ. An Orthodox theologian explains this view as

56 *Theology of christian marriage*, 30. **57** M. Schmaus, *Dogma 5: The Church as sacrament,* Sheed and Ward, London, 1975, 275. **58** Fl I, 950, GC n. 48a. **59** Fl II, 824, n. 13. **60** *The dignity of women (Mulieris dignitatem),* Veritas, Dublin, 1988, n. 24. **61** F. R. McManus, "The ministers of the sacrament of marriage in western tradition" in *Studia Canonica* 20 (1986), 85. This is stated in the *General catechetical directory,* n. 59 (Fl II, 562).

follows: "By affirming that the priest is the minister of the marriage, as he is also minister of the Eucharist, the Orthodox Church implicitly integrates marriage in the eternal Mystery, where the boundaries between heaven and earth are broken and where human decision and action acquire an eternal dimension".[62]

The *Catechism of the Catholic Church* simply states that "it is ordinarily **55** understood that the spouses, as ministers of Christ's grace, mutually confer upon each other the sacrament of matrimony by expressing their consent before the Church".[63]

The graces of the sacrament Grelot states that Christian doctrine takes ac- **56** count of the gap between sinful human nature and the ideal of Christian marriage. He adds:

> [Christian doctrine] therefore sets forth firmly as a fundamental princi-
> ple, that man would not by his own powers be capable of fully attain-
> ing the ideal of marriage...: the miracle of redemptive grace is needed.
> Only this grace can create a new man by totally renewing his whole
> being (Eph 4:22-24; Ps 50:12). By remedying in this way the natural
> injury which befell man's sexuality like all the other aspects of his
> being, it makes possible ... the sanctification of the couple.[64]

The baptised couple encounter Christ in the celebration of their mar- **57** riage; Vatican II taught that "just as of old God encountered his people with a covenant of love and fidelity, so our Saviour, the spouse of the Church, now encounters Christian spouses through the sacrament of marriage".[65] *Familiaris consortio* states that "the Spirit which the Lord pours forth gives a new heart, and renders man and woman capable of loving one another as Christ has loved us".[66] Christ dwells with them, gives them the strength to take up their crosses and so follow him, to rise again after they have fallen, to forgive one another, to bear one anther's burdens, to be "subject to one an- other out of reverence for Christ" (Eph 2:5; cf. Gal 6:2) and to love one another with supernatural, tender and fruitful love.[67]

Sacramental intention Can. 1055 §1 declares that the marriage covenant **58** has, between the baptised, been raised to the dignity of a sacrament. Can. 1055 §2 adds: "Consequently, a valid marriage contract cannot exist between baptised persons without its being by that very fact a sacrament". The equiva-

---

62 J. Meyendorff, *Marriage: an Orthodox perspective*, St Vladimir's Seminary Press, New York, 1970, 27. **63** n. 1623. Cf. U. Navarrete, "De ministro sacramenti matrimonii in Ecclesia latina et in Ecclesiis orientalibus: tentamen explicationis concordantis" in *Periodica* 84 (1995), 711-33. **64** *Man and wife in scripture*, 101. **65** Fl I, 950, GS n. 48b. **66** Fl II, 824, n. 13c. **67** *Catechism of the Catholic Church*, n. 1642.

lent canon in the Code of Canons of the Eastern Churches states: "From the institution of Christ a valid marriage between baptised persons is by that very fact a sacrament..." (Can. 776 §2). The Church's teaching in this matter can be traced back to the encyclical letter of Pope Leo XIII, *Arcanum* (1880) in which the Church taught that "in Christian marriage the contract cannot be dissociated from the sacrament; thus there can be no true legitimate contract which is not also a sacrament".[68] The challenge to that teaching since Vatican II arises from pastoral experience. More and more often clergy find themselves officiating at marriages of baptised Catholics who appear no longer to believe in or practise the Christian faith.[69] At the same time the Church teaches that the sacraments "not only presuppose faith, but by words and objects they also nourish, strengthen, and express it".[70]

59   O'Callaghan poses the theological question as follows: "If one declares that nothing other than baptism is required for sacramental marriage, has one elided the intention? If one stresses sacramental intention as essential has one debarred baptised unbelievers from validly marrying when they decline the sacrament?"[71] Having surveyed the Catholic tradition on this question[72], he concludes that "whereas an intention is necessary for the valid reception of a sacrament, faith is not so required".[73] He insists however that such an intention requires some measure of appreciation of marriage as Christians see it.[74]

---

68 *The Church teaches*, n.1822. 69 Pompedda comments that the meaning of this phrase is not precise: "[I]t does not have a univocal meaning, but refers to a datum of fact that is by its nature markedly complex: that is, behind the expression 'baptised non-believer' there are situations that run the gamut from the ignorant baptised person to the non-practising baptised person; from the baptised person who has not the faith but who holds on to a basic religiosity, to the baptised person who has lost the faith altogether; from the baptised person who does not accept the Christian plan of marriage in some of its aspects to the baptised person who contests the sacramentality, and any religious institutionalisation, of marriage" ("Faith and the sacrament of marriage" in *Marriage studies* IV, ed. J.A. Allesandro, 56). 70 Fl I, 20, SC n. 59a. 71 "Faith and the sacrament of marriage" in *Irish Theological Quarterly* 52 (1986), 161. 72 He refers to "the classic monograph": L. Villette, *Foi et sacrement*, 1: *du Nouveau Testament à Saint Augustin*; 2: *de Saint Thomas à Karl Barth* (Bloud et Gay, Paris, 1959 and 1964). 73 "Faith and the sacrament of marriage" in *Irish Theological Quarterly* 52 (1986), 172. 74 Ibid. The International Theological Commission had made this point: "The intention of carrying on what Christ and the Church desire is the minimum condition required before consent is considered to be a 'real human act' on the sacramental plane. The problem of the intention and that of the personal faith of the contracting parties must not be confused, but they must not be totally separated either. In the last analysis the real intention is born from and feeds on living faith. Where there is no trace of faith (in the sense of 'belief' - being disposed to believe), and no desire for grace or salvation is found, then a real doubt arises as to whether there is the above-mentioned general and truly sacramental intention and whether the contracted marriage is validly contracted or not. As was noted, the personal faith of the contracting parties does not constitute the sacramentality of matrimony, but the absence of personal faith compromises the validity of the sacrament" ("Propositions on the doctrine of Christian marriage"

When dealing with the relationship between sacramental intention and **60** faith, Lane distinguishes between the personal act of faith and the content of faith: "It must be pointed out that the non-practice of faith cannot be taken automatically to imply the absence of personal faith, nor can the absence of personal knowledge about the content of faith be taken to imply complete absence of personal faith".[75]

He continues: **61**

> Theology today talks about a distinction between basic primordial faith and explicit faith. This basic primordial faith ... is implicitly religious and ultimately Christian in foundation and orientation. This ... can be illustrated in particular in relation to two people who are in love and wish to marry. The love that a man and a woman have for each other, when it is authentic and selfless, when it is understood to be mutually exclusive, when it is seen as life-long and permanent, when it is understood to be open to life, then it must be said that this kind of love between a man and a woman is ultimately the creative love of God poured into the world through the spirit of Christ. The kind of personal love and commitment that the baptised spouses bring to the point of entry into the covenant of marriage can only be explained by reference to the grace of God that is co-present in the lives of people. It seems to me that a good case can be made in favour of presuming the existence of faith, however implicit or tacit or inchoate, in the lives of baptised couples who wish to marry.[76]

Pope John Paul II addresses this dilemma by stressing that marriage is   **62** rooted in the economy of creation:

> Therefore the decision of a man and a woman to marry in accordance with this divine plan, that is to say, the decision to commit by their irrevocable conjugal consent their whole lives in indissoluble love and unconditional fidelity, really involves, even if not in a fully conscious way, an attitude of profound obedience to the will of God, an attitude which cannot exist without God's grace. They have thus already begun what is in a true and proper sense a journey towards salvation, a journey which the celebration of the sacrament and the immediate preparation for it can complement and bring to completion, give the uprightness of their intention.[77]

in *International Theological Commission: texts and documents 1969-1985*, ed. M. Sharkey, Ignatius Press 1989, San Francisco, 168, 2.3). **75** Unpublished paper given to the the Annual Conference of the Canon Law Society of Great Britain and Ireland in 1990. **76** Ibid. **77** Fl II, 872, *FC* n. 68c.

63   Since these couples are baptised and show by their "right intention" that they have accepted God's plan for marriage, the Church is satisfied that they "at least implicitly consent to what the Church intends to do when she celebrates marriage".[78]

64   Many theologians are reluctant to presume that such implicit consent is present. Lawler has written:

> Today, the faith-situation of baptised persons is anything but clear, and the Church and its theologians acknowledge two kinds of baptised, believers and non-believers. The two are distinguished theologically on the basis of the presence or absence of active personal faith. They ought never, therefore, to be equated in law as easily as the Code equates them.[79]

65   However, Pope John Paul II warns against setting criteria other than baptism and "right intention", especially any that touch on the level of faith required of those to be married:

> In the first place, it would involve the risk of making unfounded and discriminatory judgements; secondly, the risk of causing doubts about the validity of marriages already celebrated, with grave harm to Christian communities, and new and unjustified anxieties to the consciences of married couples; one would also fall into the danger of calling into question the sacramental nature of many marriages of brethren separated from full communion with the Catholic Church, thus contradicting ecclesial tradition.[80]

66   He concludes however that "when, in spite of all efforts, engaged couples show that they reject explicitly and formally what the Church intends to do when the marriage of baptised persons is celebrated, the pastor of souls cannot admit them to the celebration of marriage".[81] In other words, the Church will presume the presence of an implicit sacramental intention until the contrary is clear.

---

78 Ibid., n. 68e. **79** "Faith, contract and sacrament in Christian marriage: a theological approach" in *Theological studies* 52 (1991), 720-1. Örsy writes that "it is [the] personal act of faith, however minimal, and always under the grace of God, that transforms the human being from one who can be a believer into one who is a believer ... and it is that act of faith that is required for right sacramental intention" ("Faith, sacrament and contract and christian marriage" in *Theological Studies* 43 (1982), 383).   **80** Fl II, 873, n. 68f. **81** Ibid., n. 68g.

Celibacy "for the sake of the Kingdom"

The Church traces the origins of celibacy to the New Testament. While celi-   **67**
bacy was known before then,[82] "it is only in the New Testament that a doctrine of celibacy can be found".[83] There are two texts in particular which
refer directly to it: Matthew 19:10-12 and 1 Corinthians 7:25-35, and others
which can be understood to refer to it indirectly. Matura holds that Matthew
19:12 ("there are eunuchs who have made themselves that way for the sake
of the kingdom of heaven") can be traced to Jesus himself and is probably a
justification of the celibacy practised by him, John the Baptist and some of
his disciples.[84] Luke 18:29b-30 adds "a wife" to the list of things which the
disciple of Jesus must be prepared to give up to follow his Master.[85] Marriage is subordinated to the supreme importance of the Kingdom and the
following of Jesus. Another word of Jesus – "at the resurrection men and
women do not marry" (Mt 22:30) – puts marriage in a new perspective; marriage belongs to this world but when death is overcome, it will be no more.[86]

St Paul's teaching on marriage and celibacy is dominated by the fact that   **68**
"the world as we know it is passing away" (1 Cor 7:31). The death and
resurrection of Jesus have turned the world upside-down. Marriage belongs
to the things of this world, to the fleeting realities of our present condition.[87]
The unmarried can attach themselves more easily to the things of God. Hence
in the Churches of the New Testament and the early Church celibacy emerged
as a new radical form of consecration to Christ. Barth wrote of this:

> Can we wonder that in the entourage of Jesus and the primitive Church
> and later, there seem to have been those who thought that they should
> make use of this other possibility [this second vocation known as celi-
> bacy], so that entrance into and membership of the community obvi-
> ously took the place of married life, not in opposition to marriage as
> understood and newly evaluated in the sense of Ephesians 5:31, but in
> another inference from this new appraisal, and in direct imitation of
> the pattern set by Jesus himself?[88]

82 Th. Matura, "Le célibat dans le nouveau testament" in *Nouvelle revue théologique* 97
(1975), 486: "Le célibat ... n'était pas un phénomène inconnu". **83** L. Legrand, *The biblical doctrine of virginity*, Geoffrey Chapman, London, 1963, 22. **84** Matura, 496. **85** Cf.
Matthew 19:29; Mark 10:29-30. Matura writes: "Ainsi, le fait que Luc seul ait introduit
(ou maintenu) parmi les exigences du renoncement la mention de l'épouse ... indique du
moins que le mariage, lui aussi, doit céder le pas à l'expérience du Royaume" (ibid., 498).
86 Matura, ibid.: "Malgré toute son importance humaine et religieuse, celui-ci appartient
à l'ordre actuel du monde, est lié à la mort et disparaîtra en même temps que l'un et
l'autre" (499). **87** L. Legrand, *The biblical doctrine of virginity*, 81. **88** *Church dogmat-
ics* (edd. G.W. Bromley and T. F. Torrance), vol. 3: *The doctrine of creation*; part 4, 144.
The *Catechism of the Catholic Church* also makes this point: "From the very beginning of
the Church there have been men and women who have renounced the great good of marriage to follow the Lamb wherever he goes, to be intent on the things of the Lord, to seek
to please him, and to go out to meet the Bridegroom who is coming" (n. 1618).

69   Pope John Paul II has written that marriage and celibacy for the sake of the Kingdom of God "are two ways of expressing and living the one mystery of the covenant of God with his people".[89] The celibate person anticipates in his or her person "the new world of the future resurrection".[90] By liberating the human heart in a unique way, "so as to make it burn with greater love for God and all humanity", virginity or celibacy bears witness that the Kingdom of God and his justice is that pearl of great price which is preferred to every other value no matter how great.[91] Pope John Paul II concludes: "Just as fidelity at times becomes difficult for married couples and requires sacrifice, mortification and self-denial, the same can happen to celibate persons, and their fidelity, even in the trials that occur, should strengthen the fidelity of married couples".[92]

THE ESSENTIAL PROPERTIES OF MARRIAGE

Can. 1056 The essential properties of marriage are unity and indissolubility; in christian marriage they acquire a distinctive firmness by reason of the sacrament.

Unity

70 The "unity" of marriage refers to the fact that marriage is a monogamous relationship, that is, between one man and one woman. This quality arises in the first instance from the nature of marriage. As Kasper notes, "the act in which the bride and bridegroom give and receive each other has in itself an inner tendency towards definitiveness and exclusiveness".[93] Accordingly, all forms of polygamy are excluded, whether it be polygyny, where one man has several wives, or polyandry where one woman has several men, or "group marriages" where several men "marry" several women.[94] Such practices run counter "to the plan of God ... because it is contrary to the equal personal dignity of men and women who in matrimony give themselves with a love that is total and therefore unique and exclusive".[95]

71   The Church has always taught that Christ excluded polygamy. This is clear from Matthew 19:6: "Have you not read that the creator from the beginning made them male and female and that he said: This is why a man must leave father and mother, and cling to his wife, and the two become one

---

89 Fl II, 826, *FC* n. 16a. **90** 827, ibid., n. 16c. **91** Ibid., n. 16e. **92** Ibid., n. 16g. **93** *The theology of christian marriage*, 45. **94** *The Canon Law: letter and spirit*, prepared by the Canon Law Society of Great Britain and Ireland in association with the Canadian Canon Law Society (editorial board: G. Sheehy, R. Brown, D. Kelly, A. McGrath; F.G. Morrisey, consultant editor), Veritas 1995 (hereafter *The Canon Law: letter and spirit*), 574. **95** Fl II, 829, *FC* n. 19d.

body? They are no longer two, therefore, but one body". This teaching was defined by the Council of Trent: "If anyone says that Christians may have more than one wife at once and that it is forbidden by no divine law: let him be anathema."[96]

The unity of marriage should not however be understood only in a nega- **72** tive way, that is, as excluding polygamy; it has a positive, dynamic meaning. By virtue of the covenant of married love, spouses "are called to grow continually in their communion through day-to-day fidelity to their marriage promise of total mutual self-giving".[97] The unity of marriage is exalted in a special way in the case of those who celebrate the sacrament of matrimony: "the Holy Spirit who is poured out in the sacramental celebration offers Christian couples the gift of a new communion of love that is the living and real image of that unique unity which makes of the Church the indivisible Mystical Body of the Lord Jesus".[98]

Indissolubility

John T. Noonan wrote: "the canons concerning marriage were meant to teach **73** a single lesson, to incorporate a single value – indissolubility was the *raison d'être* of the system; without it, the whole enterprise would have lacked focus, connection, energy".[99] It is important today to establish the basis of indissolubility; one of the most challenging tasks facing the Church is to uphold it in teaching and in pastoral practice. Indissolubility is increasingly regarded either as a utopian ideal or as an unreasonable burden. The right to remarry during the life-time of one's spouse is regarded as a human and civil right; it is seen as necessary to provide relief to those whose marriages have broken down.[100]

The indissolubility of marriage, like its unity, arises in the first instance **74** from the nature of marriage. It is based on the nature of marriage itself; the spouses' personal decision is accepted, protected, and reinforced by society itself, especially by the ecclesial community; this is for the good of the spouses, the good of the children and for the common good.[101] Kasper writes that "this unity and indissolubility, already an essential part of marriage as a reality of creation, are given an ultimate and unambiguous meaning in the Old Testament by the insertion of the order of creation into God's plan of salvation (see, for example, Ex 34:6; Ps 99:5)".[102] Faithfulness in marriage was

---

96 N. Tanner, *Decrees of the ecumenical councils*, vol. 2, 754. **97** Fl II, 829, *FC* n. 19b. **98** Ibid., n. 19b. **99** *Power to dissolve*, The Belknap Press of Harvard University Press, Cambridge, Massachussets, 1972, 394. **100** For a response to this argument, cf. W. Binchy, *Is divorce the answer?* Irish Academic Press, Dublin, 1984. **101** "Propositions on the doctrine of christian marriage", in *International Theological Commission: texts and documents, 1969-1985* (ed. M. Sharkey), 172, 4.3. **102** *The theology of christian marriage*, 46.

seen as an image of God's faithfulness in the covenant. It is in this context that Deuteronomy 24:1-4, which deals with drawing up a bill of divorce, must be interpreted. This text does not permit divorce; rather it prohibits remarriage of the divorced wife. It was not until the later period of Judaism that the idea of permission for divorce was derived from this passage in cases where the husband found some "scandal" in his wife.[103]

75   *Mark 10:2-12* The teaching of Jesus on the indissolubility of marriage is clearly stated. In his recent study, Collins begins with the Markan texts which he believes were written first.[104] He takes the view that "the language, style, and content of Mark 10:2-12 coalesce to suggest that the entire story, that is, the discussion with the Pharisees (vv. 2-9) and the instruction of the disciples (vv. 10-12) is a single unit of material that has been created by the evangelist".[105] He summarises his exegesis of the text as follows:

> The conflict story offers a rationale for Jesus' prophetic warning against divorce by appealing to the will of God as expressed in the creation of man and woman. A proof from Scripture had been developed in a Hellenistic-Jewish environment to demonstrate that divorce was indeed contrary to the order of creation and the will of God. Jesus' teaching on this matter creates a social division between "us", that is, Jesus and his disciples, and "you", that is those who take issue with the Christian position, represented in the Markan narrative by the Pharisees, the traditional opponents of Christians and their way of life.[106]

76   *Matthew 19:3-12* Matthew reworked the Markan text for the needs of his own community.[107] He presents Jesus as an authoritative interpreter of the Law, a teacher whose "radical demand spells out the way of life incumbent on those who would enter the kingdom".[108] This text has two sections: the teaching of Jesus (vv.3-9) and an instruction for the community (vv. 10-12). In answer to the question as to how a disciple of Jesus can live according to the rigorous teaching on divorce, "Matthew's answer, given in the instruction to the disciples, is by means of the gift of God himself".[109]

77   *Matthew 5:31-32* The context of this saying of Jesus on divorce is the Sermon on the Mount. It is characterised by a series of antitheses: "You have heard how it was said ... but I say to you". The opposition is not between Jesus and the Scriptures as such, but between the teaching of Jesus and the biblical commandment as it has been handed down in the Jewish tradition.[110] In contrast to the traditional interpretation of Deuteronomy 24:1-4, "Mat-

---

103 Kasper, ibid. **104** *Divorce in the New Testament* (Good News Studies 38), Michael Glazier, Collegeville, Minn., 1989, 66. **105** Ibid., 76-7. **106** Ibid., 102. **107** Ibid., 104. **108** Ibid., 114. **109** Ibid., 126. **110** Ibid., 161.

thew's Jesus describes any man who is involved in divorce as one who is responsible for a violation of the sixth commandment: 'anyone who divorces his wife, except on the ground of unchastity, causes her to commit adultery; and whoever marries a divorced woman commits adultery' ".[111]

An exception? Collins holds that the clauses "except on the ground of **78** unchastity" (παρεκτὸς λόγον πορνείας) (Mt 5:32) and "except for unchastity" (μη επὶ πορνεία) (Mt 19:9) probably did not belong to the earliest tradition of Jesus' sayings on divorce, but arose as a response to the particular needs of Matthew's community.[112] He insists that they are not exceptions since the teaching of Jesus, even with the exceptive clause, "is such that it must be understood as a position that was countercultural to the dominant view of marriage and divorce held by the Jewish opponents of Matthew's community, represented by his Pharisees, with their scribes".[113]

Many scholars hold that πορνεία (unchastity) in the Matthean text refers **79** to incestuous unions, that is, marriages which were within the prohibited degrees of consanguinity and affinity. Meier explains:

> All too common in the eastern Mediterranean, such marriages were forbidden by Leviticus 18:6-18. Some rabbis allowed a Gentile to maintain the incestuous union when he entered Judaism, and similar problems about these unions arose when Gentiles became Christians. The problem is mentioned in Acts 15:20, 29, 21:25, and 1 Corinthians 5:1. In all these texts πορνεία (*porneia*) is used to describe the incestuous marriage.[114]

Harrington also holds that Matthew 19:9 is not an exceptive clause: **80**

> Jesus is not abrogating the Mosaic legislation, nor is he (or a secondary editor) reducing his radical demand to something more palatable. On the contrary, he is emphasising the risks which mankind as a whole must face when the sexuality inherent in man's nature is confronted with the indissoluble reality of marriage ... Marriage is a call to a life of total sacrifice and self-giving ... if one's spouse is unfaithful, a life dedicated to him or her may have to be totally thrown away, laid down in love (since there is no possibility of enjoying another similar partnership) ... Christian love must continue faithful, even if rejected, loyal even if deserted, and abiding even if unrequited. Why? – for the sake of God's love shown in the very union of man and woman ... Jesus'

---

111 Ibid., 166-7. **112** Ibid., 186. **113** Ibid., 211. **114** J. P. Meier, *Matthew* (New Testament Message 3), Michael Glazier, Wilmington, Delaware, 1980, 51. Cf. also J. Fitzmyer, "The Matthean divorce texts and some new Palestinian evidence" in *Theological Studies* 37 (1976), 197-226.

demand is absolute and is for indissolubility in marriage ... Matthew has not softened Jesus' radicalism but underlined it.[115]

81   Collins takes the view that the teaching of Jesus on divorce was initially a prophetic saying which, after his death and resurrection, became a community regulation. As a community regulation and a moral challenge, his teaching on divorce "seems to admit of no exception: the christian husband may not divorce his wife; the christian wife may not divorce her husband".[116]

82   *St Paul: 1 Corinthians 7:12-15* Although the teaching of Jesus admits of no exception, St Paul had to deal with a situation on which the tradition gave him no guidance. When a woman who has become a Christian has an unbelieving husband and the latter desires to separate, Paul says: "Let it be so; in such a case the brother or sister is not bound. For God has called us to peace" (1 Cor 7:15). He took the view that such a marriage cannot properly be described as a "marriage in the Lord". Paul considered that the tradition of Jesus was relevant only to those marriages in which both partners were Christians. Kilgallen writes:

> It seems reasonable to conclude from Paul's words that one partner of an already existing marriage has converted to belief in Christ and that this new religious commitment has in various ways so disturbed the non-Christian partner that the latter chooses to end the marriage. Given the will of the non-Christian partner if Paul forces the marriage to continue out of an obedience which is given to a religion in which the non-believer does not believe – given all this, Paul accepts the divorce of the two partners as legitimate. Paul will not allow the marriage bond to be broken by the choice of the Christian; the decision to divorce must come from the non-believing partner.[117]

83   Differences regarding the interpretation of the scriptures are at the root of the different theologies of marriage and the different pastoral practices of the Christian Churches.[118]

---

115 *Irish Theological Quarterly* 39 (1972), 183-5. **116** Ibid., 229. **117** J. K. Kilgallen, *First Corinthians: an introduction and study guide*, Paulist Press, New York/Mahwah, 71. St Paul does not say if the Christian spouse in this situation can remarry (*Divorce in the new testament*, 63-4). In his *Decretum* Gratian commented that the "pauline privilege" does not apply if the marriage was contracted after the baptism of one of the parties or in the case of apostasy after baptism (c.XXVIII, q.2, c.2). Innocent III declared that the baptised was free to remarry not only if the baptised refused to cohabit, but if cohabitation is rendered morally impossible by blasphemies or by drawing the converted party to mortal sin (X.1.IV, t.19, c.7). Cf. W.H. Woestman, *Special marriage cases*, Faculty of Canon Law, St Paul's University, Ottawa, 1992, 36-7. **118** *Anglican-Roman Catholic Marriage*, the Report of the Anglican-Roman Catholic International Commission on the Theology

The Fathers of the Church Many of the Fathers of the Church refer to adul- **84**
tery breaking the bond of marriage. Origen speaks of a "dissolution" (λύειν)
of the marriage bond in this circumstance.[119] However it is clear that this
involves an end to the common life of the parties and that they are not free to
remarry.[120] John Chrysostom writes that after the adultery of one of the
spouses the marriage is dissolved (λέλυται) [121] but again this only refers to
a *de facto* separation and does not involve the right to remarry.[122] In reply to
a letter from the Bishop of Toulouse, Pope Innocent I made clear that any
marriage that takes place while another spouse is living is an adulterous union "although the marriage seems to have broken" (*quamvis dissociatum
videatur coniugium*).[123] St Augustine also refers to adultery as "the only
cause of the dissolution [of marriage]" (*unica causa dissolutionis*)[124] but
this does not imply a right to remarry.[125] Crouzel speaks of "the remarkable
uniformity in the Church's tradition of the early centuries of the Church" on
this point.[126] Although there are instances of tolerance shown towards di-
vorcees who have remarried, he observes that "on the subject of divorce the
first Christian centuries do not merit the scepticism with which they are sometimes regarded, because in East and West they show a real unity in the exegesis of the scriptural texts and in the discipline which results".[127]

The Middle Ages During the middle ages some local synods and penitential **85**
books seem to have permitted divorce and remarriage in certain cases.[128]

---

of Marriage, highlights the points of agreement and disagreement between both Churches
on the interpretation of the scriptural texts on marriage: "We agree on a text-critical approach; on the priority of Mark's version in this pericope (Mk 10:1-12; Mt 19:1-12; cf. Mt
5:32); that the exceptive clauses in Matthew are additions to the words of Jesus; that the
most probable interpretation of πορνεία (porneia) is as marriage within the forbidden
Jewish degrees, and that this clause is inserted not as a mitigation but to preserve the full
rigour of Jesus' words; ... that Jesus' statements are uncompromising; that Mark 10:1-9
intends to throw into relief the hardness of heart involved in making use of Deuteronomy
24 allowing a bill of divorce, and that its direct concern is with the failure of the married
couple to stay together, rather than with remarriage. We disagree, however, in that Henry
Wansborough thinks that Jesus intends to abrogate this permission, Barnabas Lindars that
he does not... We disagree, however, as to whether Jesus intended his words to be taken as
having force of law. Henry Wansborough regards them as a directive to the disciples
which would be normative for the future Christian community. Barnabas Lindars holds
that Jesus sets out neither to correct the existing law nor to establish a new law; it is a
mistaken undertaking to attempt to construct a law on the basis of Jesus' sayings; rather
the sayings of Jesus will continue to stand in judgement on any law" (15). **119** *Commentary on Matthew*, Book 14, ch.16. **120** *L'église primitive face au divorce* (Théologie
historique 13), Beauchesne, Paris, 1971, 76-7. **121** *Homily 19 on 1 Corinthians*, in *PG*
61, part 3, 155. **122** H. Crouzel, 191-2. **123** *Letter 6*, in *PL* 20, 500. **124** *De Sermone
Domini in Monte*, in *Corpus Christianorum* 35, 1/16, 50. **125** Crouzel, 321. **126** "Remarriage after divorce in the primitive Church" in *Irish Theological Quarterly* 38 (1971),
41. **127** Ibid. **128** T. Mackin, *Divorce and remarriage*, Paulist Press, New York/Ramsey,
1984, 240ff.

Separation and remarriage was permitted on certain grounds that later emerge as impediments (e.g., consanguinity, affinity, impotence) or as grounds of nullity (force and fear). In the twelfth century the scholastics counted marriage as a sacrament in the present dogmatic sense. This influenced the growing acceptance of the juridical status of a ratified and consummated marriage.[129] The Decree for the Armenians issued by the General Council of Florence (1439) stated:

> The efficient cause of matrimony is the mutual consent duly expressed in words relating to the present ... But, although it is permitted to separate on account of adultery, nevertheless it is not permitted to contract another marriage since the bond of a marriage legitimately contracted is perpetual.[130]

86 *The Council of Trent* The reformers upheld the sacredness of marriage in the order of creation, but denied that it belongs to the order of grace as a Christian sacrament in the strict sense. They permitted divorce because of adultery and other causes.[131] The Council of Trent set out the teaching of the Church in twelve canons; Can. 7 affirmed the Church's teaching on the indissolubility of marriage:

> If anyone says that the Church is in error for having taught and for still teaching that in accordance with the evangelical and apostolic doctrine (cf. Mk 10; 1 Cor 7), the marriage bond cannot be dissolved because of adultery on the part of one of the spouses, and that neither of the two, not even the innocent one who has given no cause for infidelity, can contract another marriage during the lifetime of the other; and that the husband who dismisses an adulterous wife and marries again and the wife who dismisses an adulterous husband and marries again are both guilty of adultery, *anathema sit.*[132]

87 *Teaching of the Church today* Pope John Paul II writes:

> Being rooted in the personal and total self-giving of the couple, and being required by the good of the children, the indissolubility of marriage finds its ultimate truth in the plan that God has manifested in his revelation: he wills and he communicates the indissolubility of the ab-

---

129 The distinction between intrinsic and extrinsic indissolubility which developed in the middle ages will be considered below in the context of the material on the formation of the bond of marriage. **130** *The Christian Faith*, n. 1803. **131** For a summary of Luther's theology of marriage, cf. T. Mackin, *Divorce and remarriage*, 377-85. **132** *The Christian Faith*, n. 1814.

solutely faithful love that God has for man and that the Lord Jesus has for his Church.[133]

The Church regards indissolubility as an essential property of marriage **88** by virtue of the natural law; hence every valid marriage is indissoluble in the sense that it cannot be dissolved by the parties or by any human power. The natural bond of marriage can however be dissolved in certain situations by virtue of "the power of the keys" (Can. 1142ff). The indissolubility – and unity – of marriage "acquire a distinctive firmness by reason of the sacrament" (Can. 1056). Can. 1141 states that "a marriage that is ratified and consummated cannot be dissolved by any human power or by any cause other than death".

THE FORMATION OF THE BOND OF MARRIAGE

Can. 1057 §1 A marriage is brought into being by the lawfully manifested consent of persons who are legally capable. This consent cannot be supplied by any human power.

Roman tradition

The Scriptures provide no data that answers the question: what brings about **89** the relationship of marriage? In the early Church the view current in Roman law was accepted, namely, that consent between the parties brought about the relationship of marriage: *nuptias non concubitus, sed consensus facit* (consent, not sexual intercourse, makes marriage).[134] However the mutual consent of the parties created a status which lasted only as long as the partners persevered in this agreement.[135] The involvement of the Church in the person of the bishop was motivated by a desire to ensure the pastoral care of the couple, "so that marriage may be according to the Lord and not according to desire".[136]

The teaching of the Roman Church on this question was expressed by **90** Pope Nicholas I in 866. In reply to an inquiry from the Emperor of the Bulgarians who had become a Christian, he stated that for the marriage of Chris-

---

133 Fl II, 830, *FC* n. 20. The International Theological Commission drew attention to the link between the indissolubility of marriage and its sacramentality: "A unique bond exists between the indissolubility of marriage and its sacramentality, that is, a reciprocal, constitutive relationship. Indissolubility makes one's grasp of the sacramental nature of Christian marriage easier and from the theological point of view, its sacramental nature constitutes the final grounds, although not the only grounds, for its indissolubility" (*International Theological commission: texts and documents, 1969-1985*, 167, 2.2). 134 *Digesta*, 50,17,30. 135 E. Schillebeeckx, *Marriage: human reality and saving mystery*, 241. 136 Ignatius of Antioch, cited in Schillebeeckx, 245.

tians consent was sufficient.[137] This reply implicitly criticised the Greeks who had converted the Bulgars and who placed great emphasis on the crowning and blessing by the priest.

Germanic tradition

91 When Christianity spread to the Germanic tribes, it found there a different tradition. Germanic law treated marriage as a union created by cohabitation, rather than by formal act, such as consent.[138] What was essential in bringing about marriage was consummation and no marriage was binding without it.[139] This so-called *copula* theory is reflected in the teaching of Hincmar, archbishop of Rheims (845–82), which emphasises the importance of consummation in the formation of marriage:

> A true coupling in legitimate marriage between free persons of equal status occurs when a free woman, properly dowered, is joined to a free man with paternal consent in a public wedding [followed by] sexual intercourse.[140]

92 Hincmar attributes no significance to the consent of the parties; the consent of the woman's father and the subsequent consummation of the union were the key elements; an unconsummated marriage was incomplete and hence not fully binding.

The medieval synthesis

93 During the tenth and eleventh centuries Church officials began to assert jurisdiction over marriage. Church courts acquired exclusive competence in judging if marriages were valid or not. The question of how the bond of marriage was formed had to be resolved if decisions were to be reached in individual cases. In the twelfth century, Gratian and Peter Lombard contributed significantly to the search for agreement on this question.

94 In his *Decretum* Gratian taught that marriage came into being as the result of a two-stage process; he distinguished the initiation of marriage, when

---

137 DS 643: "Sufficit secundum leges solum eorum consensus, de quorum coniunctione agitur; qui consensus si solus in nuptiis forte defuerit, cetera omnia, etiam cum ipso coitu celebrate, frustrantur, Ioanne Chrysostomo magno doctore testante, qui ait: 'Matrimonium non facit coitus, sed voluntas." The *leges* (laws) referred to in this teaching are the Roman law on marriage. **138** J. A. Brundage, *Law, sex, and Christian society in medieval Europe*, University of Chicago Press, Chicago and London, 1987, 128. **139** Brundage, 130. **140** PL 126: 137-8: "Quibus sententiis evidenter ostendit, quia tunc est vera legitimi coniugii copula, quando inter ingenuos, et inter aequales fit, et paterno arbitrio viro mulier juncta, legitima dotata, et publicis nuptiis honestata, sexuum commistione coniungitur."

the parties exchanged words signifying consent, and the completion or perfection of marriage through sexual consummation. Marriage is both a spiritual union, brought into being by consent, and a physical union, achieved by
sexual intercourse. Coitus without consent to marry is no marriage, nor is an
exchange of consent that is not followed by intercourse. Consummation transformed the union into a "sacrament" and hence made it indissoluble.[141]

Peter Lombard taught that the consent of the parties was the *sacramentum* **95**
of the unity of Christ and his Church, a symbolism that extended to sexual
intercourse. He held that the marriage bond was already established by the
parties' mutual consent. The object of this consent was the "marital community", which was more than sexual intercourse.[142]

The effect of these different views was that "the Italian ecclesiastical **96**
courts dissolved marriages (on grounds of sexual non-consummation) which
were declared by the Frankish churches to be indissoluble".[143] Finally in the
latter half of the twelfth century and the first half of the thirteenth century a
consensus was reached:

> These popes personally supported the views of the canonists who took
> their stand on Gratian's decretals, but they were realistic enough to
> recognise that the view of the Paris school afforded a clearer criterion
> and provided an easier solution in many matrimonial lawsuits. The le-
> gal security of the validity of a marriage thus made them decide in
> favour of the Paris school, while retaining the essential element in the
> teaching of the school of Bologna – namely, that marriage was a true
> and legally valid sacrament formally and exclusively by virtue of the
> partners' mutual consent to the marriage, but that marriage was dis-
> soluble if this sacrament was not consummated in sexual intercourse.[144]

The canonical synthesis arrived at during this period is as follows: mar- **97**
riage is brought into being by the consent of parties who are free to marry.
Before the marriage is consummated, the marriage can be dissolved by Church
authority. This valid marriage becomes indissoluble, both intrinsically and
extrinsically, once it has been consummated by an act of sexual intercourse.
Or, to put it another way, although consent makes a marriage perfect and
indissoluble, its indissolubility lacks a quality of absoluteness which only
consummation can give it. When a couple have given consent to marriage,
they cannot personally dissolve the bond, though the Church can in certain
circumstances. When they have consummated their union following consent, not even the Church can dissolve the bond; it is extrinsically indissoluble.

141 Brundage, 235-9. **142** E. Schillebeeckx, *Marriage: human reality and saving mystery,* 293-4. **143** Ibid., 294. **144** Ibid.

98   Kelly summarises the development of doctrine which led to the synthesis outlined above:

> Divorce and remarriage was an unchallenged fact of life and law in the Roman world in which Christ's teaching took root and spread. Yet, eleven hundred years later, despite disagreement about other aspects of marriage, both Christian writers and civil legislators all over the Western Church accepted that a consummated marriage could not be dissolved. The simple fact of this profound and far reaching change in marriage customs is a convincing argument for the existence in the Church of a constant tradition against divorce and remarriage. Only a wide-spread and firm conviction that Christ had taught that marriage is indissoluble could have inspired the sort of unwavering teaching necessary to bring about such a radical transformation in a difficult matter.[145]

THE NATURE OF CONSENT

Can. 1057 §2 Matrimonial consent is an act of will by which a man and a woman by an irrevocable covenant mutually give and accept one another for the purpose of establishing a marriage.

Consent – a juridical act

99 Can. 1057 §2 contains one of the few definitions in the Code of Canon Law; it defines matrimonial consent as "an act of the will by which a man and a woman by an irrevocable covenant mutually give and accept one another for the purpose of establishing a marriage". The description of matrimonial consent as "an act of the will" derives from Roman contract law. With the revival of Roman law in the twelfth century, the period when the Church was refining its own theory on the formation of marriage, canonists classified marriage as a contract.[146] At this period, Aristotelian categories were used to explain human acts:

> Human persons were described as composed of matter and form, that is of body and soul; the soul as operating through its distinct faculties, the mind and the will, one able to perceive the truth, the other to pursue the good ... Since marriage belonged to the category of "good", consent to marriage had to be an act of the will. Because the goodness of

145 W. Kelly, *Pope Gregory II on divorce and remarriage* (Analecta Gregoriana 203), Rome, 1976, 48. 146 L. Örsy, *Marriage in canon law*, 62.

marriage would enrich any well-disposed person, no more than some initial cooperation of the mind was required. Thus consent became fully defined as "an act of the will".[147]

In this conceptual framework, consent is "a human act" when it is carried out with deliberation: "Consequently those acts alone which lie under his control are properly called human. Now [a person] is master through his mind and will ... Therefore those acts alone are properly human which are of his deliberate willing".[148]   **100**

An act is truly human when the person is able to exert, or give effect to, his or her own will or intention. The human act is the freely willed act. It expresses the inner disposition of the person, not the disposition of another. Both reason and will are involved in it: the reason perceives a proposed course of action as good, makes a judgement (discernment) about it; the will moves freely towards it. An act is voluntary when it follows clear reflection and full consent of the will. In moral theology such an act is one for which the person is morally responsible;[149] within the juridical sphere such an act is considered "a juridical act" (Can. 124 §1). The issue is not the morality of the act, but its validity. In other words, if the act, for example, matrimonial consent, is judged to be a human act, the person will be held accountable for it and the act itself will be upheld. A recent commentary on this canon states: **101**

> The principal defining feature of the juridical act is its *voluntary* nature; it is a *deliberate* action by a subject; the object of the action is *intended* by the subject; moreover, the intention is in some way externally manifested: otherwise the act will remain purely internal, with no consequences for the social relationships between members of the Church.[150]

Today the integrity of a human act is judged on the basis of the maturity of the person. In a civil law suit which concerned the validity of a mother's consent to the adoption of her child, the Irish High Court stated: **102**

> In making that decision [the mother] subordinated her own will to that of her parents because of fear, which was a product of her upbringing, stress, anxiety, lack of maturity and deprivation of emotional support. It was not a free decision ... The evidence shows that it was not until [a later date] that the mother became capable of exerting her own will ...

---

147 Örsy, ibid. Roche argues that consent should not only be seen as an act of will, but also as a union of wills (cf. "Consent is a 'union of wills'" in *Studia Canonica* 18 (1984), 415-38). **148** *Summa theologiae*, I-II, q.1, in c. **149** F. Böckle, *Fundamental concepts of moral theology*, Paulist Press Exploration Books, New York etc., 1967, 29-32. **150** *The Canon Law: letter and spirit*, n. 256, 72.

[She] had matured and overcome her fear and became sufficiently in-dependent to exert her own will.[151]

103   Within the canonical tradition matrimonial consent is seen as a juridical act. When both spouses have consented, "there arises between the spouses a bond which of its own nature is permanent and exclusive" (Can. 1134). Örsy warns against a false interpretation of this phrase: "The expression "a bond arises" cannot mean that some new physical entity or new substance is cre-ated, either in the material or spiritual order. It can only mean that in each partner a set of new obligations arises ... A clearer way of conveying the same meaning would be to say that the spouses are bound to each other."[152]

Consent and conjugal love

104   One of the striking features of the Vatican II treatment of marriage is the emphasis on conjugal love. Conjugal love is described as a love which is "eminently human" and "involves the good of the whole person".[153] It is generous and dynamic, leading the spouses to "a free and mutual gift of themselves" and it finds expression in acts which are "noble and worthy".[154] The question arose however after the Council as to whether conjugal love entered into the formation of the bond of marriage instead of consent, or in addition to consent. Pope Paul VI addressed this issue in his address to the Roman Rota in 1976. He insisted that marriage is brought into being by the consent of the parties and added:

> We must therefore reject without qualification the idea that if a subjec-tive element – among these especially conjugal love – is lacking in a marriage, the marriage ceases to exist as a *juridical reality* ... No, this *reality*, which is juridical, continues to exist and does not depend on love ... What we have been saying is not to be understood as in any way lessening the importance and dignity of conjugal love, for the rich bless-ings proper to the institution of marriage are not limited to the juridical elements alone. Although conjugal love does not enter into the pur-view of law, it nonetheless plays a lofty and necessary role in marriage. It is a force of the psychological order and God has established as its goals the ends of marriage itself. In fact, when love is wanting, spouses lack a powerful stimulus for carrying out with mutual sincerity all the duties and functions proper to married life.[155]

151 *D.G. and M.G. v An Bord Uchtála*, 23 May 1996 (Laffoy, J), at 27. **152** *Marriage and canon law*, 203. **153** Fl I, 952, *GS* n. 49. **154** Ibid. **155** *Papal allocutions to the Roman Rota*, 136.

Different perspectives on marriage

Juridical It is clear from the statement of Pope Paul VI just cited that there **105**
are different perspectives on marriage. The first is the juridical one. Vatican
II reaffirmed the Church's teaching that the institution of marriage receives
its stability from the human act by which the partners mutually surrender
themselves to each other, that is, from consent.[156] It adds that "for the good
of the partners, of the children, and of society this sacred bond no longer
depends on human decision alone".[157] What does it mean to describe marriage as a juridical relationship?:

> Juridical relationships are made of rights and duties that are mutually
> given and accepted. That is why we speak about marriage as a cov-
> enant, as a bond. Through these mutually given and accepted rights
> and duties, two married persons are bound to one another and commit-
> ted to each other. They must strive to establish the proper psychologi-
> cal relationships between husband and wife, and must strive with the
> help of the grace of the sacrament to grow constantly in mutual love.
>
> It is a sad experience that instead of growing, the mutual love and
> affective relationship of husband and wife may actually die. Yet the
> mutual commitment, the mutual bond that is the reality of marriage
> cannot die except by the physical death of at least one of the parties.[158]

Sacramental Marriage can also be viewed from a sacramental perspective. **106**
The Church teaches that the reception of the sacrament coincides with the
moment of consent. The marriage relationship of baptised husband and wife
becomes by that very fact a redeeming force, a situation which makes God's
saving love in Christ present here and now in the family unit. It is a valid
offer of grace.[159]

Psychological Finally, marriage can be viewed from a psychological per- **107**
spective. For most couples the experience of exchanging matrimonial consent on their wedding day is a significant experience for them at the personal
level; after the years and months of courtship and preparation they are now
husband and wife. At this existential level, there is a real sense in which they
are beginning another stage of their relationship. Through the experience of
living together and sharing the joys and difficulties of life, their love and
trust in each other deepens. It is possible to say, from this perspective, that "it
takes ten years to make a genuine, fundamental, well-knit, true marriage".[160]

---

156 Fl I, 950, *GS* n. 48. **157** Ibid. **158** F. J. Urrutia, "The 'internal forum solution': some
comments" in *The Jurist* 40 (1980), 135. **159** D. O'Callaghan, "Theology forum: no
sacrament, no marriage" in *The Furrow* 26 (1975), 232. **160** J. Hanaghan, *The courage
to be married*, Mercier Press, Dublin and Cork, 1979, 13.

If the marriage relationship is neglected or subjected to severe strain, it may weaken or even die. This however does not call into question the juridical stability and firmness of the marriage bond created by matrimonial consent. Indeed the juridical stability of the relationship provides the context within which love and trust can grow and develop. This juridical framework provides the stable underpinning which can support spouses when their relationship is fraught with tensions and difficulties.[161] It is legitimate to use developmental language when dealing with couples in a pastoral context in order to emphasise the importance of continuing to work at their marriages.

108 *The use of developmental categories in the juridical sphere* The use of developmental language when dealing with the formation of the bond of marriage is contrary to the canonical tradition. To do so deprives the formation of the bond of marriage of the clarity and definiteness which it requires. The distinction between these perspectives is not maintained by some contemporary theologians. Thomas, for example, writes that a modern emphasis in the theology of marriage is "its existential dimension".[162] Because marriage as a human relationship is necessarily developmental "it is difficult to reduce christian marriage to fixed categories of analysis because the relationship is always in process or continually becoming".[163] He continues:

> Earlier theologies focused on the wedding itself, the initial public exchange of vows in the presence of the community along with the first act of sexual intercourse as essential for establishing the validity of the marriage. It was believed that the sacrament of matrimony was received at that time. Now Christian marriage is thought of as existing when there is established an adequate consciousness and awareness of the full range of relational requirements in marriage along with a serious willingness and the actual capacity to create a relationship of faithful love. Further, it is necessary to affirm the disposition of openness to the reception of new life within the marriage. All of these are qualities of a relationship which are not easily reduced to simple categories or to a single event in time.[164]

109   The juridical stability of marriage and the on-going dynamic growth of the marriage relationship are not in conflict with each other. It is wrong to make the juridical existence of a marriage dependent on its on-going growth. Vatican II taught that marriage receives its stability from "that human act by which the partners mutually surrender themselves to each other", and it added that "for the good of the partners, of the children, and of society this sacred

161 J. McAreavey, "Divorce, re-marriage and the Eucharist: a further view" in *Doctrine and Life* 45 (1995), 171-7.   **162** "Marriage" in *The New Dictionary of Theology*, 627. **163** Ibid. **164** Ibid.

bond no longer depends on human decision alone".[165] This implies that marriage does come into existence at a particular point in time; the task of the spouses thereafter is not to struggle to sustain the juridical bond of marriage in existence but to live out in daily life the demands of their vocation. The fact that the bond of marriage comes into existence at a point in time creates the framework within which spouses can strive to build their relationship. The validity of a marriage formed by consent and consummated by the sexual union of the parties is not an arcane, abstract concept; on the contrary, it recognises the irrevocable nature of the commitment given in matrimonial consent. It expresses the commitment of the Church to uphold and support the commitment of the couple. It acknowledges the fragility and hesitancy of human commitment and, in calling spouses to accountability for the serious commitment they made at the moment of consent, it provides a framework which promotes the good of the couple, the well-being of their children and the common good.

In this context one can ask what it means to speak of the validity of **110** marriage. Firstly, it means that consent has been given by parties who were legally capable, that is, there were no impediments to the marriage. Secondly, it means that the act of consent was free and informed; thirdly, it means that the marital consent was given in accordance with the formalities laid down by law and that, as a result, the matrimonial consent given by the couple has brought into being the marriage relationship desired by the couple. The opposite is true when we speak of the invalidity or nullity of consent. It means that an essential element was missing and as a result the juridical act of consent did not bring about the effect which it intended. In brief, it can be said that if matrimonial consent is valid the marriage is valid, and that if the matrimonial consent is invalid or null, the marriage is invalid or null.

Various other judgements are made about marriages which break down; **111** it is sometimes said that a marriage "did not gel", that "the chemistry was not right", that the parties were "incompatible". Even when it is clear what these statements mean, it does not follow that the matrimonial consent, and the marriage, was invalid.

Marriage before God and the Church

In the marriage rite, the official witness invites the couple "to declare before **112** God and his Church [their] consent to become husband and wife". When they have exchanged consent, the minister states: "What God has joined together man must not separate". In other words, the relationship which comes about through the mediation of the Church unites the couple before God in a bond that is indissoluble. The Church does not accept that a couple can be

---

165 Fl I, 950, *GS* n. 48a.

married "before God" and not "before the Church". The authority by which the Church regulates the celebration of the sacraments comes from God. The authority to determine what is necessary for the valid celebration of the sacraments is exercised by the Holy See (Can. 841). Hence a declaration that a couple is not married "before the Church" is a declaration that they are not married "before God".

FURTHER CONCEPTS IN THE CANONICAL DOCTRINE OF MARRIAGE

Can. 1058 The right to marry

All can contract marriage who are not prohibited by law.

113   The Church holds that every person has a natural right to marry. This is stated in the *Charter of the Rights of the Family*:

> a. Every man and every woman, having reached marriage age and having the necessary capacity, has the right to marry and establish a family without any discrimination whatsoever; legal restrictions to the exercise of this right, whether they be of a permanent or temporary nature, can be introduced only when they are required by grace and objective demands of the institution itself and its social and public significance; they must respect in all cases the dignity and the fundamental rights of the person.
> b. Those who wish to marry and establish a family have the right to expect from society the moral, educational, social and economic conditions which will enable them to exercise their right to marry in all maturity and responsibility.[166]

114   The right to marry is a natural one; restrictions of the exercise of this right must be in accordance with the law. In case of doubt, "marriage is not to be prevented" (Can. 1084 §2).

Can. 1059 The Church's competence over marriage

> The marriage of catholics, even if only one party is a catholic, is governed not only by divine law but also by canon law, without prejudice to the competence of the civil authority in respect of the merely civil effects of the marriage.

---

[166] Art.1.

Three kinds of law govern marriage: divine law, canon law and civil law. **115**
"Divine law" includes certain precepts of the natural law as well as the commandments of the gospel. The impediment of consanguinity in the direct line (Can. 1091 §1) is an example of the natural law; the impediment of an existing marriage bond is an example of a gospel precept. All marriages are subject to the divine law since "the married state has been established by the creator and endowed by him with its own proper laws".[167]

The Church exercises competence over marriages in which a catholic is **116**
a party. Although non-catholics as a general rule are not bound by "merely ecclesiastical laws" (Can. 11), I take the view of Örsy who regards this canon as an exception. He writes:

> The Church claims jurisdiction over all marriage where one of the parties is catholic. Thus, the non-catholic person, baptised or not, is brought into the orbit of our canonical legislation.[168]

Members of the Church are subject to the relevant civil requirements of **117**
the jurisdictions where they reside and where they contract marriage in matters such as domicile, notice, and registration. Those who officiate at marriages in the name of the Church are also bound to observe the relevant civil law. The "civil effects" of marriage concern issues such as citizenship, property rights, and social welfare benefits.

Can. 1060 The favour of the law

> Marriage enjoys the favour of law. Consequently, in doubt the validity of a marriage must be upheld until the contrary is proven.

If a marriage has been celebrated, it is presumed to be valid; the person **118**
who contests its validity must provide proof of the contrary. This presumption reflects the Church's commitment to the stability of marriage. Örsy observes that "if a doubt (reasonable as it may be) could cancel out the certainty generated by a seemingly legitimate performance, the life of the community would be beset with uncertainties throughout, and the stability that the law is expected to provide would be undermined".[169] For this presumption to be operative, there must at least be the appearance of a marriage; if there is a doubt as to whether the marriage took place, proof must be given that it did. An example of this presumption is given in Can. 1086 §3: "if at the time the marriage was contracted one party was commonly understood to be bap-

---

167 Fl I, 950, *GS* n. 48.   **168** *Marriage in canon law*, 64-5.   **169** *Marriage in canon law*, 66.

tised, or if his or her baptism was doubtful, the validity of the marriage is to be presumed in accordance with Can. 1060, until it is established with certainty that was person was baptised and the other was not".

119   This canon has important implications in procedural law. In a nullity case a judgement of nullity can be returned only if the evidence is sufficiently cogent to enable a Court to reach its decision with moral certitude (Can. 1608). The presumption of validity gives way to contrary proof as happens when a marriage is proved and declared to be null.[170] If there have been two successive marriage ceremonies, the presumption is in favour of the first.[171]

120   Can. 1150 states that "in a doubtful matter the privilege of the faith enjoys the favour of the law". This means that if there is doubt about such matters as the validity of the interpellations (Can. 1144 §2) the law favours the granting of the privilege of the faith.

Can. 1061 Juridical terminology concerning marriage

> §1 A valid marriage between baptised persons is said to be merely ratified, if it is not consummated; ratified and consummated, if the spouses have in a human manner engaged together in a conjugal act in itself apt for the generation of offspring: to this act marriage is by its nature ordered and by it the spouses become one flesh.
>
> §2 If the spouses have lived together after the celebration of their marriage, consummation is presumed until the contrary is proven.
>
> §3 An invalid marriage is said to be putative if it has been celebrated in good faith by at least one party. It ceases to be such when both parties become certain of its nullity.

121 *Valid/invalid* The Church holds that "since the sacraments are the same throughout the universal Church and belong to the divine deposit of faith, only the supreme authority in the Church can approve or define what is needed for their validity" (Can. 841).[172] The use of the words "valid" and "invalid" in the context of sacramental theology and sacramental law derives from contract law; it came into common use in relation to marriage.[173] For example, the Decree for the Armenians (1439) stated:

> All these sacraments are constituted by three elements: by things as the matter, by words as the form, and by the person of the minister confer-

---

170 L. de Naurois, "Matrimonium gaudet favore iuris" in *Revue de droit canonique* II-IV (1979), 70. **171** For an authentic interpretation of the Pontifical Council for the Interpretation of the Code of Canon Law in 1947, cf. *Leges ecclesiae post codicem editae* II, n. 1935, III, col. 2424. **172** *The Christian Faith*, n. 1324. **173** J. Gurrieri, "Sacramental validity: the origins and use of a vocabulary" in *The Jurist* 41 (1981), 39. **174** *The Christian Faith*, n. 1307.

ring the sacrament with the intention of doing what the Church does. And if any one of these is lacking, the sacrament is not effected.[174]

In the case of marriage, the matter of the contract is identical with the **122** matter of the sacrament. Hence anything that renders the contract invalid also renders the sacrament invalid.

When it deals with the requirements for a valid juridical act, canon law **123** distinguishes between those which are constitutive elements and those which are required purely by the positive law. If the former elements are lacking, the act is invalid because it lacks existence; if the latter are lacking, the act will exist but will have no effect. In the case of matrimonial consent, the parties must have sufficient discretion for marriage (Can. 1095, 2°). Consent given by a person who lacks this is invalid and inexistent. However, consent given by a catholic outside the canonical form will, unless a dispensation was given, be invalid by virtue of the law (Can. 1108 §1). The consent exists but will be invalid.

Nullity, or invalidity, is the ultimate sanction in canon law if a marriage is **124** celebrated in contravention of the law. However the fact that a marriage is forbidden by law is not sufficient to render it invalid. For example, Can. 1071 states that "except in a case of necessity, no one is to assist without permission of the local Ordinary" at certain marriages. If such a marriage takes place without the required permission, it will be unlawful (or illicit) but valid.[175] A law only renders a marriage invalid when this is stated explicitly, for example, "a person contracts invalidly who enters marriage inveigled by deceit ..." (Can. 1098).

Ratified   A valid marriage brought about by the consent of two baptised **125** persons is described as ratified. By virtue of baptism it is raised to the dignity of a sacrament. The marriage of two unbaptised persons becomes a "ratified marriage" when they receive baptism.[176] If a marriage has not been consummated, it is described as ratified but not consummated.

Ratified and consummated   When a marriage has been brought into being **126** by the consent of two baptised persons and has subsequently been consummated by a human act of sexual intercourse, it is described as ratified and consummated. The insistence that the act of intercourse which consummates a marriage must be performed "in a human manner" highlights the dignity of Christian marriage. Hence sexual intercourse forced by a husband against

---

175 Cf. G. Lobo, "The Christian and canon law" in J. Hite and D.J. Ward, *Readings, cases, materials in canon law*, revised edition, Liturgical Press, Collegeville, Minn., 1990, 41. 176 The corresponding canon in the 1917 Code of Canon Law (c. 1015 §3). defined the marriage of two non-baptised persons as "matrimonium legitimum".

his wife's will would not consummate the marriage.[177] When a couple have lived together it is presumed that they have consummated their union. Like other presumptions, this gives way to contrary proof.

127 *Putative* A marriage is described as putative if it was celebrated in good faith by at least one party. Such a marriage has the semblance of validity because it has been contracted in the prescribed form but is invalid, for example, because of the presence of a diriment impediment. The children born of a putative marriage are legitimate (Can. 1137); in canon law a declaration of nullity does not render the children of the marriage illegitimate.[178]

128 *Attempted* An attempted marriage (matrimonium attentatum) is one entered in bad faith, that is, by parties who are aware of a diriment impediment (cf. Cann. 1087, 1041, 3°).

Can. 1062 Engagement

§1 A promise of marriage, whether unilateral or bilateral, called an engagement, is governed by the particular law which the Bishops' Conference has enacted after consideration of such customs and civil laws as may exist.

§2 No right of action to request the celebration of marriage arises from a promise of marriage, but there does arise an action for such reparation of harm as may be due.

129 In the history of the Church's matrimonial law, promise of marriage, or engagement (*consensus de futuro*), played an important role.[179] In the Middle Ages engagement followed by the consummation of the union was accepted as one way of forming the marriage bond. Until this century there was an extensive body of general law on this matter.[180] Under the 1917 Code, engagement to marry did not admit of an action in an ecclesiastical court to force the other person to marry; however action for possible injury done by the unjust breaking of the engagement was admitted (1017). In the Code of Canon Law engagement is governed by particular law.

---

177 *Comm* 6 (1974), 191-2. For a fuller treatment of this, cf.commentary on Can. 1084 below. 178 A recent work on a medieval canonist comments on the importance of *bona fides*: "The impact of *bona fides* appears again when he explores the legitimacy of children born and raised by parents who were presumably married. For Huguccio, the offspring enjoyed all the benefits of a regular marriage, as long as the marital partners believed that they were married canonically. Moreover the same subjective standard of good conscience continued to prevail over law when only one of the spouses acted in good faith" (W. Müller, *Huguccio: the life, works, and thought of a twelfth-century jurist*, Catholic University of America Press, Washington, 1994, 142-3). 179 It was referred to in Latin as "sponsalia" or "consensus de futuro". 180 Cf. P. Gasparri, *Tractatus canonicus de matrimonio*, 1932 vol. 1, nn. 43-121.

The nature of marriage

D. Fellhauer, "The *consortium omnis vitae* as a juridical element of marriage" in *Studia Canonica* 13 (1979), 1-171.

G. Lesage, "The *consortium vitae coniugalis*: nature and implications" in *Studia Canonica* 6 (1972), 99-113.

M.F. Pompedda, "Incapacity to assume the essential obligations of marriage" in *Incapacity for marriage* (Acts of the III Gregorian Colloquium) (ed. R. Sable), Rome, 1987, 157-98.

L.G. Wrenn, "Refining the essence of marriage" in *The Jurist* 46 (1986), 532-51.

C. Burke, "The *bonum coniugum* and the *bonum prolis* ends or properties of marriage?" in *The Jurist* 49 (1989), 704-13.

P. Connolly, "Reflections on the canonical implications of the 'good of the spouses'" in *Proceedings of the Annual Conference of the Canon Law Society of Great Britain and Ireland, May 20-24 1996*, 27-33.

The sacramentality of marriage

W. Kasper, *Theology of christian marriage*, Burns & Oates, London, 1980.

P. Grelot, *Man and wife in scripture*, Burns & Oates, London, 1964.

P.J. Elliott, *What God has joined ...*, Alba House, New York, 1990.

M. Schmaus, *Dogma 5: The Church as sacrament*, Sheed and Ward, London, 1975.

T. Norris, "Why the marriage of Christians is one of the seven sacraments" in *Irish Theological Quarterly* 51 (1985), 37-51.

F.R. McManus, "The ministers of the sacrament of marriage in the Western tradition" in *Studia Canonica* 20 (1986), 85-104.

M.J. Himes, "The intrinsic sacramentality of marriage: the theological ground for the inseparability of validity and sacramentality" in *The Jurist* 50 (1990), 198-220.

G. Koch, "What is the sacramentality of marriage?" in *Theology Digest* 43 (1996), 41-5.

L. Reynolds, "Marriage, sacramental and indissoluble: sources of the catholic doctrine" in the *Downside Review* 109 (1991), 105-50.

Faith and the sacrament of marriage

D. O'Callaghan, "Faith and the sacrament of marriage" in *Irish Theological Quarterly* 52 (1986), 161-79.

R.C. Finn, "Faith and the sacrament of marriage: general conclusions from a historical study" in *Marriage Studies* III (ed. T. Doyle), 95-111.

M.F. Pompedda, "Faith and the sacrament of marriage – lack of faith and matrimonial consent: juridical aspects" in *Marriage Studies* IV (ed. J.A. Alesandro), 33-65.

J. McAreavey, "Faith and the validity of marriage" in *Irish Theological Quarterly* 59 (1993), 177-87.

M.J. Lawler, "Faith, contract, and sacrament in Christian marriage: a theological approach" in *Theological Studies* 52 (1991), 712-31.

L. Örsy, "Faith, sacrament, contract, and Christian marriage" in *Theological Studies* 43 (1982), 379-98.

D. Baudot, *L'inséparabilité entre le contrat et le sacrament de mariage* (Analecta Gregoriana 245), Rome, 1987.

J.B. Sequeira, *Tout marriage entre baptisés est-il nécessairement sacramentel? Étude historique, théologique et canonique sur le lien entre baptême et mariage* (Thèses) Éditions du Cerf, Paris, 1985.

J. Vernay, "Mariage et foi: à propos de deux thèses" in *Unico ecclesiae servitio* (edd. M. Thériault-J. Thorn), Ottawa, 1991, 213-40.

Virginity and celibacy

L. Legrand, *The biblical doctrine of virginity*, Geoffrey Chapman, London 1963.

Th. Matura, "Le célibat dans le Nouveau Testament" in *Nouvelle Revue Théologique* 97 (1975), 481-500; 593-604.

R. Cantalamessa, *Virginity*, Alba House, New York, 1995.

The essential properties of marriage

L. Ryan, "The indissolubility of marriage in natural law" in *Irish Theological Quarterly* 30 (1963), 293-310; 31 (1964), 62-77.

R.F. Collins, *Divorce in the New Testament* (Good News Studies 38), Michael Glazier Books/Liturgical Press, Collegeville, Minn. 1992.

J.B. Meier, *Matthew* (New Testament Message 3), M. Glazier, Wilmington, Delaware 1980.

W. Harrington, "Jesus' attitude towards divorce" in *Irish Theological Quarterly* 37 (1970), 199-209.

W. Harrington, "The New Testament and divorce" in *Irish Theological Quarterly* 39 (1972), 178-87.

H. Crouzel, *L'église primitive face au divorce: du premier au cinquième siècle* (Théologie historique 13) Beauchesne, Paris 1971.

H. Crouzel, "Remarriage after divorce in the primitive church" in *Irish Theological Quarterly* 38 (1971), 21-41.

D. O'Callaghan, "How far is christian marriage indissoluble?" in *Irish Theo-*

logical Quarterly 40 (1973), 162-73.

A. Schmemann, "The indissolubility of marriage: the theological tradition of the East" in *The bond of marriage* (ed. W. Bassett), University of Notre Dame Press 1968, 97-116.

The formation of the bond of marriage

J. Brundage, *Law, sex and christian society in medieval Europe*, University of Chicago Press, Chicago and London, 1987.

A. Cosgrove (ed.), *Marriage in Ireland*, College Press, Dublin, 1985.

P.C. Power, *Sex and marriage in ancient Ireland*, Mercier Press, Cork, 1976.

E. Schillebeeckx, *Marriage: human reality and saving mystery*, Sheed & Ward, London, 1965.

W. Kelly, *Pope Gregory II on divorce and remarriage* (Analecta Gregoriana 203), Rome, 1976.

J.T. Noonan, *Power to dissolve: lawyers and marriages in the courts of the Roman curia*, The Belknap Press of Harvard University Press, Cambridge, Mass., 1972.

T. Mackin, *Divorce and remarriage*, Paulist Press, New York/Ramsey 1984.

A. Cosgrove, "Consent, consummation and indissolubility: some evidence from medieval ecclesiastical courts" in the *Downside Review* 109 (1991), 94-104.

J.Meyendorff, *Marriage, an Orthodox perspective*, St Vladimir's Seminary Press, New York, 1970.

K. Ware, "The sacrament of love: the orthodox understanding of marriage and its breakdown" in the *Downside Review* 109 (1991), 79-93.

Further concepts of canonical doctrine

L. De Naurois, "Matrimonium gaudet favore iuris" in *Revue de droit canonique* 29 (1979), 53-73.

A.N. Decanay, "Matrimonium ratum: significatio termini" in *Periodica* 79 (1990), 69-89.

2

Pastoral care and the prerequisites for the celebration of marriage

131 This section of the Code deals with three issues that are related but distinct: pre-marriage preparation (Cann. 1063-65), the pre-nuptial enquiry (Cann. 1066-70), and a number of problem situations (Can. 1071).

PRE-MARRIAGE PREPARATION

Can. 1063 Pastoral care

Pastors of souls are obliged to ensure that their own church community provides for Christ's faithful the assistance by which the married state is preserved in its christian character and develops in perfection. This assistance is to be given principally:

1° by preaching, by catechetical instruction adapted to children, young people and adults, indeed by the use of the means of social communication, so that Christ's faithful are instructed in the meaning of christian marriage and in the role of christian spouses and parents;

2° by personal preparation for entering marriage, so that the spouses are disposed to the holiness and the obligations of their new state;

3° by the fruitful celebration of the marriage liturgy, so that it clearly emerges that the spouses manifest, and participate in, the mystery of the unity and fruitful love between Christ and the Church;

4° by the help given to those who have entered marriage, so that by faithfully observing and protecting their conjugal covenant, they may day by day achieve a holier and a fuller family life.

132 In July 1996 the Pontifical Council for the Family issued an instruction entitled: *Preparation for the Sacrament of Marriage*.[1] It deals extensively with the material covered in this canon. Section I stresses the importance of faith-preparation for Christian marriage. Section II distinguishes three phases in preparation for marriage: remote, proximate and immediate preparation; the final section deals with the celebration of marriage.

1 *Origins* 26 (1996), 98-109.

It presents marriage preparation as a process of evangelisation through **133** which the couple grow in personal maturity and in faith.[2] The underlying principle is stated as follows:

> The starting-point for an itinerary of marriage preparation is the aware-
> ness that the marriage covenant was taken up and raised to a sacrament
> by the Lord Jesus Christ, through the power of the Holy Spirit. The
> sacrament joins the spouses to the self-giving love of Christ, the bride-
> groom, for the church, his bride (Eph 5: 25-32) by making them the
> image and sharers in this love. It makes them give praise to the Lord, it
> sanctifies the conjugal union and the life of the Christian faithful who
> celebrate it, and gives rise to the Christian family, the domestic church,
> the "first and living cell of society" ... and the "sanctuary of life"...[3]

Marriage preparation has a wider dimension than dealing with individual **134** couples and their needs:

> [Marriage preparation] must be set within the urgent need to evange-
> lise culture – by permeating it to its roots ... – in everything that con-
> cerns the institution of marriage: making the Christian spirit penetrate
> minds and behaviour as well as the laws and structures of the commu-
> nity where Christians live ... This preparation, both implicitly and ex-
> plicitly, constitutes one aspect of evangelisation, so much so that it can
> deepen the strength of the Holy Father's affirmation: "The family is
> the heart of the new evangelisation".[4]

For the Christian couple marriage preparation is "a journey of faith which **135** does not end with the celebration of marriage but continues throughout family life".[5] The document of the Holy See distinguishes three phases in prepa-
ration for marriage: remote, proximate and immediate.

Remote preparation

Remote preparation for marriage begins in childhood: "a Christian lifestyle, **136** witnessed to by Christian families, is in itself a form of evangelisation and the very foundation of remote preparation".[6] The example given by parents can be reinforced in the teaching given in church, in school and in various forms of youth ministry.[7]

---

2 Ibid., n. 2, 99. **3** Ibid., n. 9, 100. **4** Ibid., n. 20. **5** Ibid., n. 16, 102. **6** Ibid., n. 28, 104.
7 Ibid., nn. 29-30.

Proximate preparation

137 Proximate preparation takes place during the engagement period. Couples "should also be helped to become aware of any psychological and/or emotional shortcomings they may have, especially the inability to open up to others and any forms of selfishness that can take away from the total commitment of their self-giving".[8] The document adds:

> However, the centre of this preparation must be a reflection in faith on the sacrament of marriage through the word of God and the guidance of the Magisterium. The engaged should be made aware that to become *una caro* [one flesh] (Mt 19:6) in Christ through the Spirit in Christian marriage means imprinting a new form of baptismal life on their existence. Through the sacrament, their love will become a concrete expression of Christ's love for his Church.[9]

138 This preparation usually takes place in pre-marriage courses.[10] The document says that "the pastoral usefulness of marriage preparation courses show that they can be dispensed with only for proportionally serious reasons".[11]

Immediate preparation

139 The immediate preparation for the celebration of the sacrament of matrimony should consist of the following: a summary of previous preparation (especially its doctrinal, moral and spiritual content), experiences of prayer "in which the encounter with the Lord can make them discover the depth and beauty of the supernatural life", a suitable liturgical preparation, with special attention to the sacrament of reconciliation.[12] This spiritual preparation should include all who will take an active part in the celebration of the marriage liturgy:

> It should be explained to the witnesses that they are not only the guarantors of a juridical act, but also representatives of the Christian community which, through them, participates in a sacramental act relevant

---

8 Ibid., n. 36, 105. **9** Ibid., n. 47, 106. **10** In 1993 the Bishop of Raphoe, Dr Hegarty, commissioned an evaluation of the pre-marriage courses which were held in the diocese. It was entitled *A Study and an Evaluation of Pre-Marriage Courses*. It was carried out by the Adult and Community Education Centre, St Patrick's College, Maynooth, under the direction of Rev Liam Carey. A summary of the recommendations are to be found in Appendix VI. **11** Ibid., n. 51, 107. Such courses should not be imposed on couples to the extent that attendance becomes effectively an impediment to the celebration of marriage. The danger of further alienating "nominal" Catholics has been raised by Bishop McCarthy (Austin, Texas) (cf. "On refusing sacraments to nominal Catholics" in *Origins* 22 (1992), 392-4). **12** Ibid., n. 50.

to it because a new family is a new cell of the Church. On account of its essentially social character, marriage calls for the participation of society, and this is to be expressed through the presence of the witnesses.[13]

Can. 1064 Responsibility of local Ordinary for marriage preparation

It is the responsibility of the local Ordinary to ensure that this assistance is duly organised. If it is considered opportune, he should consult with men and women of proven experience and expertise.

An earlier draft of this canon assigned responsibility for marriage prepara- **140** tion to Bishops' Conferences.[14] However the responsibility now rests with the local Ordinary to see to it that adequate preparation is provided within his diocese. This involves ensuring that those who exercise this ministry are well trained and have the opportunity and the means to continue their formation. In practice the ministry to couples preparing for marriage is carried out by lay men and women, many of them married couples, in cooperation with clergy.

Can. 1065 Sacramental preparation

§1 Catholics who have not yet received the sacrament of confirmation are to receive it before being admitted to marriage, if this can be done without grave inconvenience.
§2 So that the sacrament of marriage may be fruitfully received, it is earnestly recommended that spouses approach the sacraments of penance and the blessed Eucharist.

Confirmation The sacraments of the Church are closely inter-related; they **141** "are not seven ways in which God communicated himself to us; they are seven ways in which we receive the one self-communication".[15] The Church groups them together: baptism, confirmation and Eucharist are sacraments of initiation; penance and anointing of the sick are sacraments of healing, and orders and matrimony are sacraments at the service of communion.[16] By means of the sacraments of orders and matrimony "those already consecrated by baptism and confirmation for the common priesthood of all the faithful can receive particular consecrations".[17] Walsh explains the link between confirmation and matrimony as follows:

Confirmation reinforces the witnessing and missionary status of the

---

13 Ibid., n. 55, 107. **14** *Comm* 9 (1977), 138. **15** M.J. Himes, "The current state of sacramental theology as a background to the New Code" in *Canon Law Society of America Proceedings 1980*, 75. **16** *Catechism of the Catholic Church*, nn. 1533-5. **17** Ibid., n. 1535.

sacrament of marriage and its own meaning is made more concrete by its relationship with marriage. Marriage can build up a nuclear family, a tribe, a social class, a nation, and can cement loyalties within these groups. By that very fact it can also become [inward-looking and self-centred] ... Confirmation will not allow Christian marriage to be of this sort. The men and women who received the Spirit at Pentecost become people for whom human love sealed in marriage could never again lock them into any kind of tribal or linguistic particularism ... They will rather stand for a human love that reaches across such barriers, that keeps open house and hospitality from which no one is excluded ...[18]

142 Can. 1065 §1 addresses the situation where one – or both – of the parties is not confirmed. While it is preferable, from a theological point of view, for those who wish to marry to be confirmed, the Church does not make the reception of confirmation is an absolute condition for contracting marriage.[19] Hence, as the introduction to the Rite of Confirmation states, "if it is foreseen that the conditions for a fruitful reception of confirmation cannot be satisfied, the local Ordinary will judge whether it is better to defer confirmation until after the marriage".[20] When it is not possible to prepare a person adequately for confirmation before marriage, this should be done after the marriage has taken place.

143 *Penance* The Church desires that the celebration of matrimony be not only valid and lawful, but also fruitful. Marriage is a pivotal moment in the life of a couple and it is appropriate for the parties to celebrate this moment by being fully reconciled to God and the Church in the sacrament of penance. Couples should be reminded that matrimony is a sacrament and that they should be in a state of grace as they prepare to celebrate it. The celebration of a sacrament when a person is in a state of mortal sin is, at least objectively, a sacrilege.[21]

144 Couples are invited to receive holy communion during the nuptial Mass, if their marriage is being celebrated during Mass. Indeed they are usually invited to receive holy communion under both species. In order to receive holy communion they should be in a state of grace (Can. 916). Walsh highlights the theological and spiritual appropriateness of this:

The Eucharist provides initiation into Christian marriage in a still more intimate way. It unites the body of a Christian to the body of Christ. It is that same body that becomes one with the body of a marriage partner. It is because the bodies of Christians are seen to be made one with

18 L. Walsh, *The sacraments of initiation*, Geoffrey Chapman, London, 1988, 55.
19 *Comm* 15 (1983), 225. **20** DOL 2521. **21** *Catechism of the Catholic Church*, n. 2120.

Christ in the Eucharist that their becoming one with one another in the sexual bond of marriage becomes Christ-bearing and Christ-revealing, and can be a sacrament of the human love of Christ for his brother and sisters who form his Church.[22]

PRE-NUPTIAL ENQUIRY: COMPLETION, GATHERING AND FORWARDING, STORAGE

Can. 1066 Valid and lawful celebration

Before a marriage takes place, it must be established that nothing stands in the way of its valid and lawful celebration.

This canon states a general principle that is given practical expression in the **145** canons that follow: before a marriage takes place there is a responsibility to ensure that it will be valid and lawful. Since there is a natural right to marry (Can. 1058), there is no question of persons having to establish or prove that they are fit for marriage. The pre-nuptial enquiry is an administrative procedure whose purpose is to identify anything that would render the proposed marriage unlawful or invalid. It is entirely different in character from the judicial procedure that is necessary to establish the nullity of a marriage.

Can. 1067 Pre-nuptial enquiry, publication of banns

The Bishops' Conference is to lay down norms concerning the questions to be asked of the parties, and concerning the publication of marriage banns or other appropriate means of enquiry to be carried out as a pre-requisite for marriage. When he has carefully observed these norms the parish priest may proceed to assist at a marriage.

The task of establishing that nothing stands in the way of the valid and law- **146** ful celebration of a marriage is carried out in accordance with procedures laid down by the Bishops' Conference.[23] It is for the latter also to decide if marriage banns should be called.

Can. 1068 Danger of death

In danger of death, if other proofs are not available, it suffices, unless there are contrary indications, to have the assertion of the parties, sworn if need be, that they are baptised and free of any impediment.

22 *The sacraments of initiation*, 55. **23** The Irish Bishops' Conference decided, when issuing a new Pre-Nuptial Enquiry form in 1984, that the publication of banns which had been required by the 1917 Code (c. 1022) was no longer necessary. This decision was incorporated in the decrees which were promulgated in 1987 (cf. n. 13, *Intercom* (supplement) 18 (1987-88), 10). Can. 1067 made the marriage banns optional.

147   If one or both parties are in danger of death, it may not be possible to carry out the pre-nuptial enquiry envisaged for normal circumstances. In this situation, unless there are grounds for doubt, the assertion of the parties regarding their baptism and freedom to marry are sufficient to enable the marriage to proceed. It is important to keep in mind the norms regarding dispensation of impediments in danger of death (Can. 1079).

148   If a marriage breaks down and one of the parties applies for a declaration of nullity, the tribunal may ask to see the pre-nuptial enquiry forms. Burke writes:

> It may be that the priest who performed the wedding noticed some unusual signs, was not able to resolve the question raised in his own mind by the signs, but nevertheless, if he was prudent, made discreet note of this on the pre-nuptial forms. The pre-nuptial form is a public document of the Church and carries a great deal of force. Not all pre-nuptial papers will offer that assistance.[24]

Can. 1069 Duty of the faithful to reveal knowledge of marriage impediments

> Before the celebration of a marriage, all the faithful are bound to reveal to the parish priest or to the local Ordinary such impediments as they may know about.

149   This canon reflects the ecclesial significance of Christian marriage. The faithful have a duty "to promote the growth of the Church" (Can. 210), particularly through the stability of marriage.

Can. 1070 If a priest other than the parish priest carries out pre-nuptial enquiry

> If someone other than the parish priest whose function it is to assist at the marriage has made the investigations, he is by an authentic document to inform that parish priest of the outcome of these enquiries as soon as possible.

150   The duty of assisting at marriages is entrusted to the parish priest of the parish where the marriage takes place (Can. 530, 4°). When both parties live in the parish where the marriage will be celebrated, the parish priest or a priest of the parish will carry out the pre-nuptial enquiry. If however one of the parties lives in another parish, the pre-nuptial enquiry for that party will

---

24 "Canon 1095, 1°-2°; ... jurisprudence" in *Incapacity for marriage*, 141

be carried out in his or her parish by a priest of that parish. In this event, the priest who carries out the pre-nuptial enquiry will forward to the parish priest of the place of marriage the results of that enquiry. Normally this will be done by means of the pre-nuptial enquiry form approved for use in the region.

Preparation of other documents

Marriages involving catholics are governed by the civil law as well as by canon law (Can. 1059). Those who officiate at marriages in the name of the Church should be familiar with the requirements of civil law and should observe them.   **151**

Can. 1071 Celebration of marriages for which the permission of local Ordinary is required

§1 Except in a case of necessity, no one is to assist without the permission of the local Ordinary at:
1° a marriage of *vagi*;
2° a marriage which cannot be recognised by the civil law or celebrated in accordance with it;
3° a marriage of a person bound by natural obligations towards another party or children, arising from a previous union;
4° a marriage of a person who has notoriously abandoned the catholic faith;
5° a marriage of a person who is under censure;
6° a marriage of a minor whose parents are either unaware of it or are reasonably opposed to it;
7° a marriage to be entered by proxy, as mentioned in Can. 1105.
§2 The local Ordinary is not to give permission to assist at the marriage of a person who has notoriously abandoned the catholic faith unless, with the appropriate adjustments, the norms of Can. 1125 have been observed.

The Church has identified a number of situations in which there is no impediment to marriage but in which, for pastoral reasons, a marriage may not be celebrated unless the local Ordinary has given permission. This prohibition does not affect the validity of the marriages concerned. This list is not exhaustive; the Church in a particular area could add a particular local circumstance to it.[25]   **152**

---

25 L. Chiappetta, *Il codice di diritto canonico*, Edizioni Dehoniane, Naples, 1988, II, n. 3560, 186.

1°   *Vagi* (people with no fixed residence)

153   A *vagus* in canon law is a person "who has nowhere a domicile or quasi-domicile" (Can. 100). This provision reflects the experience of the Church, that it is difficult to establish if those who have no fixed abode are actually free to marry.[26]

2°   Marriages which cannot be recognised by the civil law or celebrated in accordance with it

154   This category includes marriages involving a person who had obtained a Church annulment but had not obtained a divorce, or the marriage of a person who obtained a foreign divorce which was not recognised by the civil law of his or her own country.

3°   The marriage of a person for whom a previous union has created natural obligations towards a third party or towards children

155   If a person wishing to celebrate a canonical marriage had previously been civilly married and divorced or was involved in an irregular union, enquiries should be made to see if he or she has any natural obligations to a previous partner or to the children of the previous union. Permission for the canonical marriage should not be given unless there is an assurance that he or she will continue to fulfil the obligations arising from the earlier union.

4°   The marriage of a person who has notoriously rejected the catholic faith

156   Pope John Paul II has written that "when in spite of all efforts engaged couples show that they explicitly and formally reject what the Church intends to do when the marriage of baptised persons is celebrated, the pastor of souls cannot admit them to the celebration of marriage".[27] The marriage of a catholic to a person who has notoriously rejected the catholic faith should be treated like a mixed marriage; as in a mixed marriage, permission will not be given unless the catholic party makes the promises regarding the practice of the faith and the baptism and education of the children (Can. 1125, 1°).

5°   The marriage of a person who is under censure

157   A person who is under the censure of either excommunication or interdict is "forbidden to celebrate the sacraments ... and to receive the sacraments"

---

26 An instruction issued by the Holy See in 1921 included refugees, exiles, and tourists. Cf. X. Ochoa, *Leges ecclesiae post codicem editae*, vol.1, n. 365, col. 400. 27 Fl II, 873, *FC* n. 68g.

(Cann. 1331 §1, 2°, 1032). When the matter is referred to the local Ordinary, he will decide if the censure can be remitted. If not, permission may be granted for the marriage only in the most exceptional circumstances. One matter to be considered in such a case is the danger to the faith of the other party.[28]

6° The marriage of a minor whose parents are either unaware of it or are reasonably opposed to it

The Church is also concerned that in the exercise of such an important right, **158** the parents of minors (in canon law, those under eighteen) be consulted.[29]

7° The marriage to be entered by proxy, as mentioned in Can. 1105

Proxy marriages are marriages in which either one or both parties are not personally present at the ceremony but are represented by a proxy in accord- **159** ance with Can. 1105. Special difficulties arise in regard to such marriages; there may be doubt as to the freedom of the parties or their preparedness for marriage; hence the reserve of the Church in their regard. Permission is given for such marriages only for very grave reasons.[30]

Marriage ban (vetitum) A further category can be added to the above, viz., a marriage where one of the parties obtained a Church annulment but **160** where a ban, or *vetitum*, was attached to the decree of nullity. This normally states that the person may not marry "without the permission of the local Ordinary". Notification of this *vetitum* is entered in the marriage register where the marriage was initially registered (Can.1680). When these cases are referred to the Chancery office, the Bishop or his delegate will make the necessary enquiries and will decide if it is prudent to remove the *vetitum*.[31]

SPECIAL SITUATIONS

Those too immature to marry

Can. 1072 Dissuade couples from marrying before the age customary in a region

Pastors of souls are to see to it that they dissuade young people from entering marriage before the age customarily accepted in the region.

28 *The Canon Law: letter and spirit*, n. 2104, 587. **29** Cf. C.F. O'Donnell, *The marriage of minors*, Washington, 1945. **30** *The Canon Law: letter and spirit*, n. 2106, 588. **31** Cf. A. Dewhirst, "The *vetitum* and *monitum* down under: a necessity, a help or a hindrance" in *CLSGBI Newsletter* 105 (1996), 41-64.

161 The Code of Canon Law states general principles which have to be applied in various cultural situations throughout the world. One such principle is that "a man cannot validly marry before the completion of his sixteenth year of age, nor a woman before the completion of her fourteenth year" (Can. 1083 §1). Can. 1083 §2 adds that "the Bishops' Conference may establish a higher age for the lawful celebration of marriage". Can. 1072 asks pastors, notwithstanding Can. 1083 §1, to take account of local custom and to discourage young people from entering marriage before the age customarily accepted in the region. Local custom in this matter may be reflected in the age at which marriage is permitted in civil law since national legislatures take account of the specific circumstances of time and place.[32]

162 The purpose of the pre-nuptial enquiry is to ensure that nothing stands in the way of the valid and lawful celebration of the marriage (Can. 1066). If the person who carried out this enquiry has serious doubts as to the capacity for marriage of (at least) one of the parties, he should refer the matter to the diocesan Bishop or his delegate. The Bishop could, if he considered it appropriate, postpone the marriage in accordance with Can. 1077 §1. Many dioceses in North America have developed procedures to deal with couples who are regarded as unprepared for marriage.[33]

One party has HIV virus, suffers from AIDS
or is a carrier of a sexually transmitted disease

163 Marriages involving a person infected with the HIV virus or who suffers from AIDS or is a carrier of a sexually transmitted disease give rise to particular problems.[34] Pastoral practice should be based on established moral and canonical principles:

> **a.** All can contract marriage who are not prohibited by law (Can. 1058).
> **b.** It is not permitted to place either one's own life or that of others in danger without good reason.[35]
> **c.** The failure of a person who has the HIV virus, suffers from AIDS or is the carrier of a sexually transmitted disease to reveal this to his or her partner would render the marriage null as it is a circumstance that "can seriously disrupt the partnership of conjugal life" (Can. 1098).
> **d.** Marriage would be permitted if the person with AIDS was in danger of death.

32 For a commentary on norms introduced in the civil law of the Republic of Ireland, cf. J. McAreavey, "The Family Law Act 1995 – implications for pastoral practice" in *The Furrow* 47 (1996), 410-5. **33** Cf. J. McAreavey, *Emotional immaturity and marriage: a canonical analysis of diocesan pre-marriage policies and ecclesiastical jurisprudence*, Rome, 1979. **34** Cf. *AIDS: Meeting the community challenge*, ed. V. Cosstick, St Paul Publications, 1987. **35** B. Häring, *The Law of Christ*, Mercier Press, Cork, 1963, III, 214.

e. It would be immoral for a person who has AIDS or another sexually transmitted disease to enter marriage with a non-infected partner with the intention of carrying on a normal sexual relationship since the inevitable outcome of such a relationship would be the death of the uninfected spouse. One canonist has stated that "it appears to be irrefutable according to catholic doctrine that a person infected with the AIDS virus cannot morally engage in sexual intercourse".[36]

Persons with learning disabilities

Today many persons with learning disabilities live in normal society rather than in hospitals or institutions. They receive education and training appropriate to their gifts and ability. The Church has adapted its approach to preparation for the sacraments to take account of their special needs.[37]   **164**

The question of the marriage of persons with learning disabilities raises important questions for both society and the Church. Jean Vanier, founder of *l'Arche*, has addressed the question on the basis of his experience over many years of living in community with men and women who had learning disabilities. He writes: "It is evident that some people with a mental handicap, especially if it is slight, are able to enter into the joys and pains of conjugal life and of a family life. However, many have been labelled 'deficient' or 'disabled'. In reality, they could have functioned quite well in society if they had received adequate support."[38]   **165**

The research of Servais[39] and the experience of *l'Arche* have led Vanier   **166**

---

36 W.A. Varvaro "Prohibition against marriage of AIDS victims", in *Roman replies and CLSA advisory opinions 1987*, 121. O'Donnell writes: "Another question sometimes asked regards the use of a condom in marital intercourse when one of the spouses has contracted AIDS ... but only for the purpose of not infecting the other spouse. Even if this were without any contraceptive intent ...it is important to note ... that the intrinsic disorder (moral malice) of condomistic intercourse in marriage derives not only from a contraceptive intention, but likewise from the fact that condomistic intercourse is simply not marital intercourse. The act itself is gravely disordered and merely a seriously sinful simulation of a marital act. As such, even without any contraceptive intention, it is seriously and intrinsically wrong, and thus cannot be justified for any purpose, however good or in any circumstances, however mitigating they might seem to be. The same would apply, of course, to any other prophylactic use of a condom (for example, to prevent the contagion of a venereal infection) even within marriage" (T.J. O'Donnell, *Medicine and Christian morality*, second revised and updated edition, Alba House, New York, 1991, 226). Whether a marriage entered on the basis that the couple would abstain from sexual relations would be valid is disputed. Regatillo, in his *Ius sacramentarium*, 3rd edition discusses the distinction between a right ("*ius radicale*") and the use of the right ("*usus iuris*") (807-8).
37 J.M. Huels, "Canonical rights to the sacraments" in *Developmental disabilities and sacramental access* (ed. E. Foley), Liturgical Press, Collegeville, Minn., 1994, 94-115.
38 *Man and woman He made them*, Darton Longman and Todd, London, 1984, 129.
39 "Jalons pour l'accompagnement au mariage des personnes handicappées", thesis presented at the University of Louvain la Neuve, 1981.

to the conclusion that "marriage is possible, but only for a minority of those with a mental handicap".[40] He cites Servais' view:

> The right to marry, an inalienable right of everyone, can only be exercised lawfully and lived fully, if its duties express the will to respect the partner of the covenant. Moreover, as with all vocations, marriage presupposes attractions and aptitudes. In contemporary society, the accent is generally put on the attraction for marriage rather than on the aptitude. Here, as elsewhere, educators must try to motivate the partners with mental handicap to take responsibility for the future. To do this, they must begin by creating a relationship of trust which engenders security, then they can bring constructive criticism and help to the two concerned.[41]

167 Servais emphasises the importance of a guide or counsellor who will support persons with learning disabilities as they face the challenges of married life. The guide "will have the task of stimulating social, friendly and familial relationships in order to keep the couple from closing in on themselves"; he or she will "serve as a reference, confidant or counsellor if requested by the couple, perhaps above all to renew confidence in times of difficulty".[42]

168 Vanier broaches the sensitive issue of whether a couple, both of whom have mental handicaps, can have children. Acknowledging the complexity of the issue, he states: "We quickly forget that some women with mental handicaps long, more than anything, to be mothers. The suffering of sterility is intolerable for them. If they are encouraged to have sexual relationships and are prevented from conceiving a child, their deepest desire is not being met".[43]

169 He admits that there are risks in this situation: a mother who has a mental handicap will be able to nurse her child, but when the child becomes irritable, difficult, anguished, there is a risk that the mother may become terribly insecure and anguished herself. At that moment, she may abandon or abuse her child. He concludes: "For a mother to bring up her child, she must have a security, a liberty, and an interior peace which is often lacking in someone with a mental handicap. It is irresponsible to let someone with a handicap to have children whom they are manifestly not able to bring up adequately."[44]

170 Particular law could include marriages involving a person with a mental handicap among those at which "no one is to assist without the permission of the local Ordinary" (Can. 1071 §1).[45]

---

40 Ibid.   41 Ibid., 129-30.   42 Ibid., 130. Further experiences are documented in R.B. Edgerton, *The cloak of competence,* University of California Press, Berkeley, 1967. 43 Ibid., 132.   44 Ibid.   45 L. Chiappetta, *Il codice di diritto canonico,* II, n. 3560, 186.

3

Matrimonial impediments

In canon law access to the sacraments is limited in various ways; for exam- **171**
ple, a candidate for confirmation must be baptised (Can. 889 §1). The authority to define what is needed for the valid celebration of the sacraments
is exercised by the supreme authority in the Church (Can. 841). The term
"impediment" however is used only in regard to the sacraments of matrimony and holy orders.

Can. 1073 Diriment impediment

> A diriment impediment renders a person incapable of validly contract-
> ing a marriage.

A diriment matrimonial impediment is a circumstance attaching to a person **172**
which, by virtue of either divine or human law, renders him or her incapable
of contracting a marriage. As an incapacitating law it takes effect even if the
parties are ignorant of it (Can. 15 §1). Since persons have a natural right to
marry (Can. 1058), limitations on its exercise must be interpreted strictly
(Can. 18). A matrimonial impediment affects marriage in its contractual
aspect, that is, it renders the matrimonial contract invalid. However anything that renders the contract invalid also renders the sacrament invalid (cf.
Can. 1055 §2).

Can. 1074 Public or occult

> An impediment is said to be public, when it can be proved in the exter-
> nal forum; otherwise it is occult.

Impediments are distinguished on the basis of whether they are public or **173**
occult. The distinction has practical implications in the context of dispensation of impediments (Cann. 1079 §3, 1081 §1, 1082) and in the context of
validation of marriage (Can. 1158). Those impediments are public which
can be proven in the external forum, for example, by means of public records
or the testimony of witnesses. The important phrase is "can be proven": a
fact may be known to very few people but if it can be proven, it is public.

Can. 1075 Authority to establish diriment impediments

> §1 Only the supreme authority in the Church can authentically declare
> when the divine law prohibits or invalidates a marriage.

§2 Only the same supreme authority has the right to establish other impediments for those who are baptised.

174   Although the Revision Commission proposed to give Bishops' Conferences authority to establish diriment impediments, the proposal was deleted during the consultation process.[1] The authority vested in the supreme authority in the Church, that is, the Roman Pontiff (Cann. 331-5) or the College of Bishops (Cann. 336-41) is twofold. This authority "can authentically declare when the divine law prohibits or invalidates a marriage" (§1). One recent commentary states in this regard:

> There is a general consensus that certain impediments have a basis in divine law, such as an existing bond of marriage, impotence, consanguinity. It is equally certain that the precise legal formulation of these, and, in some, the extent of the impediment, is of ecclesiastical law, e.g., consanguinity in the direct line is generally accepted to be of divine law, whereas in the farther degrees of the collateral line it is certainly of merely ecclesiastical law.[2]

175   The supreme authority in the Church also has the right to establish other impediments for those who are baptised (§2). Notwithstanding the reference to "the baptised", impediments of ecclesiastical law in practice bind only those "who were baptised in the catholic Church or received into it" (Can. 11).

Can. 1076 Impediment introduced by custom

> A custom which introduces a new impediment, or is contrary to existing impediments, is reprobated.

176   Customs can acquire the force of law (Can. 23) and can even derogate from existing laws (Can. 26). The effect of Can. 1076 is that no custom may acquire the force of a diriment impediment or remove the force of an impediment established by law.

Can. 1077 A marriage ban

> §1 The local Ordinary can in a specific case forbid a marriage of his own subjects, wherever they are residing, or of any person actually present in his territory; he can do this only for a time, for a grave reason and while that reason persists.

1 *Comm* 9 (1977), 80; ibid. 10 (1978), 126; ibid. 15 (1983), 226. 2 *The Canon Law: letter and spirit*, n. 2113, 590

§2 Only the supreme authority in the Church can attach an invalidating clause to a prohibition.

The local Ordinary has authority to forbid marriages in certain circumstances: **177** he may do so "in a specific case", "only for a time", "for a grave reason", and "while that reason persists". He may exercise his authority in relation to his own subjects "wherever they are residing" and all who are actually present in his territory. He can delegate this authority according to the usual laws for delegation. The effect of the ban is to render the marriage illicit, if it takes place; it does not render it invalid.[3]

Only the supreme authority in the Church can attach an invalidating **178** clause to a prohibition of marriage.

DISPENSATION OF IMPEDIMENTS

A dispensation is the relaxation of a merely Church law in a particular case **179** (Can. 85). It can be given for a just and reasonable cause when the competent authority judges that it will contribute to the spiritual welfare of those concerned (Can. 87 §1). If there is no "just and reasonable cause" the dispensation of an impediment is invalid (Can. 90 §1). The authority competent to dispense from general laws is the local Ordinary (Can. 134 §1). The latter can delegate the power to dispense to priests and deacons (Can. 137).[4] They cannot delegate this power to lay members of Christ's faithful.[5]

Can. 1078 In ordinary circumstances

§1 The local Ordinary can dispense his own subjects wherever they are residing, and all who are actually present in his territory, from all impediments of ecclesiastical law, except for those whose dispensation is reserved to the Apostolic See.
§2 The impediments whose dispensation is reserved to the Apostolic See are:
1° the impediment arising from sacred orders or from a public perpetual vow of chastity in a religious institute of pontifical right;
2° the impediment of crime mentioned in Can. 1090.
§3 A dispensation is never given from the impediment of consanguinity in the direct line or in the second degree of the collateral line.

---

3 Cf. J. M. Waterhouse, *The power of the local Ordinary to impose a matrimonial ban* (Catholic University Canon Law Studies 317), Washington, 1952. **4** *Comm* 15 (1983), 227. **5** On this disputed question I take the view outlined by F. X. Urrutia, "Delegation of the executive power of governance" in *Studia Canonica* 19 (1985), 339-55.

180 This canon distinguishes between impediments which are reserved to the Apostolic See and those which are not. Those reserved to the Apostolic See are the impediments arising from sacred orders (Can. 1087), the impediment arising from a public perpetual vow of chastity in a religious institute of pontifical right (Can. 1088), and the impediment of crime (Can. 1090).

181 A dispensation is never given when one party is descended from another in whatever degree, or when they are brother and sister, even of half-blood.

182 The local Ordinary is competent to dispense from the remaining impediments of ecclesiastical law.

Can. 1079 In danger of death

> §1 When danger of death threatens, the local Ordinary can dispense his own subjects, wherever they are residing, and all who are actually present in his territory, both from the form to be observed in the celebration of marriage, and from each and every impediment of ecclesiastical law, whether public or occult, with the exception of the impediment arising from the sacred order of priesthood.
>
> §2 In the same circumstances mentioned in §1, but only for cases in which not even the local Ordinary can be approached, the same faculty of dispensation is possessed by the parish priest, by a properly delegated sacred minister, and by the priest or deacon who assists at the marriage in accordance with Can. 1116 §2.
>
> §3 In danger of death, the confessor has the power to dispense from occult impediments for the internal forum, whether within the act of sacramental confession or outside it.
>
> §4 In the case mentioned in §2, the local Ordinary is considered unable to be approached if he can be reached only by telegram or by telephone.

183 The danger of death may come from various causes, such as serious illness, a dangerous operation, a sentence of death or warfare. In such situations the faculty conferred by the law to dispense from matrimonial impediments is wider than that which is conferred in normal circumstances, presumably because "it contributes to the spiritual welfare of the faithful" (Can. 88). The local Ordinary can dispense his own subjects, wherever they are residing, and all who are actually present in his territory, both from the form to be observed in the celebration of marriage, and from all impediments, public or occult, except the impediment arising from the sacred order of priesthood.

184 Should it be impossible to contact the local Ordinary in the circumstances envisaged above – and this is the case if he can only be contacted by telegram or by telephone (Can. 1079 §4)[6] – the powers granted to the local

---

6 The Church wishes to protect the privacy and confidentiality of the persons concerned.

Ordinary in Can. 1079 §1 are granted to the following: the parish priest (Can. 1108 §1); a properly delegated sacred minister, deacon or priest (ibid.); a priest or deacon lacking delegation who is called upon to be present (Can. 1116 §2).

In danger of death a confessor can dispense from occult impediments in **185** the internal forum, whether within the act of sacramental confession or outside it. Traditionally "occult" in this canon – and in Can. 1080 §1 – is understood in a broad sense, viz., as one that is not publicly known.[7] If a confessor dispenses from an occult impediment in the internal non-sacramental forum, he should record the fact in the secret archive of the Curia (Can. 1082).

Can. 1080 When all has been prepared

§1 Whenever an impediment is discovered after everything has already been prepared for the wedding and the marriage cannot without probable danger of grave harm be postponed until a dispensation is obtained from the competent authority, the power to dispense from all impediments, except those mentioned in Can. 1078 §2 n. 1, is possessed by the local Ordinary and, provided the case is occult, by all those mentioned in Can. 1079 §§2-3, the conditions prescribed therein having been observed.

§2 This power applies also to the validation of a marriage when there is the same danger in delay and there is no time to have recourse to the Apostolic See or, in the case of impediments from which he can dispense, to the local Ordinary.

Two elements are necessary to create the emergency situation envisaged in **186** this canon: when most of the preparations for a marriage are completed it is discovered that there is an impediment (of ecclesiastical law) to the marriage *and* "the marriage cannot without probable danger of grave harm be postponed until a dispensation is obtained from the competent authority". In this situation the following power is conferred by the canon:

a. the local Ordinary can dispense from all impediments except those arising from sacred orders and a perpetual vow of chastity in a religious institute of pontifical right;
b. the parish priest, a sacred minister properly delegated to assist at the marriage, the priest or deacon who assists in accordance with Can. 1116 §2: the above have the same power as the local Ordinary, provided the latter cannot be contacted and the case is not publicly known.[8]

---

7 *The Canon Law: letter and spirit*, n. 2128, footnote 2. **8** L. Chiappetta, *Il codice di diritto canonico*, I, n.3591, 198.

c. the confessor may dispense from occult impediments for the internal forum, whether within the act of sacramental confession or outside it.

187   The same persons have the same powers when it is a matter of validating a marriage already contracted invalidly if there is the same danger in delay and there is no time to have recourse to the Apostolic See or, in the case of impediments from which he can dispense, to the local Ordinary.

Can. 1081 Notification of dispensation

> The parish priest or the priest or deacon mentioned in Can. 1079 §2, is to inform the local Ordinary immediately of a dispensation granted for the external forum, and this dispensation is to be recorded in the marriage register.

188   In the event of the parish priest or the priest or deacon mentioned in Can. 1079 §2 granting a dispensation for the external forum, he must inform the local Ordinary that he has done so. This obligation must be fulfilled immediately. The dispensation must be recorded in the marriage register of the parish where the marriage took place.

Can. 1082 Dispensation of occult impediment

> Unless a rescript of the Penitentiary provides otherwise, a dispensation from an occult impediment granted in the internal non-sacramental forum, is to be recorded in the book to be kept in the secret archive of the curia. No other dispensation for the external forum is necessary if at a later stage the occult impediment becomes public.

189   The Apostolic Penitentiary is competent to grant dispensations for the internal forum.[9] When it dispenses from an occult impediment in the internal non-sacramental forum, a record of the fact is to be kept in the secret archive of the Curia. Such a dispensation is effective and is recognised only within the internal forum. If the impediment becomes public, no other dispensation for the external forum is necessary; it is sufficient to produce the document kept in the secret archive in order for the dispensation from the previously occult impediment and given for the internal forum to be recognised in the external forum.[10]

---

9 *Pastor bonus*, art.118. 10 F.J. Urrutia, "Internal forum – external forum: the criterion of distinction", in *Vatican II: assessment and perspectives*, vol. 1, edited by R. Latourelle, Paulist Press, New York and Mahwah, 1988, 643.

Summary of the above material

What authority has the *local Ordinary* to dispense from impediments? **190**

In normal circumstances   He may dispense from all impediments of eccle- **191**
siastical law with the exception of four: the impediment of orders arising
from diaconate and priesthood, the impediment arising from a public perpetual vow in an institute of pontifical right, and the impediment of crime.

In danger of death   He may dispense from all impediments of ecclesiasti- **192**
cal law, except that arising from priesthood.

When all is prepared   He may dispense from all impediments, except those **193**
arising from diaconate or from priesthood, or from a public perpetual vow.

What authority has a parish priest, a delegated minister (priest/deacon), **194**
or – in their absence – a priest or deacon who is present to dispense from
matrimonial impediments?

In normal circumstances   No authority (Can. 89); **195**

In danger of death   If the local Ordinary cannot be approached, a parish **196**
priest, a delegated minister (priest/deacon), or – in their absence – a priest
or deacon who is present can dispense from all impediments of ecclesiastical law, except that arising from priesthood.

In danger of death a confessor may dispense from occult impediments in **197**
the internal forum. He can use this authority immediately and is not under
duty to inquire if the Ordinary can be reached.

When all is prepared   If the local Ordinary cannot be approached, a parish **198**
priest, a delegated minister (priest/deacon), or – in their absence – a priest
or deacon who is present can dispense from all occult impediments, except
those arising from sacred orders (diaconate or priesthood) or from a public
vow of chastity in an institute of pontifical right.

INDIVIDUAL DIRIMENT IMPEDIMENTS

Can. 1083   Age

§1 A man cannot validly enter marriage before the completion of his
sixteenth year of age, nor a woman before the completion of her fourteenth year.
§2 The Bishops' Conference may establish a higher age for the lawful
celebration of marriage.

199   The impediment of age has a double purpose: firstly, it is designed to ensure that the parties to marriage have the capacity for sexual intercourse; secondly, it is designed to ensure that they have attained the level of discretion necessary to realise what marriage involves.[11] The age fixed in the Code is sixteen years for a man and fourteen years for a woman. The ages fixed in this canon are too low for many countries; this canon should be read in conjunction with Can. 1072 which states that "pastors of souls are to see to it that they dissuade young people from entering marriage before the age customarily accepted in the region".

200   A Bishops' Conference may establish a higher age for the lawful celebration of marriage. The Canadian Bishops' Conference fixed the age for lawful celebration of marriage at eighteen for both parties;[12] the Bishops' Conference for England and Wales decreed that for marriages in their jurisdiction "the civil requirements concerning age are to be observed" (age 16);[13] the Philippines Bishops' Conference decreed that "the age for the licit celebration of marriage shall be twenty [20] years for the bridegroom and eighteen [18] for the bride".[14] This age may not be constituted into an impediment.

201   As noted above (cf. commentary on Can. 1059), catholics are obliged to observe the civil law of the jurisdiction in which their marriage takes place. This includes stipulations regarding age. It should be noted however that the failure to observe the civil law does not affect the canonical validity of the marriage.

Can. 1084   Impotence

> §1 By reason of its very nature, marriage is invalidated by antecedent and perpetual impotence to have sexual intercourse, whether on the part of the man or on that of the woman, whether absolute or relative.
> §2 If the impediment of impotence is doubtful, whether the doubt be one of law or one of fact, the marriage is not to be prevented nor, while the doubt persists, is it to be declared null.
> §3 Without prejudice to the provisions of Can. 1098, sterility neither forbids nor invalidates a marriage.

202   The historical development of the impediment of impotence must be understood in the context of the medieval dispute on the formation of the bond of marriage. Proponents of the *copula* theory regarded impotence as "a *de facto* situation which prevented the actual formation of the marriage, rather than an impediment of law preventing the transferral of rights and obligations

---

11 F.X. Wernz, *Ius decretalium*, IV: *Ius matrimoniale*, 119, n. 319. **12** *Code of Canon Law annotated*, edd. E. Caparro, M. Thériault and J. Thorn, Wilson & Lafleur, Montréal, 1993 (hereafter *Code of Canon Law annotated*), 1327. **13** Ibid., 1337. **14** Ibid., 1404.

which otherwise would have arisen from a valid act of consent".[15] Peter Lombard, who promoted the *consensus* theory, saw impotence as "a vice, lack or defect which vitiates the act of consent by which marriage comes into being".[16] Canonists came to the view that "only perpetual impotence is a clear proof of the nullity of a marriage because it is only perpetual impotence that prevents the ends of marriage from *ever* being attained".[17] In the medical field, impotence is seen as a condition whose origin may be physical or psychological. In the canonical field, however, it is a juridical concept; it consists in "the moral inability to assume rights and obligations to place acts which of themselves are apt for the generation of children" (*actos per se aptos ad prolis generationem*).[18]

Impotence means the inability to perform the sexual act. In canonical   **203** terms, sexual intercourse involves three essential elements: the erection of the penis, at least partial penetration of the vagina[19] and ejaculation within the vagina. It has long been disputed if vasectomised men are canonically impotent or not. The debate took on a special urgency in 1930s when the Nazi regime in Germany imposed sterilisation on certain categories of men. The Holy Office permitted the celebration of marriages involving these men; however the Roman Rota declared them null on the grounds of impotence if they broke down.[20] This debate was resolved by a decree of the Congregation for the Doctrine of the Faith in May 1977; it is now the accepted doctrine that persons who have undergone vasectomy are free to marry.[21]

Impotence renders a marriage invalid only if it is antecedent, perpetual   **204** and certain. It is antecedent if the condition was present at the time of the marriage. If it arises after the marriage has been celebrated, for example as the result of an accident or an illness, it does not affect the validity of the marriage. It is perpetual if it cannot be cured by ordinary means.[22] These are means which do not involve a probable danger to life or a serious threat to the health of the person. The means must also be accessible to the person.

15 K.E. Boccafola, *The requirement of perpetuity for the impediment of impotence* (Pontificia Universitas Gregoriana, Facultas Iuris Canonici, Roma, 1975), 17. **16** Ibid., 26. **17** Ibid., 33. **18** Ibid., 63. **19** For a 1941 decree on this issue, cf. *Leges ecclesiae post codicem editae*, 1, n. 1599, col. 2050. **20** For a detailed account of this debate, cf. A. McGrath, *A controversy concerning male impotence* (Analecta Gregoriana 247), Rome, 1988. **21** CLD 8, 677: "... the Fathers of this Sacred Congregation ... decided that the questions proposed to them must be answered as follows: 1. Whether the impotency which invalidates marriage consists in the incapacity to complete conjugal intercourse which is antecedent, of course, and perpetual, either absolute or relative? 2. Inasmuch as the reply is affirmative, whether for conjugal intercourse the ejaculation of semen elaborated in the testicles is necessarily requisite? To the first question: in the affirmative; to the second: in the negative. **22** For an exposition of the distinction between the concept of ordinary and extraordinary means, cf. B.M. Ashley and K.D. O'Rourke, *Healthcare ethics*, 3rd edition, 380-4 or T. J. O'Donnell, *Medicine and christian morality*, second revised and updated edition 1991, 50-64.

205   Impotence is certain when it is not subject to any serious doubt. If the matter is in doubt "whether the doubt be one of law or one of fact, the marriage is not to be prevented nor, while the doubt persists, is it to be declared null" (Can. 1084 §2).

206   Impotence can be organic or functional. It is organic if it is caused by the absence of, or deformation in, the physical organs required for intercourse. It is functional when the organs are anatomically intact but intercourse is impossible due to psychological or neurological problems.[23] This can arise in the case of paraplegics. Paraplegia (paralysis of the lower extremities of the body resulting from disease or injury to the central nervous system) may render intercourse impossible. Wrenn cites an American canonist to the effect that "about 70% of paraplegics are capable of erection but only 10% are capable of ejaculation".[24]

207   Impotence can be absolute or relative. It is absolute if a person is incapable of sexual intercourse with any partner, for example, a man lacking a penis. It is relative if a person cannot have sexual intercourse with one person but can do so with another.

208   The impediment of impotence is commonly held to be of divine natural law as "marriage and married love are by nature ordered to the procreation and education of children".[25]

209   Can. 1084 §3 refers to sterility, that is, the inability to beget children. Sterility does not forbid marriage nor make it invalid. It can however be the basis of a nullity claim if a person, knowing that he or she was sterile, deceived his or her partner in order to secure that person's consent to marriage (Can. 1098).

210   Although Vatican II stressed the importance of procreation in marriage, it pointed out that "even in cases where despite the intense desire of the spouses there are no children, marriage still retains its character of being a whole manner and communion of life and preserves its value and indissolubility".[26] The Church teaches that "marriage does not confer on spouses the right to have a child, but only the right to perform those acts which are *per se* ordered to procreation".[27] *Donum vitae* continues:

> A true and proper right to a child would be contrary to the child's dignity and nature. The child is not an object to which one has a right, nor can he be considered as an object of ownership: rather, a child is a

---

23 Cf. G. Sheehy, "Male psychical impotence in judicial proceedings" in *The Jurist* 20 (1960), 253-94; R.C. Bauhoff and A. Mendonça, "Psychic impotence" in *Studia Canonica* 24 (1990), 205-40; 293-334. **24** L. Wrenn, *Annulments*, 6th edition, Canon Law Society of America, Washington DC, 1996, 9. Cf. J. Brenkle, *The impediment of male impotence with special application to paraplegia,* Catholic University of America Press, Washington, 1963, 156-7. **25** Fl I, 953, *GS* n. 50; *Comm* 15 (1983), 228. Cf. B. David, *L'impuissance est-elle un empêchement de droit natural ou positif?* (Analecta Gregoriana 220), Rome, 1981. **26** Fl I, 954, *FS* n. 50. **27** *Donum vitae,* n. 8.

gift, "the supreme gift" (*GS* n. 50) and the most gratuitous gift of marriage, and is a living testimony to the mutual giving of his parents.[28]

On the basis of Can. 1084 §2, marriage is permitted even if there is doubt as to the capacity of the parties to consummate their union. If however a marriage breaks down and it was not consummated due to the impotence of one of the parties, either party may petition for the annulment of the marriage on the grounds of impotence. The proofs will consist in the declarations of the parties, testimony of lay witnesses and medical reports (Can. 1680). **211**

In the course of a nullity case it may be established that a marriage was not consummated but it may not be possible to establish the incurability of the condition. When this situation arises, the petitioner may "seek the favour of a dispensation from a ratified and unconsummated marriage" (Can. 1697). **212**

Can. 1085 Existing bond or *ligamen*

§1 A person obliged by the bond of a previous marriage, even if not consummated, invalidly attempts marriage.
§2 Even though the previous marriage is invalid or for any reason dissolved, it is not thereby lawful to contract another marriage before the nullity or the dissolution of the previous one has been established lawfully and with certainty.

A person bound by the bond of a previous marriage is prevented from contracting a second valid marriage as long as his or her original partner is alive. The "bond of marriage" is the relationship brought about between persons who have exchanged valid matrimonial consent. It arises "from the human act by which the partners mutually surrender themselves to each other (and which) for the good of the partners, of the children, and of society ... no longer depends on human decision alone".[29] **213**

Sacramental bond

The bond of marriage formed between persons who are baptised is called a "sacramental bond". This bond cannot be dissolved when it has been contracted between two baptised persons and was subsequently consummated by a sexual act. In certain circumstances - which will be considered below - a marriage may be declared null. A marriage that has not been consummated "can be dissolved by the Roman Pontiff for a just reason, at the request of both parties or of either, even if the other is unwilling" (Can. 1142). **214**

---

28 Ibid. **29** Fl I, 950, *GS* n. 48.

The sacramental bond of marriage ceases only on the death of one of the parties or when a dispensation is granted for non-consummation or dissolution in favour of the faith.

215   The Catholic Church recognises marriages contracted by members of other Churches or ecclesial communities as valid and sacramental. This obtains regardless of the form in which the marriage was celebrated since members of other Churches are not bound by the canonical form (Can. 1117).

216   The status of marriages involving a member of the Orthodox Church is more complex. According to current jurisprudence, "a marriage involving an Orthodox party which would be judged invalid according to the rules of that particular Church will also be invalid in our law".[30] The Orthodox Churches regard a marriage between an Orthodox christian and a member of the reformed Churches as invalid due to defect of form if it is not blessed by an Orthodox priest.[31]

Natural bond

217   The bond of marriage between persons who are not baptised, or between a baptised person and an unbaptised person is called a natural bond. This bond has a sacred character, but it lacks the indissolubility which a sacramental marriage enjoys; in certain circumstances it can be dissolved (Cann. 1142-9).[32]

Defect of form: procedure

218   Certain marriages appear *prima facie* to be invalid due to defect of form, for example, the marriage of a catholic in a registry office. The question as to how the status of such marriages was to be established was raised with the Pontifical Council for the Interpretation of Legislative Texts. The Council was asked if in such cases the documentary process mentioned in Can.1686 must be used, or if a pre-nuptial enquiry would suffice. It replied on 11th July 1984 that the task of establishing the freedom of such persons can be carried out in the pre-nuptial enquiry.[33] In pastoral practice, marriages involving a party whose who was previously married and whose partner is still alive should not be arranged until careful enquiries are made concerning the status of the previous marriage.

Can. 1086 Disparity of cult

§1 A marriage is invalid when one of the two persons was baptised in

---

30 Decision of the Southwark tribunal in *CLSBGI Newsletter* 74 (1988), 55. **31** Ibid. **32** Cf. also commentary below on Privilege of the Faith cases (572-3). **33** AAS 76 (1984), 747.

the catholic Church or received into it and has not by a formal act defected from it, and the other was not baptised.

§2 This impediment is not to be dispensed unless the conditions mentioned in Cann. 1125 and 1126 have been fulfilled.

§3 If at the time the marriage was contracted one party was commonly understood to be baptised, or if his or her baptism was doubtful, the validity of the marriage is to be presumed in accordance with Can. 1060, until it is established with certainty that one party was baptised and the other was not.

This impediment arises when a member of the catholic Church or who has **219** been received into it – and who has not defected from it by a formal act – wishes to marry a person who is not baptised. It reflects the Church's concern for the difficulties which a catholic spouse may encounter in practising his or her faith or in having the children of the marriage baptised and raised in the catholic faith.

The concept of "defecting from the Church by a formal act" has been **220** introduced into the present Code. It remains to be clarified what kind of action would constitute such a defection.[34] Most canonists agree that leaving the catholic Church and joining another Church would constitute "defecting from the Church by a formal act".[35] It is not enough for a person to lapse from the practice of the catholic faith.

For the impediment to exist, the non-catholic party must either never **221** have received any baptism or have received one that was invalid. Catechumens come into this category.[36]

It is important to distinguish two situations: the marriage of a Catholic **222** and a non-baptised person and an inter-Church marriage, that is, a marriage between a Catholic and a baptised member of another Church or ecclesial communion. Although in the past it was customary to baptise conditionally members of other Christian Churches who were being received into the catholic Church, this is no longer done.[37] The *Ecumenical directory* (1967) recommended that "ecumenical commissions should hold discussions [regarding mutual recognition of baptism] with churches or councils of churches in various regions and, where convenient, come to a common agreement in this matter".[38]

---

34 *Comm* 10 (1978), 96-7. Cf. V. De Paolis, "Alcune annotazioni circa la formula 'actu formali ab Ecclesia catholica deficere'" in *Periodica* 84 (1995), 579-608. **35** Cf. L. Chiappetta, *Il codice di diritto canonico*, II, n. 3617, 207.   **36** *Comm* 9 (1977), 363. **37** The *Ecumenical Directory* (1967) stated: "Indiscriminate conditional baptism of all who desire full communion with the Catholic Church cannot be approved"(Fl I, 489 n. 14). **38** Fl I, 16, n. 16. For example, in Ireland meetings between the principal Churches led to the issuing of a joint statement: "As a result of joint discussions already held, we specifically wish it to be understood by our clergy and people that baptism administered in accordance with the liturgical rites and prescriptions of the Church of Ireland, the

223   There are some "christian" bodies which do not practice baptism, e.g., the Quakers. When dealing with members of smaller sects, it is necessary to establish whether they baptise their members and their form of baptism.

224   If, before a marriage takes place, there is a doubt as to the fact or validity of baptism, a dispensation from this impediment should be sought as a precaution.

225   This impediment is of ecclesiastical law and can be dispensed. The local Ordinary is not to grant the dispensation unless the conditions laid down in Can. 1125 are fulfilled:

> 1° the catholic party is to declare that he or she is prepared to remove the dangers of defecting from the faith, and is to make a sincere promise to do all in his or her power in order that all the children be baptised and brought up in the catholic Church;
>
> 2° the other party is to be informed in good time of these promises to be made by the catholic party, so that it is certain that he or she is truly aware of the promise and of the obligation of the catholic party;
>
> 3° both parties are to be instructed about the purposes and essential properties of marriage, which are not to be excluded by either contractant.

226

If at the time the marriage was contracted one party was believed to be baptised, or if his or her baptism was doubtful, the validity of the marriage is presumed in accordance with Can. 1060 until it is established with certainty that the person concerned was not baptised. This impediment ceases on the reception of baptism by the unbaptised person.

Can. 1087 Sacred orders

Those who are in sacred orders invalidly attempt marriage.

227   The tradition of priestly celibacy has its roots in the practice of perfect continence that was observed by ordained ministers in the early Church.[39] The Second Lateran Council (1139) enacted the first general law making orders a diriment impediment to marriage. Stickler writes:

> A special importance attaches to the Council of Pisa (1135), attended by many prelates from the whole of Europe and under the presidency

Methodist Church in Ireland, and the Presbyterian Church in Ireland is to be presumed valid. This prescription should not be set aside unless there is evidence of departure from the prescribed Church practice in a given case or by a particular minister" (*Directory for ecumenism in Ireland*, 1976). **39** Cf. C. Cochini, *The apostolic origins of priestly celibacy*, Ignatius Press, San Francisco, 1990; R. Cholij, "The *lex continentiae* and the impediment of orders" in *Studia Canonica* 27 (1993), 217-60.

of the pope. They declared notably, and for the first time explicitly, that a marriage contracted by a bishop, a deacon, a sub-deacon, a cleric in regular orders or a monk, was not a marriage, *matrimonium non esse*. This ruling was reiterated and extended to nuns by the Second Lateran Council (1139).[40] Thus *ordo* [orders] as well as *votum* [a vow] was proclaimed as an obstacle invalidating marriage.[41]

This discipline was confirmed by the Council of Trent[42] and by the 1917 Code of Canon Law (c. 1072). **228**

In 1972 Pope Paul VI restored the permanent diaconate in the Latin Church.[43] A short time later he stated that "the special consecration of celibacy observed for the sake of the kingdom of heaven and its obligation for candidates to the priesthood and for unmarried candidates for the diaconate are indeed linked with the diaconate".[44] Candidates for the diaconate and the priesthood in the Latin rite promise "as a sign of [their] interior dedication to Christ, to remain celibate for the sake of the kingdom and in lifelong service to God and mankind".[45] The impediment of orders arises on the reception of diaconate (Can. 266 §1). **229**

The discipline regarding permanent married deacons who wish to re-marry after the death of their spouse was considered at great length by the Revision Commission. *Ad pascendum* had decreed that "in accordance with the traditional discipline of the Church, a married deacon who has lost his wife cannot enter a new marriage".[46] The Revision Commission proposed that permanent deacons who were widowed would not be bound by this impediment.[47] The issue was raised again at the Plenary Meeting of the Revision Commission in October 1981.[48] In the event the Code remained silent on the matter; hence the current law is as stated in *Ad pascendum:* a permanent deacon whose wife dies must – if he wishes to remarry – request a dispensation from the Holy See (Can. 1078 §2, 1°; cf. also Can. 291). **230**

The dispensation from the impediment arising from the diaconate is reserved to the Apostolic See (Can. 1078 §2, 1°). In danger of death it can be **231**

---

40 Cf. Can. 7, cf. *Decrees of the Ecumenical councils* (ed. Tanner), I, 198. **41** A. M. Stickler, "The evolution of the discipline of celibacy in the western Church from the end of the patristic era to the Council of Trent" in *Priesthood and celibacy*, Ancora, Milan and Rome, 1970, 548-9. Schillebeeckx comments: "The eastern church chooses its bishops almost entirely from monks; moreover, the eastern as well as the western church denies marriage to those already ordained who continue to exercise their ministry ... In this respect the attitude of the universal church is uniform" (*Clerical celibacy under fire*, Sheed & Ward, London, 1968, 117). **42** *Decrees of the ecumenical councils* (ed. Tanner), II, 755. **43** *Sacrum Diaconatus Ordinem*, DOL 2533-46. **44** *Ad pascendum*, Fl I, 439. **45** *De ordinatione episcopi, presbyterorum et diaconorum*, second editio typica, n. 200. **46** Fl I, 439, Norm 6. **47** *Comm* 9 (1977), 365; 15 (1983), 229-30. **48** Pontificium Consilium de Legum Textibus Interpretatandis, *Congregatio plenaria diebus 20-29 octobris 1981 habita*, Typis Polyglottis Vaticanis, 1991 (hereafter *Congregatio plenaria*), 138-49.

dispensed by a parish priest, a properly delegated minister, and by the priest or deacon who assists at the marriage in accordance with Can. 1116 §2. However even in danger of death, the dispensation from the impediment arising from priesthood is reserved to the Apostolic See (Can. 1079 §1).

Can. 1088 Public vow of chastity

> Those who are bound by a public perpetual vow of chastity in a religious institute invalidly attempt marriage.

232   A vow of chastity gives rise to this impediment if three conditions are fulfilled: the vow must be public, perpetual, and be taken in a religious institute. A vow is *public* "if it is accepted in the name of the Church by a lawful Superior" (Can. 1192 §1); it is *perpetual* if it is taken for life. It must be *taken in a religious institute*. Therefore a vow of chastity taken in a secular institute does not constitute an impediment to marriage.[49] If the institute in which the vow was taken is "of pontifical right", dispensation from it is reserved to the Apostolic See (Can. 1078 §2, 1°); if it is "of diocesan right", the impediment can be dispensed by the local Ordinary. When a religious is also a cleric, there is a double impediment. A dispensation of this impediment automatically involves the loss of the religious state.[50]

Can. 1089 Abduction

> No marriage can exist between a man and a woman who has been abducted, or at least detained, with a view to contracting a marriage with her, unless the woman, after she has been separated from her abductor and established in a safe and free place, chooses marriage of her own accord.

233   While this impediment seldom arises today, historically it was very important. In Carolingian France, for example, abduction was one of the four crimes involving blood law.[51] The concern was not simply for the freedom of the woman; she was often a willing victim! The difficulty arose from the fact that if she was already promised to another man, he was entitled to have her as his wife. If he did not wish to marry her, the woman's relations still had the right to give her in marriage to anyone they liked. The concern of

---

49 *Comm* 15 (1983), 230. **50** L. Chiappetta, *Il codice di diritto canonico*, II, n. 3626, 210. Chiappetta comments that what is at issue here is a dispensation from the vow; when the vow ceases to bind, the impediment ceases automatically. **51** G. Duby, *The knight, the lady and the priest* (Penguin, London, 1985), 38.

the law was "to prevent the defrauded family of the intended bridegroom from attacking the family of the abductor".[52] The purpose of the impediment is to ensure the freedom of the abducted person.

The canon states that marriage cannot take place between a man and a   **234**
woman who has been abducted, or at least detained, with a view to contracting a marriage with her, unless, after she has been separated from abductor and established in a safe and free place, the woman chooses marriage of her own accord. The impediment does not affect a man who has been abducted.

Can. 1090 Crime

§1 One who, with a view to entering marriage with a particular person, has killed that person's spouse, or his or her own spouse, invalidly attempts this marriage.
§2 They also invalidly attempt marriage with each other who, by mutual physical or moral action, brought about the death of either's spouse.

This canon envisages three situations. The first is when a person murders   **235**
his or her own spouse in order to marry another person. The murder that is the cause of the impediment must actually have been carried out, though it is irrelevant whether it was carried out personally or through the agency of another person. The second situation is when a person murders another person's spouse in order to marry that person. The third arises when two people conspire jointly to bring about the death of the spouse of either, even if marriage is not the motive of the murder. In the latter case, the impediment arises from the intent to murder, not from the intent to marry.

This impediment is of ecclesiastical law only. The impediment never   **236**
ceases of itself because it arises from a fact. Dispensation from the impediment is reserved in normal circumstances to the Apostolic See (Can. 1078 §1, 2°). It can be dispensed in the case of danger of death (Can. 1079 §1), and, when he cannot be approached, by the parish priest, a curate, and by the priest or deacon mentioned in Can. 1116 §2. If the impediment is discovered after everything has been prepared, it can be dispensed by the local Ordinary, and, if it is occult, by those clerics mentioned in Can. 1079 §2.

Can. 1091 Consanguinity

§1 Marriage is invalid between those related by consanguinity in all degrees of the direct line, whether ascending or descending, legitimate or natural.

---

52 Duby, ibid.

§2 In the collateral line, it is invalid up to the fourth degree inclusive.
§3 The impediment of consanguinity is not multiplied.
§4 A marriage is never to be permitted if a doubt exists as to whether the parties are related by consanguinity in any degree of the direct line, or in the second degree of the collateral line.

237 The impediment of consanguinity is based on blood relationship. The restrictions contained in the law reflect a concern regarding the genetic implications of marriage between persons who are related by close family ties. The canon also reflects a concern for the sanctity of marriage. The terminology used to describe blood relationship is found in Can. 108. Consanguinity is the natural relationship between two persons based on blood; they share a common ancestry and, to that extent, the same blood; hence the expression "blood relations". This relationship is computed in lines and degrees. The line of consanguinity refers to the series of persons from whom the persons concerned are descended. A man is related to his parents or grandparents in the direct line since he is descended directly from them. When persons are descended from the same common stock but not from each other, the line of consanguinity is collateral. Siblings in the same family, for example, are related to each other by consanguinity in the collateral line. This applies also to cousins, uncles and aunts, nephews and nieces. The degree of consanguinity refers to the closeness or distance between two persons in either the direct or the collateral line.

238 To determine the relationship between two persons who are related in the direct line of consanguinity, one counts the number of generations involved or else the number of persons, not reckoning the common ancestor. A woman is related to her father in the first degree of the direct line; she is related to her grandfather in the second degree of the direct line (cf. Can. 108 §2).

239 In order to compute the relationship between two persons who are related by consanguinity in the collateral line, it is necessary to count the number of persons in the direct lines of both persons and omit the common ancestor. Hence a brother and sister are related by consanguinity in the second degree; a niece and uncle are related by consanguinity in the third degree; first cousins are related by consanguinity in the fourth degree.

240 According to Can. 1091, marriage is invalid between those related by consanguinity in all degrees of the direct line. It is also invalid between those related up to the fourth degree of the collateral line (i.e., first cousins). Consanguinity is based on descent from a common ancestor, for example, the same mother or the same father or both. A half-blood relationship, that is, between a man and woman who have only one ancestor in common, alters neither the computation of degrees nor the existence of the impediment. A man is related to his half-sister in the collateral line in the second degree, and hence he cannot marry her. It is to prevent this situation that the

Church recommends the use of the more detailed form of the baptismal certificate when pre-marriage papers are being prepared.[53]

The rule that where there is a doubt of fact a dispensation can be given **241** (Can. 14) does not obtain in the case of the impediment of consanguinity if the doubt concerns the possibility of a relationship in the direct line to any degree or in the second degree of the collateral line (Can. 1078 §3). The local Ordinary may dispense from the third degree of the collateral line, but in practice this dispensation is given only for very grave reasons.[54] Dispensations involving the fourth degree of the collateral line, that is, marriage between first cousins, is given more readily. When requests for dispensations in this area arise, the parties concerned should obtain medical advice.

Can. 1092 Affinity

Affinity in any degree of the direct line invalidates marriage.

Whereas the relationship of consanguinity arises from descent from a com- **242** mon ancestor, or common ancestors, the impediment of affinity arises from marriage. So the relationship of affinity arises between a man and the blood relations of his wife, and vice versa. In non-technical language they are "in-laws".

St Paul castigated the Corinthians for their toleration of a man living **243** with his father's wife [that is, his stepmother], something which "must be unparalleled even among pagans" (1 Cor 5:1). His attitude reflects the attitude of Roman law to such marriages. The detailed regulations of Roman law were accepted into the canon law. In the medieval period the impediment arose from intercourse (*ex coitu*), not from marriage.

Medieval canonists and theologians held that the impediment was of **244** natural or divine law; they made an exception however in the case of a man who wished to marry the widow of a brother who died without offspring.[55] The authority in the *Corpus iuris canonici* was a letter of Innocent III, *Deus qui Ecclesiam.*[56] In this letter Innocent gave a ruling to the hierarchy of Livonia that pagans who, in obedience to the law of Moses, had married the widows of brothers who had died without children were not to be separated from their wives on reception into the Church. Their marriages were to be

---

53 For details of an exceptional dispensation in a case involving a half-brother and half-sister, cf. X. Ochoa, *Leges ecclesiae post codicem editae*, V, n. 4488, col. 7288. **54** Cf. Instruction of Sacred Congregation of the Sacraments issued in 1931 (AAS 23 (1931), 413; CLD 1, 514-6. **55** J.J. Scarisbrick, *Henry VIII*, Eyre Methuen, London, 1968, 173. In this work, the author outlines the canonical case made by the King for the nullity of his marriage to Catherine of Aragon and the reasons why it failed (163-197). For a fuller treatment of this celebrated case, cf. H. A. Kelly, *The matrimonial trials of Henry VIII*, Stanford University, Stanford, CA, 1976. **56** Cf. Migne, 216, cols. 1183ff.

declared valid.[57] It was on the basis of this authority that Henry VIII's petition to have his marriage declared null failed.[58]

245   The 1917 Code changed the basis of the impediment to a valid, ratified marriage, even if not consummated (c. 97). The impediment rendered invalid marriage in any degree of the direct line and in the collateral line to the second degree inclusively (c. 1077); this meant, for example, that a man could not marry his deceased brother's wife or a woman her deceased sister's husband. It was possible however to dispense the impediment.

246   The relationship of affinity arises only between a man and the blood relations of his wife, and between a woman and the blood relations of her husband (Can. 109). Can. 1092 states that the impediment of affinity arises between a party and all those related to his or her spouse in any degree of the direct line; it arises between a man and his wife's mother, or between a woman and her husband's father. It also arises between a woman and her husband's son (by another woman) and between a man and his wife's daughter (by another man). The impediment no longer arises in the collateral line, that is, for example, between a man and his deceased brother's wife.[59]

247   The impediment is of ecclesiastical law only and applies to "those who were baptised in the catholic Church or [were] received into it" (Can. 11).

248   It may be helpful to trace the relationships mentioned above in the following family tree. John and Mary Kelly are the common ancestors and the relationships between the various parties arise from this fact. Following this schema, Can. 1091 means that marriage between father/daughter (2-4) is invalid; marriage between brother/sister, uncle/niece (1-4), first cousins (3-4) is invalid. Following this schema, Can. 1092 means that the impediment of affinity arises between a father-in-law and his daughter-in-law (1-3°); no impediment arises between a man and his sister-in-law or between a woman and her brother-in-law (1-2°).

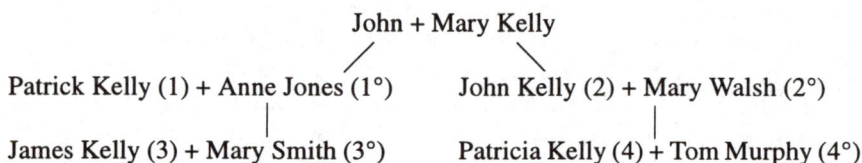

John + Mary Kelly

/ \

Patrick Kelly (1) + Anne Jones (1°)   John Kelly (2) + Mary Walsh (2°)

| |

James Kelly (3) + Mary Smith (3°)   Patricia Kelly (4) + Tom Murphy (4°)

Can. 1093 Public propriety

> The impediment of public propriety arises when a couple live together after an invalid marriage, or from a notorious or public concubinage. It invalidates marriage in the first degree of the direct line between the man and those related by consanguinity to the woman, and vice versa.

57 Cf. J. J. Scarisbrick, *Henry VIII*, 178. 58 Scarisbrick writes: "Innocent was a catastrophe for Henry" (op. cit., 178). 59 *Comm* 9 (1977), 368.

Whereas the impediment of affinity arises from marriage, the impediment **249** of affinity arises from situations which are closely related to marriage. There are two situations where it arises: firstly, when a man and a woman have lived together after an invalid marriage, for example, a civil marriage which is invalid due to defect of form and, secondly, from a notorious or public concubinage. "Concubinage" is a sexual relationship which has a degree of stability. The effect of the impediment of public propriety is that on the break-up of these relationships, the man cannot validly marry his former partner's mother or daughter and the woman cannot marry her former partner's father or son.

Can. 1094 Adoption

> Those who are legally related by reason of adoption cannot validly marry if their relationship is in the direct line or in the second degree of the collateral line.

The 1917 Code had no impediment of its own arising from legal adoption. It **250** stated that those who by the civil law are declared incapable of marriage on account of legal adoption cannot under canon law validly contract marriage (c. 1080). The Revision Commission decided that it was no longer appropriate to "canonise" the civil law and it introduced its own norms.[60]

Under the current canon law marriage is invalid between an adopted **251** person and his or her adoptive parent. It is also invalid between those related in the second degree of the collateral line, that is, a brother or sister. An adopted daughter cannot marry a boy adopted by the same parents even if he is not her blood-brother; neither can she marry the natural son of her adoptive parents.[61] An adopted daughter is not barred from marriage to her parents' brothers, viz., her uncles, or from marriage to the children of her aunts or uncles, viz., her first cousins.

---

60 *Comm* 15 (1983), 230. Cf. J. Prader, "De impedimento matrimoniale adoptionis et tutelae in iure condito et in iure condendo" in *Periodica* 65 (1976), 141-58. **61** Marriage between an adopted son and the illegitimate daughter of his adoptive father is invalid (E. Garcia, "Impediment of legal adoption" in *Bolletín ecclesiastico de Filipinas* 70 (1994), 778-9).

4

Matrimonial consent

Can. 1095 Inability to give valid consent for psychological reasons

The following are incapable of contracting marriage :

1° those who lack sufficient use of reason;
2° those who suffer from a grave lack of discretion of judgement concerning the essential matrimonial rights and obligations to be mutually given and accepted.
3° those who because of causes of a psychological nature, are unable to assume the essential obligations of marriage.

252 Most of the canons in this section correspond to canons in the 1917 Code; this is not the case with Can. 1095. It is based on jurisprudence which developed from natural law principles,[1] reflecting "a developing understanding of the nature of marital consent".[2] The Revision Commission stated that "although the principles regarding the incapacity to give valid marriage consent are contained implicitly in the current law, it was seen as advantageous that [they] be expressed more clearly in the new law".[3]

Can. 1095, 1° Lack of the sufficient use of reason[4]

253 Can. 1095, 1° deals with those who are incapable of contracting marriage "due to a lack of the sufficient use of reason". In canon law a person is presumed to have reached the use of reason at the age of seven (Can. 97 §2); hence it is unusual for an adult to lack sufficient use of reason. The "lack of sufficient use of reason" may arise from an habitual mental state, such as severe mental handicap; but those who habitually lack the use of reason seldom undertake marriage. It is more common in practice for this state to

---

1 A. Mendonça, "The incapacity to contract marriage: canon 1095" in *Studia Canonica* 19 (1985), 260.   **2** J.H. Provost, "Canon 1095: past, present, future" in *The Jurist* 54 (1994), 83. Cf. P. Gasparri, *Tractatus canonicus de matrimonio* 1932, vol. II, n. 783. **3** *Comm* 3 (1971), 77. Translation is by R. Burke (cf. below). **4** For an English translation of the cases given as sources to Can.1095, 1° – along with a commentary – in *Codex Iuris Canonici fontium annotatione et indice analytico-alphabetico auctus* (1989), cf. J.H. Provost, "Cases: Sources for canon 1095, 1°" in *The Jurist* 54 (1994), 257-333; 629-747.

arise as a temporary condition, for example, when persons who are normally *sui compos* are so affected by drug or alcohol consumption that, at the moment of consent, they do not know where they are or what they are doing.[5]

Lack of the use of reason renders marriage null; the use of reason alone however is not sufficient for valid matrimonial consent. Canon law has fixed the age for marriage at sixteen for a man and fourteen for a woman to ensure that those entering marriage have reached puberty and have attained the maturity of judgement necessary to realise what is involved in marriage.[6] It is accepted in Rotal jurisprudence that "the only measure of sufficient consent is the discretion of judgement proportionate to marriage".[7] For this reason, some commentators feel that Can. 1095, 1° is unnecessary: **254**

> For the sake of aesthetics, it would have been much better to use the text of Can. 1095, 2° alone, i.e., "who lacks the discretion of judgement sufficient or proportionate to the rights and obligations of marriage [is incapable]". The existence of Can. 1095, 1° does not harm anything, but it is contained already in Can. 1095, 2°.[8]

Can. 1095, 2° Grave lack of discretion of judgement (see page 96)

Although lack of due discretion does not appear in the 1917 Code of Canon Law, the concept was well known in the canonical and theological traditions. St Thomas, for example, had taught that more discretion was required for religious profession than for marriage.[9] Commentators on the Code refer to *"discretio seu maturitas iudicii"* (discretion or maturity of judgement) as something that affects a person's capacity to understand what marriage means. Gasparri includes it in his commentary on c. 1082 which deals with ignorance about marriage.[10] In a 1919 decision c. Prior, lack of due discretion was introduced into rotal jurisprudence as a ground of nullity;[11] in the 1940s Wynen held that "evaluative knowledge" was necessary for valid matrimonial consent[12] and in the decades that followed the understanding of discretion continued to develop in jurisprudence.[13] This development was possible **255**

---

5 For an example of a case heard on the grounds of lack of the use of reason, cf. decision c. Egan, 2 April 1981, SRR decis. 73 (1981), 210-7. **6** F.X. Wernz, *Ius decretalium*, IV, *Ius matrimoniale*, n. 319, 119. **7** Decision c. Sabattani, 24 February 1961, *SRR decis.* 53 (1961), 118, n. 4. **8** R. Burke, "Canon 1095, nn. 1-2" in *Incapacity for marriage*, 125. **9** III, suppl., q.58, a.5, ad.1. **10** *Tractatus canonicus de matrimonio*, 1932, II, n. 783; cf. Wernz, Vidal and Aguirre, *Ius canonicum*, V, *Ius matrimoniale*, ed. 1946, 588, n. 456; I. Chelodi, *Ius canonicum de matrimonio*, 1947, 132, n. 109. **11** SRR decis. 11 (1919), 174, n. 6. **12** SRR decis. 33 (1941), 144-68. **13** A. Mendonça, "The incapacity to contract marriage: canon 1095" in *Studia Canonica* 19 (1985), 267-78.

because incapacity to consent invalidates marriage by virtue of the natural law.[14] Its inclusion as a ground of nullity in the Code will give further impetus to its development. In his Address to the Roman Rota in 1984 Pope John Paul II stated:

> There still remain canons of great importance in matrimonial law, however, which have been necessarily formulated in a generic way and which await further determination, to which especially the expert jurisprudence of the Rota could make a valuable contribution. I am thinking, for example, of the determination of the grave lack of discretion ... mentioned in Can. 1095.[15]

256   Since an exposition of this ground involves the use of qualifying adjectives such as "due", "sufficient" or "proportionate" it is important to establish a number of principles. Since "all can contract marriage who are not prohibited by law" (Can. 1058), the Church cannot require a level of maturity which would impede a substantial number of persons from entering marriage.[16] After all, as Haughton observed, "most couples are nowhere near emotionally mature when they marry... Either or both are likely to be in some degree still dependent or 'un-grown-up'".[17] What the Church requires is that parties have reached a level of maturity proportionate to the seriousness of the commitment involved. Haughton's comment highlights another issue, viz., the meaning of maturity. Versaldi observes that the word does not have the same meaning in canon law as it has in psychology:

> In psychology, maturity is understood to be the end-point of human development: an individual is conscious and free in what he/she does in conformity with his/her ideals ... In canon law, however, maturity is the minimal starting-point necessary both to intend and to implement the object of matrimonial consent, even when difficulties and obstacles create conditions of distress because of bad will ... or even if there are unconscious conflicts in the parties.[18]

257   The maturity required in those entering marriage relates specifically to "the essential matrimonial rights and obligations to be mutually given and

---

14 Decision c. Pinto, October 28, 1976 in SRR decis. 68 (1976), 384-5. **15** *Papal allocutions to the Roman Rota*, 185, n. 7. **16** O. Fumagalli Carulli, *Intelletto e volontà nel consenso matrimoniale in diritto canonico*, Vita e Pensiero, Milan, 1974, 285, n. 149. **17** R. Haughton, "Growth in marriage" in J. Marshall (ed.), *The future of christian marriage*, G. Chapman, London, Dublin and Melbourne, 1969, 86. **18** "The dialogue between psychological science and canon law" in *Incapacity for marriage*, 118. Cf. Address of Pope John Paul II to the Roman Rota in 1987 in *Papal allocutions to the Roman Rota*, 194, n. 6.

accepted".[19] The fact that a person is able to fulfil obligations in commercial or professional life is not of itself proof of capacity to appreciate the true significance of marriage.[20]

258 The canonical concept of lack of due discretion is separate from ignorance (Can. 1096) and error about marriage (Can. 1099). In a recent judgement Pompedda outlined its essential elements: "sufficient intellectual understanding of marriage (1); sufficient critical judgement about marriage in itself, the reasons for getting married or the personal implications of getting married (2); sufficient internal freedom to weigh up the reasons for and against marriage, and to overcome internal impulses"(3).[21]

259 Those entering marriage must have an understanding of the essential elements that constitute marriage; they must know that it involves a permanent partnership between a man and a woman and which is characterised by a fundamental equality (Can. 1135); moreover they must know that it is ordered to the procreation of children and involves "some form of sexual co-operation" (Can. 1096). O'Neill puts it as follows: "Discretion must include conceptual or abstract thinking: the ability to grasp such concepts as right and duty, permanence, and exclusive sexual partnership in its unitive and procreative aspects; in a word, all that pertains to the essence of marriage. It would not be necessary that a person should be able to express these ideas in precise language, but the ideas must exist".[22]

260 The discretion necessary for matrimonial consent includes the ability to assess the consequences of marriage and a realisation of the implications it will have for each of the parties. One of the most important prerequisites for marriage is the ability to separate from parents. This is spelt out in the Scriptures: "This is why a man leaves his father and mother and joins himself to his wife, and they become one body" (Gen 2:24). Stankiewicz, in a Rotal decision, held that the abnormal attachment of a man to his mother prevented him from developing the critical faculty which would enable him to appreciate the practical implications of marriage.[23]

261 In order to grasp the covenantal or mutual nature of marriage, they must have overcome "the immaturity of egocentricity".[24] O'Neill writes: "[Discretion] must involve ... the ability to overcome the immaturity of egocentricity, to have a sensitivity for the rights and needs of others, the ability to adjust one's life and behaviour to meet these needs, the basic ability to see things from the other's point of view."[25]

---

19 The nature of marriage was considered above in relation to Can. 1055 §1; it will be considered below in relation to Can. 1095, 3°. **20** Decision c. Anné, 22 July 1969 in SRR decis. 61 (1969), 865, n. 4. Serrano writes that capacity for marriage "is a unique capacity" ("Suggestions for the interpretation of canon 1095, 2°" in *CLSGBI Newsletter* 93 (1993), 26). **21** 14 November 1991 in SRR decis. 83 (1991), 728, n. 4. **22** "A basic look at lack of due discretion" in *CLSGBI Newsletter* 33 (1977), 43. **23** 11 July 1985 in SRR decis. 77 (1985), 354-63. **24** O'Neill, 43. **25** Ibid.

262   Since marriage is fundamentally relational, the capacity of those entering marriage to grasp the relational nature of marriage is fundamental. O'Neill observes that "it is not simply intelligence or a high IQ that leads to the acquisition of such concepts but progress in experience that comes naturally with the passing of the years".[26] In the area of moral development, authors acknowledge that an understanding of moral principles and values is not sufficient for an adolescent to develop into a moral person; empathy is also important. Hence "being a moral person means not only being someone who understands, but also someone who feels, and ... this experience must be accorded significant weight when coming to understand the moral life".[27] The capacity to empathise with another person, to identify with him or her, to see life from his or her perspective is essential not only for moral sensitivity and moral decisions; it is an important component in the awareness which a person brings to the decision to marry; it allows the person to grasp the human implications of the decision for him– or herself and for the partner. A person who has not grasped what it means to be a friend, to care for a person, to be a person-in-relationship will be out of his or her depth when deliberating on an irrevocable covenant in which a man and a woman mutually give and accept one another for the purpose of establishing a marriage (cf. Can. 1057 §2).

263   Matrimonial consent is an act of the will (Can. 1057 §2). The capacity of a person to consent is normally assured by the proper functioning of the intellect, as outlined above. However, discretion for marriage also involves internal or psychological freedom. This is not the absence of internal pressures – these are always present to some degree; rather it is the ability of the person, notwithstanding such pressures, to choose between alternative courses of action. A person who is sufficiently self-possessed to be able to weigh up the reasons for and against a particular course of action can act with freedom.

264   Internal freedom also concerns the ability to "take the plunge", to make a decision. There are, for example, people who are intelligent and who have experience of life and relationships but who are paralysed by doubt when faced with a decision or commitment:

> The obsessive or compulsive individual most strikingly illustrates this point since he cannot make a choice in spite of having reviewed every issue a number of times and in great detail. Such decisions and commitments are impossible for him because of his need for absolute guarantees and certainties regarding the consequences of his actions. As a result these individuals are forced to make decisions impulsively or only when external forces compel them to overcome the enormous

---

26 Ibid. **27** C. M. Shelton, *Morality of the heart*, Crossroad, New York, 1990, 61.

anxieties implicit in making the wrong choice. When such decisions turn out to be wrong they cannot take responsibility for them since they must insist that the decision was forced on them by others. Thus, every decision is a conditional one, lacking full commitment and resolution and rarely based on positive issues of love, intimacy or care.[28]

The maturity necessary to make a free and informed judgement about marriage to a particular person at a particular time requires more than intellectual gifts. In assessing if a person had the capacity to make such a commitment, judges must take into account "not only the intellectual and cognitive capacities of the individuals involved, but also their emotional and psychic integrity".[29] The process by which a person attains a sufficient degree of personal integration is complex. One psychologist has written: **265**

> During the teenage years particularly, physical, intellectual, emotional and spiritual development occurs in a pronounced fashion. Physical maturity refers ... specifically to the process of reproduction – puberty. A child begins to reason at a very early age but peaks intellectually at fifteen or sixteen years. The emotions vary in quality and quantity. Emotional maturity is the last state to be arrived at and many never fully reach it.[30]

When a couple come to arrange their marriage and they are over the ages fixed in Can. 1083 – and even more so if they are at the age when most couples marry in their region (Can. 1072) – it is presumed that they have sufficient maturity for marriage, unless they have shown by their behaviour that they are irresponsible and unreliable. This presumption also holds when a party applies for a declaration of nullity on the grounds of lack of due discretion (cf. Can. 1060). Experience shows however that the presumption or appearance of discretion is not always justified. Chronological age is an indicator of personal maturity, not a guarantee. The process of growth towards maturity may be delayed by various factors and circumstances, such as youthfulness, educational deprivation, low intelligence, emotional deprivation and lack of experience.[31] Shelton gives some examples: "Child abuse and domestic violence can, for example, foster in children such deep-rooted emotional reactions – like the inability to trust, character disorders, and crippled emotional lives – that one's heart is forever compromised".[32]   **266**

It is necessary to presume that those mentioned above have sufficient maturity of judgement to give valid consent when they present themselves   **267**

---

28 L. Salzman, "Commitment to and in marriage" in the *Catholic Lawyer* 21 (1975), 165. 29 Ibid., 163. 30 Dr P. Walsh, "Adolescent judgement concerning marriage" (1982), unpublished paper. 31 Cf. decision c. Mc Grath, 17 October 1989, *Matrimonial Decisions of Great Britain and Ireland* 26 (1990), 64, n. 11. 32 *Morality of the heart*, 86.

for marriage and so lack of discretion must be proven when either party seeks a declaration of nullity on that ground. Various psychological states may be adduced as the source of lack of due discretion: mental illnesses such as schizophrenia,[33] personality disorders,[34] and emotional immaturity.[35] Regardless of the cause, it is essential to determine in each case the effects of the psychological condition on the capacity of the person to consent to marriage. Burke concludes: "Schizophrenia in its fundamental characteristic, the loss of personal unity, prevents the unitary action of intellect and will in the practical judgement of marriage consent, the discretion of judgement proportionate to marriage ... The degree to which schizophrenia causes lack of discretion of judgement depends on the stage at which the illness has arrived".[36]

268   The same author states as a general principle that "a person who has attained a certain age when ordinarily this discretion of judgement for marriage is present and yet does not enjoy the said discretion, either temporarily in the moment of consent or as a habitual condition, must suffer from some pathology, temporary or chronic".[37] "Pathology" in this context must be understood in a canonical rather than in a medical or psychological sense.[38]

269   There is however a difficulty in this area: how can a Court judge whether a person lacked due discretion if there is no objective yard-stick to measure the degree of maturity that is necessary?[39] Sabattani resolved this difficulty as follows:

> I thus propose that the "dynamic criterion" be adopted in the place of the static criterion. That means: I do not know if this particular consent has the sufficient and necessary weight to be valid; I do not have the unit of measure. I can, however, try to see how this consent was produced, what its components were, if in the "assembly line" there was a faulty manoeuvre, an inadmissible omission. Thus, without knowing its objective weight, I can declare that this product is not legitimate because the forces which produced it ... were not the normal ones.[40]

---

33 R. L. Burke, *Lack of due discretion of judgement because of schizophrenia: doctrine and recent rotal jurisprudence* (Analecta Gregoriana 237), Rome, 1986. **34** A. Mendonça, "The effects of personality disorders on matrimonial consent" in *Studia Canonica* 21 (1987), 85-105. **35** J. McAreavey, *Emotional immaturity and marriage*, Rome, 1979. Cf. E. Colagiovanni, "Immaturità: per un approccio interdisciplinare alla comprensione ed applicazione del Can. 1095, 2° e 3°" in *Monitor ecclesiasticus* 113 (1988), 337-59; *L'immaturità psico-affettiva nella giurisprudenza della Rota Romana* (Studi Giuridici XXIII), Libreria Editrice Vaticana, Rome, 1990. **36** Burke, ibid., 139-40, **37** Ibid., 116.   **38** Cf. decision c. Burke, 22 June 1995, *Studia Canonica* 31 (1997), 237, n. 5. **39** J. McAreavey, *Emotional immaturity and marriage*, 96. **40** A. Sabattani, "L'évolution de la jurisprudence dans les causes de nullité de mariage pour incapacité psychique" in *Studia Canonica* 1 (1967), 150 (translation in A. Mendonça, "Consensual incapacity for marriage" in *The Jurist* 54 (1994), 498.

In reaching a judgement in cases where lack of due discretion is pleaded **270** as a ground of nullity, Courts will use the services of a psychologist or a psychiatrist "unless from the circumstances this would obviously serve no purpose" (Can. 1680). It will be the task of the expert witness to throw light on the psychological processes that produced the act of consent.

Grave concern has been expressed about the over-use of lack of due dis- **271** cretion in tribunals at the present time. Burke observed that "today some tribunals have come to consider this ground of nullity the easiest to establish and, therefore, have the tendency to view every *factispecies* [case history] ..., first of all, through the optic of the serious lack of discretion of judgement".[41] This may be due to a lack of clarity regarding the meaning of lack of due discretion; it might also point to a failure to understand the other classical grounds of nullity.

Can. 1095, 3° Inability to assume and fulfil the essential obligations of marriage (see page 96)

Like Can. 1095, 2°, the inability to assume and fulfil the essential obliga- **272** tions did not appear in the 1917 Code. It developed in the jurisprudence of the Roman Rota on the basis of natural law principles.[42] The earliest cases dealt with psychosexual disorders, a fact that left its mark on the process of formulating the present section.[43] The Revision Commission was also influenced by a current of thought that saw inability to assume and fulfil the obligations of marriage as an extension of the impediment of impotence rather than as something that affected the capacity of a person to consent.[44]

Inability to assume and fulfil the essential obligations of marriage on the **273** part of a party to marriage renders that person's consent invalid; it is distinguished from Can. 1095, 1° and 2° as follows: whereas the latter refer to an incapacity to elicit the psychological act of consent – due to a lack of the use of reason or a lack of sufficient discretion of judgement – 3° concerns an incapacity to carry out the essential duties of marriage. Some authors distinguish between a defect in the act of consent and a defect of the object of consent. In each instance however the incapacity lies totally in the subject: "Can. 1095 is not speaking of marriages that cannot be undertaken, but of persons who cannot consent to marriage."[45]

---

41 Cited in A. Mendonça, "Consensual incapacity for marriage" in *The Jurist* 54 (1994), 478. **42** Among the cases cited as the sources of this canon, the earliest rotal decision is a decision c. Sabattani, 21 June 1957. **43** J.H. Provost, "Canon 1095: past, present, future" in *The Jurist* 54 (1994), 101. **44** Cf. *Comm* 7 (1975), 49-50. This tradition continues in the jurisprudence and writings of one Rotal judge (cf. J.M. Pinto Gómez, "Incapacitas assumendi matrimonii onera" in *Dilexit iustitiam (Studia in honorem Aurelii Card. Sabattani)* (eds. Grocholewski and Cárcel Ortí), Libreria Editrice Vaticana, Rome, 1984 (hereafter referred to as *Dilexit iustitiam*), 17-37. **45** C. Burke, "The distinction between 2° and 3° of canon 1095" in *The Jurist* 54 (1994), 230.

"The essential obligations of marriage"

274 In order to interpret Can. 1095, 3° it is necessary to ascertain what constitutes the essential obligations of marriage. I will review the various schemata which have been formulated in Rotal jurisprudence and canonical doctrine. Various attempts have been made to formulate these elements. Pinto writes:

> It seems the essential elements of marriage mentioned in Can. 1101 of the new code are to be derived from Can. 1055. The mind of the Consultors in formulating this canon was "to determine in what does marriage consist". The good of offspring and the good of spouses have already been established by the very Creator of nature as *fines operis*. Even if the end of a created thing is outside its essence, the ordination of offspring is essential to marriage, and in this ordination the good of the spouses is also indicated as its substance. Consequently, according to the norm of the new code the essential obligations of marriage are those which concern the good of offspring, the good of the spouses, the good of fidelity, and the good of sacrament. The partnership of the whole of life is "by its very nature" ordered to the first two (Can. 1055 §1); the last two are the "essential properties of marriage" (Can. 1056).[46]

275 Pompedda argues on the basis of Can. 1055 §1 there are three elements: (1) a *consortium* between a man and a woman, which is ordered (2) to the good of the spouses and (3) to the generation and upbringing of children. He adds that unity and indissolubility are essential properties (Can. 1056).[47] Stankiewicz holds that matrimonial consent generates two main obligations: "(1) obligation to the gift of conjugal love, ordered to procreate and educate the child, to be shared with the partner in a human way, perpetually and exclusively ... (cf. *Familiaris consortio*, n. 11) ...; (2) obligation to constitute and preserve conjugal communion which is characterized by unity and indissolubility".[48]

276 Mendonça takes *Familiaris consortio*, n. 11 as his starting-point and lists the essential elements as follows: (1) marriage is an interpersonal relationship, which is (2) heterosexual, (3) ordered to the good of offspring and (4)

---

46 *Dilexit iustitiam*, 23, n. 9 (translation in A.Mendonça, "Consensual incapacity for marriage" in *The Jurist* 54 (1994), 511. **47** SRR decis. 77 (1985), 54-5, n. 6. In 1986 Pompedda expressed his mind on this matter as follows: "... we can therefore say that the essence of matrimony is ... 1) a *consortium* between a man and a woman; 2) a consortium of the whole of life; 3) perpetual and exclusive; 4) directed toward the good of the spouses; 5) directed toward the generation and raising of offspring" in *Incapacity for marriage*, 190. **48** 16 December, 1982, in *Ephemerides Iuris Canonici* 39 (1983), 258-9, n. 9 (translated in Mendonça, "Consensual capacity for marriage" in *The Jurist* 54 (1994), 513-4.

the good of the spouses and (5) is characterised by fidelity. I will follow this structure.[49]

Contemporary doctrine on marriage emphasises the interpersonal nature **277** of marriage. Mendonça writes that "the capacity and willingness on the part of both spouses for ... an intimate interpersonal relationship is essential for the very being of marriage from the beginning".[50] He adds that "a substantial lack of this capacity, for whatever reason, would result in the denial of a right essential to marriage".[51] Some personality disorders have the effect of rendering persons incapable of sustaining a stable relationship. The narcissistic personality disorder[52] and paranoid personality disorder are examples of disorders that can render persons unable to assume and fulfil the essential obligations of marriage.[53]

Marriage is a relationship in which sexual intimacy plays an important **278** part. It is essentially a heterosexual relationship. Giannecchini writes: "Since sexuality is a means of union "by which man and woman give themselves to one another through the acts which are proper and exclusive to spouses" ... it follows that without sexuality, or with a sexuality which is permanently and seriously abnormal, mutual and complete gifting of spouses becomes impossible".[54]

In a rotal decision Anné wrote that "the abnormal conditions in the per- **279** son marrying which ... obstruct the beginning of any communion of married life [include] the following: a very serious distortion and perversion of the sexual drive, for example, cases of overt homosexuality, if and inasmuch as the homosexuality extinguishes the activity of the heterosexual drive ..."[55]

The parties to marriage must also be responsible in the generation and **280** raising of children.[56] It will be for evolving doctrine and jurisprudence to determine what capacity is required in those who marry from the perspective

---

49 Mendonça also includes "sacramental dignity". Of this he writes: "... The Code Commission resisted to the end to yield to any tendency to define the exact juridic nature of the sacramental dignity. In other words, the question remains open to doctrinal and jurisprudential developments concerning the theological and juridical nature of sacramental dignity" ("Consensual incapacity for marriage" in *The Jurist* 54 (1994), 525). For this reason, I will not deal with this topic in this context. **50** "Consensual incapacity for marriage" in *The Jurist* 54 (1994), 515. **51** Ibid. **52** Cf. R.J. Sanson, "Narcissistic personality disorder: possible effects on the validity of marital consent" in *Monitor ecclesiasticus* 113 (1988), 541-81; ibid., 114 (1989), 405-24; A. Mendonça, "Narcissistic personality disorder: its effects on matrimonial consent" in *Studia Canonica* 27 (1993), 97-144. **53** For a description of this disorder and the behaviour associated with it, cf. DSM IV, 634-8. **54** 19 July 1983 in SRR decis. 75 (1983), 454, n.2 (cited in Mendonça, "Consensual incapacity for marriage" in *The Jurist* 54 (1994), 516-7. Cf. Mendonça, "Recent rotal jurisprudence on the effects of sexual disorders on matrimonial consent" in *Studia Canonica* 28 (1992), 211-21. **55** Cf. L. Wrenn, *Decisions*, Toledo, 1980, 101, n. 19. **56** M.F. Pompedda, "Incapacity to assume the essential obligations of marriage" in *Incapacity for marriage*, 192.

of responsible parenthood and to determine the conditions that would render a person incapable of assuming the responsibilities of parenthood.[57]

281   Marriage is ordered to the good of the spouses; hence a person who marries must be able to sustain a conjugal relationship which – to put it negatively – is not destructive of his or her own good and the good of his or her spouse. Pompedda states that it will be for jurisprudence and further study to determine how this should be applied in practice; he cautions however that "we must not confuse what is essential with what is non-essential in this conjugal good".[58] There is little doubt that conditions such as alcoholism, compulsive gambling or substance addiction which undermine the capacity for responsibility – if they are present at the time of consent – can render those afflicted by them unable to assume and fulfil the obligations of marriage.

282   Finally, marriage is characterised by fidelity. In marrying a person gives his or her spouse the right to an exclusive sexual relationship. This person must be able to sustain this aspect of the marriage relationship. This capacity for fidelity can be rendered impossible by hypersexuality. Male hypersexuality is known in psychiatry as Don Juanism or satyriasis; female hypersexuality is known as nymphomania. In both cases sexual activity is marked by its compulsive and unsatisfying nature.[59] In a recent rotal decision Stankiewicz wrote: "[O]ne whose mind is so obscured and will so weakened by the force of violent sexual drive that he or she irresistibly and insatiably seeks sexual relationship and indulges self thoughtlessly and promiscuously, cannot validly contract marriage because of an incapacity to assume the obligations of maintaining fidelity which falls within the scope of the willpower."[60]

283   The elements outlined above constitute the essence of marriage; the personality disorders cited and the behaviour associated with them can in serious cases render persons incapable of assuming the duties of married life. It would be wrong however to conclude that there is a simple equation, as if one could say, "X suffers from this condition, therefore his or her marriage is invalid". It must be established in each specific case whether a person suffered from a psychic disorder which was so severe in his or her case as to render that person unable to assume the essential obligations of marriage. Pompedda writes "that this moral impossibility [must be] proven by a psychological or psychiatric examination, by a consideration of all the circum-

57 A. Mendonça, "Consensual incapacity for marriage" in *The Jurist* 54 (1994), 518. 58 "Incapacity to assume the essential obligations of marriage" in *Incapacity for marriage*, 92. 59 J. Yager, "Clinical manifestations of psychiatric disorders" in *Comprehensive textbook of psychiatry/V*, vol.1, 558, cited in A. Mendonça, "Recent rotal jurisprudence on the effects of sexual disorders on matrimonial consent" in *Studia Canonica* 26 (1992), 222. 60 14 November 1985, SRR decis. 77 (1985), 487, n. 5 (translated in Mendonça, "Recent rotal jurisprudence on the effects of sexual disorders on matrimonial consent" in *Studia Canonica* 26 [1992], 225-6).

stances and by [a study of] the actual behaviour of the spouse".[61] Pope John Paul II made this clear in his Address to the Roman Rota in 1987:

> For the canonist the principle must remain clear that only incapacity and not difficulty in giving consent and in realising a true community of life and love invalidates marriage. Moreover, the breakdown of a marriage union is never in itself proof of such incapacity on the part of the contracting parties ... The hypothesis of real incapacity is to be considered only when an anomaly of a serious nature is present, which, however it may be defined, must substantially vitiate the capacity of the individual to understand and/or to will.[62]

"Causes of a psychological nature"

Can. 1095, 3° states that "those who, because of causes of a psychological **284** nature, are unable to assume the essential obligations of marriage" are incapable of contracting marriage. What does the phrase "causes of a psychological nature" mean? Provost holds that this refers to factors that are "beyond the will or control of the affected party".[63] Pompedda states that the Legislator wanted to refer to the personality of the contractant[64] and adds:

> It is only when there is something that impedes the capacity in the psyche or in the psychic constitution of the person that once can affirm that the person is incapable ... A person can be held incapable to the extent that he /she is found to have something rooted in his/her concrete existence which impedes the assumption of these obligations.[65]

While the "psychological cause" normally arises from a mental illness **285** or personality disorder, Pompedda interprets the phrase to include the situation of a man who, due to deeply ingrained habits, is unable to be faithful to his spouse. This person may not suffer from a pathological condition in the clinical sense; however sexual promiscuity has become "second nature" to him and renders him unable to sustain an exclusive heterosexual relationship.[66]

Several further considerations arise in regard to the psychological causes **286** mentioned in the canon. Firstly, the psychological condition must be grave. The criterion for judging the gravity of the condition is whether it "impaired the proper functioning of the intellect and of the will in judging and making

---

61 "Incapacity to assume the essential obligations of marriage" in *Incapacity for marriage*, 200. **62** *Papal allocutions to the Roman Rota*, 194, n. 7. **63** "Canon 1095: past, present and future" in *The Jurist* 54 (1994), 99. **64** "Incapacity to assume the essential obligations of marriage" in *Incapacity for marriage*, 197. **65** Ibid. **66** Ibid.

the decision".[67] The issue of gravity will normally be determined with the help of evidence from an appropriate expert witness. Secondly, the psychological condition must be present at the time of consent.[68] Thirdly, it must be certain.[69] Fourthly, the question of the requirement of perpetuity in regard to the psychological cause has been raised. Bruno, a rotal judge, has written that "after some initial hesitation, the consolidated jurisprudence of the Rota *passim* teaches that it is not at all necessary to insist on perpetual incapacity".[70] However the obligations of marriage are perpetual and parties to marriage must be able to undertake them. The final question is whether incapacity to assume the obligations of marriage can be understood in a relative sense. Rotal jurisprudence and canonical doctrine have not reached a uniform position on this issue.[71] Mendonça argues that incompatibility of personalities is "a psychological fact"; he agrees however that "only when real psychopathology, and not merely character differences, underlies such an incompatibility in a concrete situation can we admit true 'relative incapacity' for assuming the essential obligations of marriage".[72] If a real psychopathology is not present, there is a danger that a simple clash of personalities would be regarded as sufficient to declare a marriage null.[73]

Relationship between Can. 1095, 3° and Can. 1095, 2°

287   Jurisprudence and canonical doctrine acknowledge that Can.1095, 3° is an autonomous ground of nullity. It deals with an incapacity *vis-à-vis* the object of consent (the essential obligations) whereas lack of discretion affects the act of consent. However both incapacities are rooted in the unity and capacity of the same person, and in practice evidence that proves the existence of one ground often proves the existence of the other. Stankiewicz argues that if it is proven with moral certainty that, due to psychological causes, a person marrying was incapable of understanding and weighing sufficiently the

67 Decision c. Lanversin, 20 January 1981, SRR decis. 73 (1981), 25, n. 3 (cited in Mendonça, "Consensual incapacity for marriage" in *The Jurist* 54 (1994), 531). **68** M.F. Pompedda, "Incapacity to assume the essential obligations of marriage" in *Incapacity for marriage*, 203. **69** Decision c. Bruno, 19 July 1991, SRR decis. 83 (1991), 466, n. 6. **70** 19 July 1991, SRR decis. 83 (1991), 466, n. 6 (cited in Mendonça, "Consensual incapacity for marriage" in *The Jurist* 54 (1994), 532-3). **71** Pinto, who sees incapacity mentioned in Can. 1095, 3° as similar to impotence, holds that relative incapacity can be admitted as a form of incapacity (cf. "Incapacitas assumendi matrimonii onera" in *Dilexit iustitiam*, 27). Serrano accepts it also on the basis of the unique interpersonal nature of each marriage (decision of 15 November 1977, in SRR decis. 69 (1977), 460, n. 9). Pompedda states that "to this point in time, a juridic foundation for such a 'relative' incapacity has not been found" ("Incapacity to assume the essential obligations of marriage" in *Incapacity for marriage*, 206). Burke is also opposed to it ("Some reflections on canon 1095" in *Monitor ecclesiasticus* 117 (1992), 142). **72** Mendonça, ibid., 540. **73** M. Manning, "Essential incompatibility. A valid ground of nullity?" in *Studia Canonica* 13 (1979), 339-63.

essential rights and duties of marriage and of giving and receiving the same
rights and duties with a sufficient degree of internal freedom of choice, then
there is no need to pursue the question concerning that person's incapacity to
assume the essential obligations of marriage.[74]

The ground of nullity expressed in Can. 1095, 3° derives from the natural   **288**
law principle that a person cannot contract marriage who is incapable of
assuming the essential obligations that arise from marital consent. Its immediate source is the jurisprudence of the Roman Rota and the Apostolic
Signatura. The annotated version of the Code makes this clear by providing
a list of significant cases as its sources. While the central principles relating
to "inability" are stated in the canon and have been elaborated over several
decades, significant areas remain to be clarified. It will be for jurisprudence
and canonical doctrine to continue to work at the significance and practical
application of the canon.[75]

Can. 1096 Ignorance

§1 For matrimonial consent to exist, it is necessary that the contracting
parties be at least not ignorant of the fact that marriage is a permanent
partnership between a man and a woman, ordered to the procreation of
children through some form of sexual cooperation.
§2 This ignorance is not presumed after puberty.

According to Can. 126, "an act is invalid when performed as a result of   **289**
ignorance ... concerning the substance of the act". Can. 1096 applies this
principle to matrimonial consent. It states the level of knowledge which those
wishing to marry must possess. Since the right to marry is a natural right, the
amount of knowledge required is pitched at a minimal level.

The equivalent canon in the 1917 Code stated that "matrimonial consent   **290**
cannot be given unless the contracting parties know at least that marriage is
a permanent union between a man and a woman for the purpose of generat-
ing offspring" (c. 1082 §1).[76] Can. 1096 states that couples must not be
ignorant of the fact that the procreation of children involves "some form of
sexual cooperation". An earlier draft referred to "some form of bodily coop-

74 Mendonça, ibid., 546-7. 16 December 1982, SRR decis. 74 (1982), in *Ephemerides
Iuris Canonici* 39 (1983), 259-60, n. 10. Egan also takes this view (2 April 1981, *SRR
decis.* 73 (1981), 210-7. Pompedda writes: "It is absurd to think that a person can oblige
oneself either morally or juridically, or that a person can assume an obligation whether
it be moral or juridic, when this same individual is not capable of either understanding
or of deciding freely" ("Incapacity to assume the essential obligations of marriage" in
Incapacity for marriage, 172). 75 Cf. Address of Pope John Paul II to the Rota in 1984,
in *Papal allocutions to the Roman Rota*, 185, n. 7. 76 Cf. R. Zera, *De ignorantia in re
matrimoniali*, Rome, 1978.

eration".[77] Those contracting marriage must be aware that there is a connection between the interaction of their sexual organs and the conception of a child. Canestri held that a person who thought that a child could be conceived by kissing could not validly marry.[78]

291   The level of knowledge required for valid consent is minimal and cases where a person does not possess it are rare. Such ignorance is not presumed after puberty. There have however been instances where a young person raised in an over-protective environment had not attained even this minimum level of knowledge.[79]

Can. 1097 Error of person

> §1 Error of person renders a marriage invalid.
> §2 Error about a quality of the person, even though it be the reason for the contract, does not render a marriage invalid unless this quality is directly and principally intended.

292   The canonical tradition distinguishes between various kinds of error, some of which renders consent invalid whereas others do not.[80] The 1917 Code distinguished four kinds of error: error of person, error of quality, error of quality that amounts to an error of person and error concerning servile condition. Error of person rendered marriage invalid.[81] Error about a quality of the person, even if it led to the marriage, rendered it null in two circumstances: if the error of quality amounted to an error of person or if a person contracted marriage with a slave believing him or her to be free.

293   The broad principles are clear: error about the identity of a marriage-partner renders consent invalid; error about a quality of the person does not. A person might, for example, believe that his or her prospective spouse is wealthy, honest, sober, healthy or hard-working; the fact that he or she is mistaken about this does not affect the validity of the consent. This applies even if the mistaken belief about his or her prospective partner is the reason why the person was attracted to him or her. Leaving aside "error of servile condition" which has not featured much in recent jurisprudence, the principal exception to this principle arose when there was error of person that

---

77 *Comm* 15 (1983), 232. Örsy states that "a meticulously precise rendering of the Latin *sexualis* in this context should be 'genital'" (*Marriage in canon law*, 133). **78** SRR decis. 35 (1943), 607, n. 17. **79** *Matrimonial decisions of Great Britain and Ireland* 24 (1988), 34-7. **80** Gratian wrote: "Verum est quod non omnis error consensum excludit; sed error alius est personae, alius fortunae, alius condicionis, alius qualitatis. Error personae est, quando hic putatur esse Virgilius et est Plauto. Error fortuna, quando putatur esse dives et est pauper, vel e converso. Error condicionis, quando putatur esse liber qui servus est. Error qualitatis quando putatur esse bonus qui malus est" (C.19, q.1). **81** An instance of this is found in Gen 29: 15-30.

"amounted to an error of person". After Vatican II a body of jurisprudence began to develop around this concept and it began to be interpreted more expansively.[82] It was against this background that the new laws concerning error were drafted.[83]

Can. 1097 deals with three kinds of error: error of person, error of quality **294** that is "directly and principally intended" and error about a quality that is not "directly and principally intended".[84] The first renders a marriage invalid, as we saw above. However, the question arises: what does it mean to say that an error of quality was "directly and principally intended"? After all, men and women do not marry qualities, but a person whom they hope and believe – rightly or wrongly – to be endowed with certain qualities. A pointer to the interpretation of this phrase is given in Can. 126; it states that "an act is invalid when performed as a result of ... error which ... amounts to a condition *sine qua non*". This means that if a person made his or her consent to marry X conditional on X possessing a certain quality, then that quality is "directly and principally intended". The focus of the law has changed from the objective importance of the quality, viz., one that "amounted to an error of person" to the intention of the person. Doyle explains:

> The quality must be directly and principally intended, to the extent that the principal reason for the marriage is the quality and not the other person. This quality need not be unique to the person, but even if common to many, must be of such subjective magnitude in the mind of the person marrying, that it almost completely overshadows the person of the other party.[85]

One author illustrates what this might mean in practice: **295**

> A pregnant woman may mistakenly tell a man that he is the father of her child. If he marries her and later alleges invalidity when he discovers that the child is not his, again in this case, the question of paternity would have to be examined to see if it was directly and principally intended. There will be other cases dealing with conditions such as virginity, fertility, nationality, wealth, etc., where such qualities could have been intended.[86]

82 Decision c. Canals, SRR decis. 62 (1970), 370-5. **83** *Handbuch des katholischen Kirchenrechts* (herausgegeben von J. Listl-H. Muller-H. Schmitz), Verlag Pustet, 1983, 771. **84** This phrase, a technical one, is the third of three rules developed by St Alphonsus Liguori (*Theologia moralis*, lib.VI, tractatus VI, cap. III, dubium II, n. 1016). It was substituted for "error qualitatis redundans in errorem personae" (error of quality that amounts to error of person) at a late stage in the drafting process; even in 1981 the latter phrase was still included in the Can. 1051 §2 (now Can. 1098) (*Comm* 15 (1983), 232). **85** *The Code of Canon Law: a text and commentary* (edd. Coriden, Green and Heintschel), Paulist Press, New York/Mahwah, 1985 (hereafter *The Code of Canon Law: a text and commentary*), 780. **86** P. Hennessy, "Canon 1097: a requiem for error redundans?" in *The Jurist* 49 (1989), 175.

296   The condition need not be posited explicitly; in fact persons may not be aware of the condition until they discover that the quality which they erroneously assumed to be present is in fact absent. Hence the strongest evidence of the existence of such an implicit condition is the reaction of the person on discovering the truth. In some instances a party has been known to leave the marriage on the spot. Hennessy holds that "it would not be fair to demand absolutely the end of the marriage on the discovery of the error";[87] however it would be difficult – though not impossible – to establish that the presence of the "quality" was a condition *sine qua non* for the contracting of a marriage if the common life of the couple continued after its absence was noticed.

Can. 1098 Deceit

A person contracts invalidly who enters marriage inveigled by deceit, perpetrated in order to secure consent, concerning some quality of the other party, which of its very nature can seriously disrupt the partnership of conjugal life.

297   There was no reference to deceit as a ground of nullity of marriage in the 1917 Code. However since "error about a quality that amounts to an error of person" could scarcely occur without deception, some authors take the view that "deception is contained in [the 1917 Code] by implication".[88] In the years before and during Vatican II, canonists observed that c. 1083 – which dealt with error of person – did not protect innocent persons against those who were prepared to bring about a marriage by deceitful means.[89]

298   Can. 125 §2 outlines the effect of deceit (*dolus*) on the validity of juridical acts. In this context – in penal law it has a different meaning – it refers to "the deliberate manipulation of another by telling lies or concealing the truth so that the other is persuaded to perform a juridical act".[90] One such juridical act is matrimonial consent.

299   In order to invalidate marriage deceit must be carried out with the aim of obtaining the agreement of the other person to marry. It presupposes a belief on the part of the deceiver that if the truth were known the other party would not proceed with the marriage. The means used to carry out the deceit do not matter. A person might, for example, create a tissue of lies in order to create a false impression of his or her life, background, career, education, social circumstances, personal circumstances, health, age and so on. Alternatively, a person might, by remaining silent, allow a partner to continue to believe

---

87 Hennessy, ibid., 176. **88** M. Ahern, "Error and deception as grounds for nullity" in *Studia Canonica* 11 (1977), 246. **89** K. W. Vann, "*Dolus*: canon 1098 of the revised Code of Canon Law" in *The Jurist* 47 (1987), 378. **90** *The Canon Law: letter and spirit*, n. 259, 73.

something that was false. In this case silence is as effective in deceiving the partner as the positive deception in the former case. What matters is that the deception, whether positive or negative, was intended to bring about a marriage by fraud and was effective. Although the deceiving party will typically be the person who wishes to marry, the law does not exclude the possibility that the deceit might be carried out by someone else. This might occur in circumstances where a third party was seeking to arrange a marriage and resorted to deceit to bring it about.

Deceit renders marriage invalid only when it concerns "a quality of the other party, which of its very nature can seriously disrupt the partnership of conjugal life". This provides to some extent an objective test for deceit: it must be of such a nature that it impinges in a serious way on the partnership of marriage.[91] The example of sterility given in Can. 1084 §3 reveals the sense of the law; it is objectively serious and "can seriously disrupt the partnership of conjugal life". It will be for canonical doctrine and jurisprudence to determine if other such "qualities" come within the meaning of the canon.[92] One commentary offers the following list of possible "qualities": "ongoing psychiatric illness or personality disturbance, serious medical conditions such as syphilis, AIDS, pregnancy by someone else, a criminal record or immoral lifestyle, a previous marriage whether canonically valid or not".[93]   **300**

Canonists are agreed about the meaning and invalidating force of Can. 1098; however they dispute whether the reason for it is of natural or positive law. The Revision Commission did not agree on the point and the growing body of jurisprudence on the topic has not reached a consensus on the issue.[94] Funghini, a rotal judge, holds that the invalidating force of deceit arises from the Vatican II teaching on the dignity of the person; deceit prevents the mutual self-giving of the couple and undermines the stable community of conjugal life.[95] Stankiewicz and Doran, on the other hand, see it as an expression of canonical equity.[96] Navarrete holds that error renders a marriage invalid because it limits the internal freedom of a person, whether the error is caused by deceit or not.[97] Örsy regards Can. 1098 as a way of protecting an innocent person "from wilful deception".[98] This is not a purely academic issue: if this canon is rooted in the natural law, for example, because it impedes the freedom of consent, it can be used retrospectively and can apply to marriages that took place prior to 1983. If however it is of   **301**

---

91 *Comm* 9 (1977), 372: "est graviter perturbativa consortii vitae coniugalis". **92** *Comm* 15 (1983), 233. **93** *The Canon Law: letter and spirit*, n. 2200, 615. There are qualities which do not impinge on marriage, for example, the fear of heights or colour-blindness. **94** *Comm* 3 (1977), 77. **95** *Monitor ecclesiasticus* 111 (1989), 456. **96** SRR decis. 75 (1983), 49; *Monitor ecclesiasticus* 116 (1991), 384. For a full discussion of this issue, cf. J. Gressier, "La nullité du mariage conclu sous l'effet du dol qualifié du canon 1098 est de droit naturel" in *Studia Canonica* 30 (1996), 343-70. **97** "Canon 1098 de errore doloso estne iuris naturalis an iuris positivi ecclesiae?" in *Periodica* 76 (1987), 166. **98** *Marriage in canon law*, 140.

purely positive law it can only apply to marriages that took place since the 1983 Code was promulgated.

302   The nature of Can. 1098 was discussed at a Consultation which was held by the Pontifical Council for the Interpretation of Legislative Texts on December 13, 1985. It concluded:

> The Consultation is inclined to regard the wording of Can. 1098 as of merely positive law and consequently as non-retroactive. Given, however, the great variety of cases which the canon could embrace, one could not rule out the possibility that some of those cases could involve nullity deriving from the natural law, in which case it would be legitimate to render an affirmative decision. It is therefore the task of the judge who is in possession of all the possible facts, to determine whether the case at bar involves a type of error invalidating not by the positive dispositions of Can. 1098 but by force of the natural law, as was the case in certain sentences that predated the promulgation of the Code ...
>
> In the absence of an authentic interpretation which favours the non-retroactivity of Can.1098, there obviously remains a doubt about the prescript of Can. 1098 – and consequently a doubt about whether the canon may or may not be applied to marriages celebrated before 27 November 1983. In view of this doubt one should, of course, keep in mind Can.1060 which indicates that "in doubt the validity of a marriage is to be upheld.[99]

303   The Revision Commission considered – and rejected – a proposal that cohabitation after discovery of deceit be presumed to indicate a renewal of consent by the deceived party.[100]

Can. 1099   Error concerning the nature of marriage

> Provided it does not determine the will, error concerning the unity or the indissolubility or the sacramental dignity of marriage does not vitiate matrimonial consent.

304   Cann. 1097-8 deal with error concerning the person. Can. 1099 deals with errors concerning the essential qualities of marriage; it has traditionally been dealt with under the rubric *error iuris* (error of law). The 1917 Code stated that "simple error concerning the unity, indissolubility or sacramental dignity of marriage, does not annul matrimonial consent, even if such error

---

[99] Cf. L. Wrenn, *Annulments*, 6th ed., 223. **100** *Comm* 5 (1973), 90. **101** *Comm* 9 (1977), 373.

caused the consent" (c. 1084). Some members of the Revision Commission wanted to change the doctrine in this canon; they argued that where a person was in error about the unity or indissolubility of marriage, his or her matrimonial consent could be presumed to be flawed;[101] the Commission decided however to retain the traditional doctrine.[102]

Can. 1099 affirms that people who have a view of marriage which is not **305** in accordance with the teaching of the catholic Church can contract a valid, sacramental marriage. These includes, for example, those who hold that marriage is not indissoluble.[103] Since marriage was "established by the Creator"[104] people instinctively marry as God intended. The canonical doctrine on this point is based on two principles. The first is the distinction between an act of the intellect and an act of the will. In the 1917 Code error was called "simple" if it remained in the intellect and did not condition the choice made by the will (c. 1084). A commentary on this canon stated that "in these cases there is a so-called conflict of intentions and the problem is to determine the prevailing intention".[105]

The second principle derives from scholastic philosophical psychology: **306** "*nihil volitum quin praecognitum*" (nothing can be willed unless it is first known). Since persons commit themselves to a course of action as they perceive it, an erroneous perception will influence the choice they make. Ecclesiastical jurisprudence takes the attitude that the more deeply-rooted an erroneous view of marriage is, the more likely it is to have conditioned that person's consent.[106] An example of this was a man who joined a hippy circle and followed the hippy life-style for some years. He accepted the hippy view of marriage and free-love. When his girl-friend became pregnant he married her but the marriage soon fell apart. It was declared null at the Roman Rota on the grounds of error on the basis that the man had applied his own erroneous views on marriage when he went through the marriage ceremony.[107]

---

102 Ibid. "Consultores autem tenent doctrinam traditionalem in qua fundatur hic canon, scilicet de compossibilitate erroris simplicis in mente, qui non determinet voluntatem, quia in casu voluntas versatur circa matrimonium prout communiter habetur, id est unum et indissolubile". **103** U. Navarrete, "De sensu clausula dummodo non afficiat voluntatem" in *Periodica* 81 (1992), 479. **104** Fl I, 950, *GS* n. 48. **105** T. L. Bouscaren and A. C. Ellis, *Canon Law: a text and commentary*, Bruce, Milwaukee, 1947, p.503. In deciding this question, Navarrete has written that the objective criterion is the kind of love that the parties had for each other; when a person consents to marry out of a genuine love for his or her spouse, he or she instinctively gives him- or herself in a perpetual and faithful union which is open to children, and they do so regardless of his or her theoretical views on marriage ("De sensu clausula dummodo non determinet voluntatem Can. 1099" in *Periodica* 81 (1992), 484). **106** c. Felici, SRR decis. 46 (1954), 616, n. 4. Cf. A. Stankiewicz, "De errore voluntatem determinante (Can. 1099) iuxta rotalem iurisprudentiam" in *Periodica* 79 (1990), 441-94; I. Parisella, "De pervicaci seu radicato errore circa matrimonii indissolubilitatem" in *Ius Populi Dei* (Miscellanea in honorem Raymundi Bidagor) III, Pontificia Università Gregoriana, Rome, 1972, 513-40. **107** For summary, cf. CLD 10, 178.

307   The crucial question in such cases is not what views a person had about marriage or how deeply he or she held them. The issue is what he or she committed him– or herself to in matrimonial consent?[108] If a person who sees marriage as impermanent gives a provisional kind of consent ("I'll see how it works out"), the marriage will be null on the grounds of *error iuris*. In his address to the Roman Rota on 29 January 1993, Pope John Paul II stated, by way of an example:

> Thus ... it would cause serious harm to the stability of marriage and so to its sacred nature, if the fact of simulation was not formulated concretely on the part of the alleged simulator in a "positive act of the will" (cf. Can. 1101 §2), or if the so-called *error iuris* regarding an essential property of marriage or its sacramental dignity did not acquire such intensity as to condition the act of will, thus causing the consent to be null (cf. Can. 1099).[109]

308   In his historical analysis of the interpretation of error, Campbell concludes:

> Up until now all the discussion on error of law regarding the essential properties of marriage had to take place within the ambit of the canon on simulation ... Only by being subsumed into simulation could this error have any relevance at all to marriage consent, even if this relevance was only indirect. The whole development of the notion of this error in the jurisprudence of the Rota in the years 1918-1983 necessarily had to take place under the ground of the exclusion of *bonum sacramenti*.[110]

309   When one is dealing with "error affecting the will" as an autonomous ground of nullity the omission of an essential element of consent is implicit; the person in error marries spontaneously according to his or her own concept of marriage.[111] This ground must however be distinguished from simulation:

> The institution of marriage in both cases is nominated: in simulation it is nominated and yet denied because of a contrary act of the will; in

---

108 U. Navarrete, "De sensu clausulae *dummodo non determinet voluntatem*" (Can. 1099) in *Periodica* 81 (1992), 485-6; Z. Grocholewski, "De errore circa matrimonii unitatem, indissolubilitatem et sacramentalem dignitatem" in *Periodica* 84 (1995), 412. 109 *CLSGBI Newsletter* 93 (1993), 8-9. This ground of nullity has already been formulated in a case c. Stankiewicz, 25 April 1991, n. 20 (*Monitor ecclesiasticus* 118 (1993), 388: "... constare de matrimonii nullitate, in casu, ob errorem determinantem voluntatem tantum circa matrimonii indissolubilitatem ex parte mulieris conventae". 110 "Canon 1099: the emergence of a new juridic figure"? in *Studio rotale* V, 57. 111 A. Stankiewicz, "L'errore di diritto nel consenso matrimoniale e la sua autonomia giuridica" in *Periodica* 83 (1994), 667.

error determining the will ... it is also nominated, but the act of exchanging consent is evacuated of value on account of the fact that the will of one of the parties is not directed to the proper act on account of error.[112]

The 1917 Code listed "the sacramental dignity of marriage" among the **310** essential properties of marriage (c. 1084). In the first draft of Can. 1099, it was omitted. At the request of the Congregation for the Doctrine of the Faith the phrase was restored in 1981.[113] The current discussion of faith and the sacramentality of marriage has focused attention on it.[114] The traditional view, stated in c. 1084, was that error about ... [the] sacramental dignity [of marriage] did not render consent invalid provided there was a general will to contract a true marriage; and because of the *favor iuris* it was presumed that such a general will existed and the sacramental bond was formed.[115] Pompedda argues that it is not possible today to presume the presence of an intention whose presupposed basis is faith (the intention "to do what the Church does").[116] He writes:

> The lack of faith on the juridic level ... is precisely a situation of error, and an error specifically about the essential element of the object of the conjugal pact between two baptised persons ... Error about the sacramental dignity of marriage must be considered analogously to error about the essential qualities, since the sacramentality of marriage is not merely an element "tacked on" to thc cssence of marriage, but is instead a component which, without destroying it, transforms and perfects that essence itself.[117]

This opinion has not been widely accepted. Most judges and authors **311** hold that it is more appropriate to deal with defects of consent in this area under the heading of simulation (Can. 1101 §2).[118] This will be considered in more detail in the commentary on Can.1101.

---

112 Campbell, ibid., 58. **113** *Comm* 15 (1983), 233. Cf. *Congregatio Plenaria*, 452-60. **114** This debate was considered in Chapter 1. **115** P. Gasparri, *Tractatus canonicus de matrimonio*, II, n. 807, 28. **116** M.F. Pompedda, "Faith and the sacrament of marriage, lack of faith and matrimonial consent: juridical aspects" in *Marriage Studies* IV, 53-4. **117** Ibid. **118** A. Stankiewicz, "Errore circa le proprietà e la dignità sacramentale del matrimonio" in *La nuova legislazione matrimoniale canonica* (Studi giuridici X), Libreria Editrice Vaticana 1986, 130-32; D. Faltin, "The exclusion of the sacramentality of marriage with particular reference to the marriage of baptised non-believers" in *Marriage Studies* IV, 94-104; G. Versaldi, "Exclusio sacramentalitatis matrimonii ex parte baptizatorum non credentium: error vel potius simulationis?" in *Periodica* 79 (1990), 435-6.

Can. 1100 Knowledge or opinion about nullity

> Knowledge of or opinion about the nullity of a marriage does not necessarily exclude matrimonial consent.

312 This fact that a person knows or believes, rightly or wrongly, that his or her marriage is null due to an undispensed impediment or a defect of canonical form does not of itself render his or her consent invalid. This principle has an important application in the context of validation of marriage. For example, a person can give consent which is naturally sufficient but juridically ineffective because of the presence of an impediment. The marriage can be validated without a renewal of consent, provided that the consent given initially persists (e.g., Can. 1163).

Can. 1101 Simulation

> §1 The internal consent of the mind is presumed to conform to the words or the signs used in the celebration of a marriage.
> §2 If, however, either or both of the parties should by a positive act of will exclude marriage itself or any essential element of marriage or any essential property, such party contracts invalidly.

313 Matrimonial consent is an act of the will (Can. 1057 §2); of its nature it cannot be perceived. The law requires that it be expressed in words or, if this is not possible, in equivalent signs (Can. 1104 §2). Can. 1101 §1 states the legal presumption that what spouses inwardly intend corresponds to what they say in words or signs. If this is not the case, the onus of proof falls on the person who makes this claim. This presumption concerns canonical marriage; the extent to which it applies to marriages contracted without canonical form by parties who are not members of the Church must be judged in each case.[119]

314   When couples celebrate the sacrament of marriage they must marry "as the Church intends"; they are not at liberty to marry on their own terms. The Church's teaching on the essence of marriage is summarised in the marriage rite[120] and, more succinctly, in Can. 1055 §1: "The marriage covenant, by which a man and a woman establish between themselves a partnership of their whole life, and which of its own very nature is ordered to the well-being of the spouses and to the procreation and upbringing of children, has, between the baptised been raised by Christ the Lord to the dignity of a sacrament".

---

119 J. J. García Faílde, "Observationes novae circa matrimonium canonicum simulatum et coactum" in *Periodica* 75 (1986), 194. **120** OCM 1991, n. 59.

Can. 1056 describes unity and indissolubility as "essential properties of **315** marriage". Can. 1101 §2 states that "if ... either or both of the parties should by a positive act of the will exclude marriage itself or any essential element of marriage or any essential property, such party contracts invalidly".

The present text of Can. 1101 §2 is the product of a long and complex **316** drafting process. The Revision Commission took as its starting-point c. 1086 §2 (1917 Code) which stated that "if either or both parties by a positive act of the will exclude marriage itself, or all right to the conjugal act, or any of the essential qualities of marriage, they contract invalidly".[121] In the first draft of the new canon, the Revision Commission wished to incorporate Vatican II's description of marriage as "an intimate partnership of life and love"; it stated that "if either or both parties by a positive act of the will exclude marriage itself or the right to the communion of life or the right to the conjugal act, or any essential property of marriage, they contract invalidly".[122] The phrase "right to a communion of life" was deleted on the grounds that it would constitute a danger to the stability of marriage;[123] it was replaced by the phrase "the right to those things that essentially constitute the communion of life".[124] In 1980 this phrase in turn was deleted for the same reason, viz., that it would endanger the stability of marriage.[125] The omission of this, and the earlier phrase reflected the difficulty the Revision Commission had in defining exactly what they amounted to in practice. It believed that something substantial had been added to the definition of marriage at Vatican II; however the Revision Commission, rather than include an unclear concept in the law, decided to leave it to canonical doctrine and jurisprudence to further develop the concept.[126]

A second issue arose regarding the wording of this canon: the reference **317** to "the sacramental dignity of marriage" was also included in this canon.[127]

---

121 "At si alterutra vel utraque pars positivo voluntatis actu excludat matrimonium ipsum, aut omne ius ad coniugalem actum, vel essentialem proprietatem, invalide contrahit". **122** "At si alterutra vel utraque pars positivo voluntatis actu excludat matrimonium ipsum aut ius ad vitae communionem, aut ius ad coniugalem actum, vel essentiales aliquam matrimonii proprietatem, invalide contrahit" (*Comm* 9 (1977), 375). Cf. J.-M. Serrano-Ruiz, "Le droit à la communauté de vie et d'amour conjugal comme object du consentement matrimonial: aspects juridiques et évolution de la jurisprudence de la Sacrée Rote Romaine" in *Studia Canonica* 10 (1976), 271-302. **123** *Comm* 9 (1977), 375. **124** "At si alterutra vel utraque pars positivo voluntatis actu excludat matrimonium ipsum aut ius ad ea quae ad vitae communionem essentialiter constituunt, aut ius ad coniugalem actum essentialem aliquam matrimonii proprietatem, invalide contrahit". **125** *Comm* 15 (1983), 233. **126** "Ita auferuntur difficultates circa clausulam 'aut ius ad ea quae vitae communionem essentialiter constituunt' et, etsi generico modo, relatio exprimitur necessaria ad ea quae essentialia matrimonii sunt, quae quidem a doctrina et iurisprudentia determinanda sunt, habita ratione definitionis Can. 1008 §1 [now Can. 1055 §1] necnon totius legislationis et doctrinae, sive iuridicae sive theologicae" (*Comm* 15 (1983), 233-4). **127** "At si alterutra vel utraque pars positivo voluntatis actu excludat matrimonium ipsum aut matrimonii essentiale aliquod elementum vel essentialem proprietatem vel sacramentalem dignitatem, invalide contrahit".

In 1981 Cardinals Höffner and Ratzinger asked that it be omitted in case it created difficulties in ecumenical relations. The phrase was omitted, but this does not indicate a change in doctrine.[128]

Simulation: total or partial

318 Jurisprudence and canonical doctrine distinguish total simulation and partial simulation. The former exists when "marriage itself" is excluded; the latter exists when "any essential element of marriage or any essential property" is excluded from matrimonial consent.

Total simulation

319 A person "excludes marriage itself" when he or she goes through a marriage ceremony without the intention of entering the marriage state as such. On the face of it, this is an unusual situation and rotal jurisprudence takes the view that the person who does this must be aware that he or she is doing something abnormal.[129] The law on this point was stated in a decision c. Jullien:

> But it can happen that someone in celebrating marriage intends other objects, extrinsic to marriage... whether honorable, such as in order to establish peace between families, to preserve honor, to preserve health, or base, such as from a vicious greed for riches, for vain glory, or from lust. Such objects extrinsic to marriage can be found in the mind of the contracting party in two ways: 1) the extrinsic end can be [found] as a secondary end, more or less as a reason for deciding to marry, although without it the marriage would not take place... 2) The extrinsic end can be ... the principal and final cause of contracting ... and therefore it excludes the intention of marrying, which is to say it excludes marriage itself.[130]

320 The morality of the extraneous motivation for marriage is not the issue; the issue is "whether the extrinsic goal so occupies the subject's consciousness that there is no room left for genuine marital intention".[131] Examples of different motivations for marriage include the following: a case where a man

---

128 Cardinal Ratzinger described the doctrine that the exclusion of sacramentality renders a marriage invalid as well founded ("in se ipsa fundata est") (*Congregatio Plenaria*, 458). 129 Cited in J.G. Johnson, "Total simulation in recent rotal jurisprudence" in *Studia Canonica* 24 (1990), 390-1. He adds: "If one properly investigates the nature of human acts, it will become clear that no one simulates unless she self-consciously desires and intends to persuade others through external signs that she wants a certain thing when she herself desires in her heart something altogether contrary and opposite" (ibid., 391). 130 Ibid. 394. 131 Ibid.

married a young woman so that she could be released from reform school, the celebration of a marriage so that the man could get a residence permit in the country where he worked, and the celebration of a marriage so that a child would be legitimated.[132] The law was stated in a case before the Birmingham Marriage Tribunal:

> Where the evidence in a case shows that a person willingly and deliberately goes through a ceremony of marriage, but at the same time has the intention of not entering upon a common life in any sense of the word; and where it is clear that such a ceremony can in no sense whatever be looked upon as the entrance to a living, interpersonal relationship ..., then the decision of a tribunal must be (that) ... there is full and total simulation of Christian marriage itself.[133]

The total simulation of matrimonial consent can also arise from the beliefs of the party to a marriage. In the case involving the hippy referred to above, Stankiewicz wrote that "anyone who totally rejects marriage as an institution because of pervasive opinions regulating his lifestyle thereby rejects marriage as a communion of the whole of life or as a permanent *consortium*".[134] Johnson summarises the nature of total simulation: "The person who simulates totally does not want a relationship, period".[135]   **321**

It is necessary to distinguish between motivation for marriage and marital intention. Some motivations are more laudable than others, but the reasons why people marry each other is a matter of personal choice. As long as the parties do not exclude marriage itself or some element of marriage, their motivation is of no juridical relevance.[136]   **322**

There are two kinds of proof where total simulation is concerned, direct and indirect. Direct proof involves the confession of the simulating party; indirect proof relies on evidence concerning the reasons for simulating and the circumstances implying that simulation occurred. Ideally, these approaches complement each other.[137] Johnson gives several examples of indirect proof: **323**

> Serrano found that a woman's extreme attachment to her personal freedom demonstrated that she had never offered her husband any "rights" over her person. Ferraro held that a man's habitual promiscuity combined with an admission that he lacked the capacity to be a faithful husband constituted proof of simulation. Ragni decided that the beha-

---

132 Ibid., 396. 133 c. Humphries, 23 April 1971, *Matrimonial decisions of England and Wales* 5 (1971), 8-11. 134 Johnson, 401. For a detailed study of this "hippy" case, cf. L. Robitaille, "Simulation, error determining the will, or lack of due discretion?" in *Studia Canonica* 29 (1995), 397-432. 135 Ibid., 405. 136 O. Fumagalli Carulli, *Intelletto e volontà nel consenso matrimoniale in diritto canonico*, Vita e Pensiero, Milan, 1974, 133, n. 63. 137 Johnson, 410.

viour of a baptised Anglican who had received no religious education and who lived a life totally at odds with Christian values manifested a non-verbal rejection of marriage as the Church understands it.[138]

Partial simulation

324　In the section dealing with the canonical doctrine, we referred to the conceptual frameworks which are found in the canonical tradition regarding marriage. One of these is the three goods of marriage (*bona matrimonii*): fidelity (*bonum fidei*), the good of children (*bonum prolis)* and good of perpetuity (*bonum sacramenti*).[139] This framework is used in tribunal practice in cases of simulation; a marriage may be null, for example, on the grounds of an intention *contra bonum fidei* on the part of the respondent.

Exclusion of the "right to children"

325　As was noted above in the commentary on Can. 1084, there is no strict "right to a child".[140] In matrimonial consent couples give to and receive from each another the right to acts which are apt by their nature for the procreation of children (1917 Code, c. 1081). The *bonum prolis* consists in the generation, birth, support and physical, moral and spiritual education of children.[141] The *bonum prolis* can be excluded in several ways.

326　　The right to a sexual relationship with one's spouse is one of the rights which is given and received in matrimonial consent; the absolute refusal of a person to consummate his or her marriage would point to an exclusion of the *bonum prolis*.[142]

327　　The relationship of husband and wife involves the right to sexual acts which are *per se* apt for the procreation of children. The intention of a person to carry on a sexual relationship in a way that would exclude entirely the possibility of conception invalidates consent. This is the case regardless of the means used, whether they are artificial or natural.[143] The decision of a

138 Ibid., 414. 139 Fidelity means that one refrains from sexual contact outside the marriage bond; offspring, that (the child) is lovingly received, tenderly nurtured, religiously brought up; the sacrament, that the marriage is not broken and the abandoned spouse marry another, not even for the sake of having children. This can be considered the rule of marriage, by which natural fecundity is adorned and the baseness of sexual disorder (*De genesi ad litteram*, lib. 9, Can. 7, n. 12). 140 *Donum vitae*, n. 8. 141 P. Huizing, "Bonum prolis ut elementum essentiale obiecti formalis consensus matrimonialis" in *Gregorianum* 43 (1962), 658. 142 Ibid., 714. 143 Ibid., 716/720. Pope Pius XII stated: "If in contracting marriage at least one of the parties had the intention to restrict the matrimonial right, and not simply its use, to the sterile periods in such a way that on the other days the other partner would not even have the right to ask for the act, this would amount to an essential defect in the matrimonial consent which in turn would mean that the marriage is null" (*AAS* 43 (1951), 845).

couple to postpone starting their family does not render their consent invalid. Jurisprudence distinguishes in this area between the exclusion of the right and the exclusion of the use of the right. One canonist comments: "More recent jurisprudence demands that for nullity to be proved the right itself must be excluded. Recent jurisprudence sees the temporary exclusion as the denial of the use of the right and so has held that in such cases the marriage is not invalid"[144]

In addition to the avoidance of conception, the positive intention to omit what is necessary for the physical survival of a child renders also represents an intention *contra bonum prolis*. The following intentions fall under this heading: the intention to use the "morning-after" pill to completely avoid conception, the intention to abort any child conceived, the intention to kill at birth any children born, the intention not to feed any children born or to expose them so that they will die.[145] The exclusion "by a positive act of the will" which Can. 1101 §2 requires does not have to be expressed in words; actions which reveal intentions such as those mentioned speak louder than words.[146]   **328**

There are four ways of proving such an exclusion: a) the declarations of the parties; b) the testimony of witnesses regarding the intentions of the person concerned; c) motives or circumstantial evidence; d) presumptions. The kind of motive which lends credence to allegations of an intention *contra bonum prolis* would, for example, be an inordinate fear of child-birth, an aversion to children or a single-minded attachment to a career. In some cases the continuing reluctance of one of the parties to have children masks an underlying determination never to do so.   **329**

Exclusion of the right to fidelity

The *bonum fidei* concerns the exclusive nature of the rights given and exchanged in marriage. Fidelity is defined in *Casti connubii*:   **330**

> The second of the blessings of matrimony mentioned by St Augustine is fidelity, that is, the mutual faithfulness of husband and wife in observing the matrimonial contract. This implies that the right which in virtue of this divinely ratified agreement belongs exclusively to each companion will neither be denied by the one to the other nor granted to any third party; and, moreover, that no concession will be made even to one of the contracting parties if it is contrary to the rights and laws of God and incompatible with matrimonial fidelity itself.[147]

144 A. Arena, "The jurisprudence of the Sacred Roman Rota: its development and direction after the Second Vatican Council" in *Studia Canonica* 12 (1978), 280. **145** Huizing, 717. **146** Decision c. Felici, 24 April 1956 in SRR decis. 48 (1956), 403. **147** *The Christian Faith*, n. 1828.

331   The exclusive nature of the conjugal relationship can be omitted in a number of ways and not simply by the intention to have more than one spouse. A person might intend to have only one spouse but might reserve the right to commit adultery; such a person has not given to his or her spouse an exclusive right to sexual relations or a right to an exclusive conjugal partnership.[148] Jurisprudence has identified a number of ways in which the *bonum fidei* can be excluded: the keeping on of a previous lover and the liberal (free-love) mentality. The firm intention of a person who is marrying to continue to have relations with a former or concurrent lover is a strong indication that this person has not assumed the obligation of fidelity.[149] Evidence that a person lived a promiscuous life-style before marriage and continued to live in this way from the start of married life can be "very pertinent in proving the non-assumption of the obligation of fidelity even when there is no self-confession by the guilty party".[150] Other examples include a promise to be faithful to a third party and the intention of a man to put his wife out for prostitution and to live of the earnings.[151] It must be stressed that infidelity in marriage does not of itself amount to a denial of the fundamental right.

332   Rotal jurisprudence does not accept that the *bonum fidei* is excluded when a spouse reserves a right to homosexual relations.[152] Cases involving homosexuality are normally heard on other grounds, such as Can. 1095, 3°.

Exclusion of the right to perpetuity

333   Can. 1056 states: "The essential properties of marriage are unity and indissolubility; in christian marriage they acquire a distinctive firmness by reason of the sacrament". Indissolubility is one of those "essential properties" whose exclusion by a positive act of the will renders consent invalid. It arises from the total self-giving of the spouses which is expressed in their matrimonial consent; it is not simply an obligation imposed on them by the Church:

> Being rooted in the personal and total self-giving of the couple, and being required by the good of the children, the indissolubility of marriage finds its ultimate truth in the plan that God has manifested in his revelation: he wills and communicates the indissolubility of marriage as a fruit, a sign and requirement of the absolutely faithful love that God has for man and that the Lord Jesus has for the Church.[153]

---

148 U. Navarrete, "De iure ad vitae communionem: observationes ad novum schema canonis 1086 §2" in *Periodica* 66 (1977), 250.   **149** Arena, 271-2.   **150** Ibid., 274.
151 T. Doyle, "A new look at the bonum fidei" in *Studia Canonica* 12 (1978), 16-7.
152 L. De Luca, "The new law on marriage" in the *Catholic Lawyer* 30 (1985), 87. For a fuller discussion of this point, cf. W. J. Tobin, *Homosexuality and marriage*, Catholic Book Agency, Rome, 1964, 227-39. **153** Fl II, 830, *FC* n. 20c.

This ground of nullity must be considered in the context of current trends **334** in civil legislation regarding divorce in many parts of the world. Binchy comments:

> This brief review of the divorce law in other jurisdictions shows that no-fault divorce has swept the modern world over the past decade or so. Its basic philosophy is that a marriage should be terminated, not only where both spouses desire it but even where one spouse does not wish to be divorced. Although the legislation frequently speaks of the "irretrievable breakdown of marriage", the blunt truth is that this is not a question that is investigated by the Court; the fact that one spouse seeks a divorce is in practice conclusively presumed to prove the existence of an irretrievable breakdown of the marriage.[154]

Indissolubility can be excluded in two ways: in the first case, a spouse **335** who knows the Church's teaching on the indissolubility of marriage enters marriage while reserving the right to dissolve the marriage bond; in the second, a spouse whose view of marriage is that marriage is dissoluble enters marriage on that basis.[155] This latter ground is closely related to error concerning indissolubility that determines the will (Can. 1099).[156]

Men and women marry with the hope that their married life will be happy **336** and stable; few marry with the explicit intention of excluding the indissolubility of marriage. Some however marry with the proviso that if the marriage does not work out, they will leave the marriage and seek a civil divorce. Rotal jurisprudence holds that, for consent to be invalid, "it suffices that [a person] reserves to him– or herself the possibility of getting a divorce".[157]

Exclusion of sacramentality

Pius IX taught that "there is no contract if the sacrament is excluded, that is **337** the sacrament in christian matrimony is not accessory to the contract, nor can it be separated from it".[158] This teaching is implicit in Can. 1055 §2. In order for a valid sacramental marriage to be possible the parties must be baptised and intend to do what Christ and the Church intend.[159] Canonists

---

154 *Is divorce the answer?* Irish Academic Press, Dublin, 1984, 17. **155** Decision c. Pompedda, 1 July 1969 in SRR decis. 61 (1969), 691, n.3. **156** Villeggiante holds that cases of error concerning indissolubility that determine the will (Can. 1109) can be reduced to intentions contra bonum sacramenti, but the corollary is not the case "L'esclusione del bonum sacramenti" in *La simulazione del consenso matrimoniale canonico*, 211-2. **157** Decision c. Massimi, 21 December 1927 in SRR decis. 19 (1927), 536, n. 2: "... satis est ut facultatem sibi servat divortii faciendi". This was stated in a recent case c. Palestro, 5 April 1989 (prot. no. 15.503): "... cum satis sit ut considerent matrimonium tali positiva limitatione celebratum tamquam non existens atque semetipsum veluti nunquam vinculo ullo copulatum". **158** *DS* 1766. **159** On the link between faith

accept that sacramentality can be excluded in the same way and with the same effects as the exclusion of unity and indissolubility.[160] This typically occurs in the case of those who, though baptised, have lapsed from the catholic faith:

> If the denial of faith is understood as an ideological opinion and a moral depravity as a "life-choice" which seizes and shapes the total person, in a manner of thinking, acting and being itself then one can legitimately ask if the contractant in such a situation is capable of contracting a valid sacramental marriage ... In certain candidates for matrimony there lives a spirit of total indifference, even of hostility and aversion which is almost visceral, towards Christ and the Church, creating in them a psychological irreversible obstacle, it is then difficult to hold that ... they are capable of contracting sacramental marriage.[161]

338   From a procedural perspective, Flatten argues that the ground of nullity in such cases is not "lack of faith" but "exclusion of sacramental dignity" or "a defect of intention of receiving the sacrament".[162] On 18 April 1986 the Roman Rota gave a favourable decision in a case pleaded on this ground.[163]

Exclusion of the consortium totius vitae (sharing of the whole life)

339   After Vatican II strenuous efforts were made to re-define the object of matrimonial consent in the light of the conciliar vision of marriage. Anné attempted this in a landmark decision:

> [Matrimonial consent is] an act of the will by which a man and a woman constitute between themselves a mutual covenant, or by an irrevocable consent constitute a perpetual and exclusive community of conjugal love, ordained by its very nature to the generation and education of

and this sacramental intention, the International Theological Commission stated: "The intention of carrying out what Christ and the Church desire is the minimum intention required before consent is considered to be a 'real human act' on the sacramental plane. The problem of the intention and that of the personal faith of the contracting parties must not be confused with one another, but they must not be totally separated either. In the last analysis, the real intention is born from and feeds on living faith" ("Propositions on the doctrine of Christian marriage" in *International Theological Commission: texts and documents 1969-1985*, ed. M. Sharkey, 168, 2.3). **160** Z. Grocholewski, "Crisis doctrinae et iurisprudentiae rotalis circa exclusionem dignitatis sacramentalis in contractu matrimoniali" in *Periodica* 67 (1978), 292-5. **161** D. Faltin, "The exclusion of the sacramentality of marriage with particular reference to the marriage of baptised non-believers" in *Marriage Studies* IV (ed. J.A. Alesandro), Canon Law Society of America, Washington, 1990, 99. **162** Ibid., 102. **163** SRR decis. 78 (1986), 278-98.

children. Thereby the formal substantial object of this consent is found not only in the perpetual and exclusive *ius in corpus*, but it also includes the right to a communion of life, or a community of life which, properly speaking, is matrimonial, and gives rise to an "intimate conjunction of persons and works" by which they complete each other and associate their action to God in the procreation and education of new lives.[164]

The difficulty of defining this "right to a communion of life" was clear from the outset. Navarrete wrote: **340**

> It seems that the essential object of this right and obligation [right to a communion of life] cannot be other than an undefined and undefinable unity of attitudes, of behaviour and of activities ... without which it is impossible to establish or conserve the *personarum communio* [communion of persons] required for achieving the essential purposes of marriage... The object must be the attitudes, behaviour and activities which can be directly commanded by the will and which by their nature are necessary in order than marriage can achieve at the existential level its institutional ends, especially the *vita melior atque beatior* [the better and happier life] of the spouses.[165]

The attempt to integrate this value into Can. 1101 §2 ended in 1980; the   **341**
Revision Commission left it to ecclesiastical jurisprudence to find ways of giving expression to this aspect of the conciliar teaching on marriage.[166] It is not yet clear if it will become an autonomous ground of nullity or if it will be integrated into jurisprudence in another way; so far "exclusion of the *consortium totius vitae*" has not been accepted by the Roman rota as an autonomous ground of nullity.[167] Faílde has written that a person who at the time of consent was resolved never to cohabit with his or her spouse would rule out the exercise of rights and obligations without which the *consortium vitae coniugalis* could not be achieved.[168]

---

164 Decision c. Anné, 25 February 1969 in SRR decis. 61 (1969), 183, n. 16.
165 "Problemi sull'autonomia dei capi di nullità del matrimonio per difetto di consenso causato da perturbazioni della personalità" in *Perturbazioni psichiche e consenso matrimoniale nel diritto canonico* (Studia et documenta iuris canonici VII), Catholic Book Agency, Rome, 1976, 135. **166** *Comm* 15 (1983), 233. **167** J.-M. Serrano-Ruiz, "L'esclusione del *consortium totius vitae*" in *La simulazione del consenso matrimoniale canonico*, 119. Sheehy has argued that there is no reason why a tribunal should reject a petition which included the grounds of "exclusion of the *ius ad vitae consortium*" ("Animadversiones quaedam in matrimonii essentiale aliquod elementum" in *Periodica* 75 (1986), 126). **168** "Observationes novae circa matrimonium canonicum simulatum et coactum" in *Periodica* 75 (1986), 190. De Luca has investigated this theme from another perspective in "L'esclusione del *bonum coniugum*" in *La simulazione del consenso matrimoniale canonico*, 125-37.

Can. 1102 Condition

> §1 Marriage cannot be validly contracted subject to a condition concerning the future.
>
> §2 Marriage entered into subject to a condition concerning the past or the present is valid or not, according as whatever is the basis of the condition exists or not.
>
> §3 However, a condition as mentioned in §2 may not lawfully be attached except with the written permission of the local Ordinary.

Future condition

342   The 1917 Code had detailed regulations regarding the placing of a condition prior to matrimonial consent; c. 1092, 3° stated that a condition, once placed and not revoked, suspended the validity of a marriage. Although consent was given in the marriage ceremony subject to a future condition, the marriage did not come into existence until the condition was fulfilled.[169]

343   The Revision Commission decided not to permit the contracting of marriage under a future condition.[170] The idea of consent made under a future condition does not sit easily with the understanding of matrimonial consent as "an act of will by which a man and a woman by an irrevocable covenant give and accept one another for the purpose of establishing a marriage" (Can. 1057 §2). In this decision, the Church, in the judgement of Robitaille, "left tradition behind and legislated in favour of the public good".[171]

Past and present conditions

344   Can. 1102 §2 states that "marriage entered into subject to a condition concerning the past or the present is valid or not, according as whatever is the basis of the condition exists or not". Örsy writes that "it is almost impossible to reconcile [the idea of conditional consent] with the nature of the marriage covenant".[172] The law however takes account of the human reality that individuals on occasion place a condition on their consent. They can do so implicitly; for example, a man may agree to marry a woman who he has been told is expecting his child. He harbours some doubts and when the baby is born he becomes aware that he is not in fact the father of the child and leaves the family home immediately, never to return. Pinto has written:

> Jurisprudence, even Rotal jurisprudence, has sometimes held that a

---

169 L. Robitaille, "Conditioned consent: natural law and human positive law" in *Studia Canonica* 26 (1992), 77. 170 *Comm* 3 (1971), 77. For a further discussion of this principle, cf. *Comm* 15 (1983), 234. 171 "Conditioned consent: natural law and human positive law" in *Studia Canonica* 26 (1992), 94. 172 *Marriage in canon law*, 146.

true condition can only be placed by a person who is aware of its invalidating effect. But this is not true. People are generally unaware of such legalities and in no way realise that entering marriage conditionally results in invalidity. All they know is that on occasion a particular circumstance is so important to them that they rate it higher than marriage itself and that, if they cannot have the circumstance or quality, they cannot have the marriage either.[173]

This circumstance is similar to a quality which is "directly and principally intended" (Can. 1097 §2). One of the best proofs of the existence of a true condition is "the quickness of terminating the marriage ... once it is realised that the condition has not been fulfilled".[174]   **345**

Although a past or present condition may be attached to matrimonial consent, it may not lawfully be done "except with the written permission of the local Ordinary" (Can. 1101 §3). The latter must judge if it is prudent for the marriage to take place under a specific condition.[175]   **346**

Can. 1103 Force and fear

A marriage is invalid which was entered into by reason of force or of grave fear imposed from without, even if not purposely, from which the person has no escape other than by choosing marriage.

This canon deals with marriage entered into by reason of force or of grave fear. Force is an impulse from without which cannot be resisted; it can be either physical or moral. Fear means the trepidation of mind that a person feels when facing an impending evil. It has also been defined "as a disturbance of the mind caused by impending present or future danger".[176] It can be the result of moral or physical coercion; this is why it is linked to force. Can. 125 §2 states that an act performed as a result of fear which is grave and unjustly inflicted is valid, "unless the law provides otherwise". The present canon is an instance where the law does so. Human dignity and the interpersonal nature of marriage render abhorrent and contradictory the concept of life-long marriage being undertaken only to escape a threatened evil.   **247**

Fear is a human emotion which admits of infinite degrees. For it to invalidate consent, two conditions must be fulfilled: it must be "grave", and it must be "imposed from outside". Fear is objectively grave if it arises from a threatened evil that would intimidate any reasonable person, for example, the threat of death, serious injury, disinheritance or loss of reputation. It is subjectively grave if the subjective dispositions of the person make him or   **348**

---

173 Decision of 26 June 1971, in SRR decis. 63 (1971), 560 cited in L. Wrenn, *Annulments*, 6th ed., 156. **174** Wrenn, 116. **175** *Comm* 3 (1971), 78. **176** *The Canon Law: letter and spirit*, n. 259, 73.

her particularly vulnerable to intimidation. Such dispositions would include youthfulness, parental dependence, or a nervous disposition. The essential point is that the fear is such that it leads to the marriage.[177]

349   The law requires that fear be "imposed from outside, even if not purposely". Retaining the phrase means that it is not necessary to prove that the person who was the source of the fear intended to pressurise the other party into marriage. The essential point is that a person finds a set of circumstances so threatening that he or she is prepared to enter marriage in order to avoid them.[178]

350   Jurisprudence dealing with subjectively grave fear recognises that there are situations in which the pressure on a person to marry arises from a personal relationship with a parent or respected superior. Hence the distinction between common fear and reverential fear. Whereas common fear is caused by threats "made by a hostile or brutal person",[179] fear is described as reverential when the pressure arises from the fear of arousing the anger of the respected superior. It is this anger or disapproval – rather than any particular threatened evil, which is the specific object of reverential fear.[180] In such situations this reverential fear on the part of the younger person is subjectively grave rather than objectively grave. Although in contemporary society relationships between parents and children are normally less severe than in past generations, there are still instances when a son or daughter will not dare to face the anger or disapproval of a parent.[181]

351   Proof of aversion is normally required to establish that a marriage took place out of fear and not just with fear. Evidence of this would be crying, sadness and denial of the signs of affection in the period before and after the marriage takes place. The aversion is to marriage with this person at this time.

352   Within the canonical tradition it has long been disputed whether force invalidates marriage by virtue of natural law or merely by virtue of positive law.[182] Notwithstanding that dispute, the Pontifical Council for the Interpretation of Legal Texts has stated that Can. 1103 applies to the marriages of non-catholics as well as to the marriages of catholics. This interpretation implies that the canon is of natural law.[183] It is clear that the Church places great value on the freedom of the parties. Navarrete comments: "The ultimate reason why fear has invalidating force ... is that marriage itself is, by

---

177 Decision c. Canals, 9 July 1964, in SRR decis. 56 (1964), 594: "Quidquid sit de absoluta gravitate violentiae, si causa matrimonii tribuenda est timori in subjecto passivo, profluenti a violentia seu minis a subjecto activo, certe metus gravis dicendus est." **178** Navarrete, ibid., 589.   **179** *The Canon Law: letter and spirit*, n. 2116, 619. **180** Jurisprudence assumes that women are more susceptible to such pressure than men. **181** Decision c. Palazzini, 8 July 1964, in SRR decis. 56 (1964), 566.   **182** For a brief discussion of this tradition, cf. U. Navarrete, "Responsa Pontificiae Commissionis CIC authentice interpretando" in *Periodica* 77 (1988), 497-503.   **183** *Comm* 19 (1987), 148. Cf. *CLSGBI Newsletter* 74 (1988), 77-8.

divine institution, a communion of life and love between the spouses. Where there is not love, but hatred, the fundamental element of this communion of life and love is missing. Freedom from serious coercion is demanded by the nature of marriage."[184]

Can. 1104 Manifestation of consent

§1 To contract marriage validly it is necessary that the contracting parties be present together, either personally or by proxy.
§2 The spouses are to express their matrimonial consent in words; if, however, they cannot speak, then by equivalent signs.

Cann. 1104-6 deal with the manifestation of consent. For consent to be valid, **353** the parties must normally be physically present. The law provides for the exchange of consent by proxy, that is, consent can be given on behalf of an absent party by a person authorised to act in their name. In principle, it is possible for both parties to be absent and to be represented by proxies. The safeguards necessary for such a procedure are laid down in Can. 1105.

Consent must be expressed either in words or, if a person cannot speak, **354** in equivalent signs. If consent is expressed in signs, these should be unambiguous and clearly understandable.

Can. 1105 Consent by proxy

§1 For a marriage by proxy to be valid, it is required:
1° that there be a special mandate to contract with a specific person;
2° that the proxy be designated by the mandator and personally discharge this function.
§2 For the mandate to be valid, it is to be signed by the mandator, and also by the parish priest or local Ordinary of the place in which the mandate is given or by a priest delegated by either of them or by at least two witnesses, or it is to be drawn up in a document which is authentic according to the civil law.
§3 If the mandator cannot write, this is to be recorded in the mandate and another witness added who is to sign the document; otherwise, the mandate is invalid.
§4 If the mandator revokes the mandate, or becomes insane, before the proxy contracts in his or her name, the marriage is invalid, even though the proxy or the other contracting party is unaware of the fact.

184 "Opportetne ut supprimatur verba 'ab extrinseco et iniuste incussum' in Can. 1087?" in *Ius Populi Dei: Miscellanea in honorem R. Bidagor*, III, Rome, 1972, 591 (my translation).

355 Can. 1105 lays down the conditions for the valid exchange of consent by proxy. The party who is unable to be present must designate the person who will represent him or her by a special document. This must state clearly the function of the proxy, that is, to express matrimonial consent on behalf of the mandator; it must state both the identity of the proxy and the intended spouse. The proxy must carry out the mandate personally.

356 Marriages by proxy are generally not permitted in countries which belong to the Common Law tradition.[185] Canon law stipulates that such marriages be celebrated only with the permission of the local Ordinary (Can. 1071 §1, 7°).

357 Since the validity of a marriage by proxy depends on the validity of the mandate, Can. 1105 §2 has strict requirements for this document. It can be a purely ecclesiastical document which is to be signed by the mandator and by the parish priest or the local Ordinary of the place where the mandate is given or by a priest delegated by either of these or by at least two witnesses. Or, where the civil law allows such marriages, it can be prepared as an authentic document in accordance with that law.

358 If a person who wishes to marry by proxy is unable to write, this fact must be stated in the mandate and another witness added who is also to sign the document. This is required for the validity of the mandate.

359 Since the consent of the mandator is required to contract the marriage, the marriage is invalid if he or she revokes the mandate or becomes insane before the marriage is contracted.

Can. 1106 Use of interpreter in celebration of marriage

> Marriage can be contracted through an interpreter, but the parish priest may not assist at such a marriage unless he is certain of the trustworthiness of the interpreter.

360 The services of an interpreter can be used for the celebration of a marriage. For example, if the officiating priest is unable to understand the language of the couple who are marrying, he will be unable to receive their consent as required by Can. 1108 §2. In order to be able to do so, he may seek the help of an interpreter. The law requires that he may not assist at such a marriage "unless he is certain of the trustworthiness of the interpreter".

Can. 1107 Consent presumed valid

> Even if a marriage has been entered into invalidly by reason of an impediment or defect of form, the consent given is presumed to persist until its withdrawal has been established.

---

185 *The Canon Law: letter and spirit*, n. 2222, 621.

This canon states an important presumption: consent which is naturally suf-   **361**
ficient to bring a marriage into being is presumed to be valid until the contrary is established. This applies even if the naturally sufficient consent lacks
legal force due to an impediment or a defect of form. On the basis of this
presumption, a marriage can be validated even without the renewal of consent (cf. Can. 1163 §1).

BIBLIOGRAPHY   **362**

General works on declarations of nullity

R. Brown, *Marriage annulment in the catholic Church*, 3rd edition, Kevin
  Mayhew, Bury St. Edmunds, 1990.
H.F. Doogan (ed.), *Catholic Tribunals: marriage annulment and dissolu-
  tion*, E.J. Dwyer, Sydney, 1990.
L.G. Wrenn, *Annulments*, 6th edition, Washington, 1996.
L. Örsy, *Marriage in Canon Law*, Michael Glazier, Wilmington, Delaware,
  1986.
The Canon Law: letter and spirit, Veritas, Dublin, 1995 (Commentary on
  Cann.1095-1107) nn. 2183-2227, 610-22.
I. Gramunt, J. Hervada and L.A. Wauck, *Canons and commentaries on Mar-
  riage*, Liturgical Press, Collegeville, Minnesota, 1987.
B.A. Siegle, *Marriage according to the New Code of Canon Law*, Alba
  House, New York, 1986.

Lack of discretion of judgement

J. O'Neill, "A basic look at lack of due discretion" in *CLSGBI Newsletter* 33
  (1977), 40-44.
A. Sabattani, "L'évolution de la jurisprudence dans les causes de nullité de
  mariage pour incapacité psychique" in *Studia Canonica* 1 (1967), 143-
  61.
J.B. Keating, *The bearing of mental illness on the validity of marriage*
  (Analecta Gregoriana 136) Rome, 1963.
N. Picard, "L'immaturité et le consentement matrimonial" in *Studia
  Canonica* 9 (1975), 37-56.
R.L. Burke, *Lack of discretion of judgement because of schizophrenia: doc-
  trine and recent rotal jurisprudence* (Analecta Gregoriana 237), Rome,
  1986.
G. Versaldi, "The dialogue between psychological science and canon law"
  in *Incapacity for marriage*, 25-78.
R.L. Burke, "Canon 1095, nn. 2-3", in *Incapacity for marriage*, 79-156.

Inability to assume and fulfil the essential obligations of marriage

A. McGrath, "On the gravity of causes of a psychological nature in the proof of inability to assume the essential obligations of Marriage" in *Studia Canonica* 22 (1988), 67-76.

J.H. Provost, "Canon 1095: past, present, future" in *The Jurist* 54 (1994), 81-112.

A. Mendonça, "The role of experts in 'incapacity to contract' cases (canon 1095)" in *Studia Canonica* 25 (1991), 417-50.

A. Mendonça, "Recent jurisprudence on the effects of mood disorders and neuroses on matrimonial consent" in *Unico servitio ecclesiae* (ed. Thériault and Thorn), Ottawa, 1991, 148-79.

A. Mendonça, "The incapacity to contract marriage: canon 1095" in *Studia Canonica* 19 (1985), 259-326.

A. Mendonça, "Recent trends in rotal jurisprudence" in *Studia Canonica* 28 (1994), 167-230.

A. Mendonça, "Narcissistic personality disorder: its effects on matrimonial consent" in *Studia Canonica* 27 (1993), 97-144.

A. Mendonça and N. Sangal, "Effects of anorexia and bulimia nervosa on marital consent" in *Monitor ecclesiasticus* 121 (1996), 539-610.

M.F. Pompedda, "Incapacity to assume the essential obligations of marriage" in *Incapacity for marriage*, 157-218.

R.J. Sanson, "Narcissistic personality disorder: possible effects on the validity of marital consent" in *Monitor ecclesiasticus* 113 (1988), 541-81; ibid., 114 (1989), 405-24.

Error regarding a quality "directly and principally intended"

P. Hennessy, "Canon 1097: a requiem for *error redundans?*" in *The Jurist* 49 (1989), 146-81.

W. Dalton, "*Error redundans*: a look at some recent jurisprudence" in *CLSGBI Newsletter* 50 (1981), 9-33.

Deceit

K.W. Vann, "*Dolus*: Canon 1098 of the revised Code of Canon Law" in *The Jurist* 47 (1987), 371-93.

P. Sumner, "*Dolus* as a ground for nullity of marriage" in *Studia Canonica* 14 (1980), 171-94.

G. Gressier, "La nullité du mariage conclu sous l'effet du dol qualifié du canon 1098 est de droit naturel" in *Studia Canonica* 30 (1996), 343-70.

J.G. Johnson, "On the retroactive force of canon 1098" in *Studia Canonica* 23 (1989), 61-83.

J. Cuneo, "Deceit/error of person as a *caput nullitatis*" in CLSA, *Proceedings of 45th Annual Convention* 1983, 154-67.

E. Kneal, "A proposed *in iure* section for the new statute of fraud" in *The Jurist* 42 (1982), 215-22.

Error concerning the nature of marriage

D.M. Campbell, "Canon 1099: the emergence of a new juridic figure?" in *Studio rotale* V, 35-72.

Decision c. Gabiola [error determining the will: Can. 1099] in *CLSGBI Newsletter* 106 (1996), 29-43.

M.F. Pompedda, "Faith and the sacrament of marriage, lack of faith and matrimonial consent: juridical aspects" in *Marriage Studies* IV, 33-65.

J.H. Provost, "Error as a ground in marriage nullity case" in CLSA, *Proceedings of the 75th Annual Convention*, 1995, 306-24.

Simulation

J.G. Johnson, "Total simulation in recent rotal jurisprudence" in *Studia Canonica* 24 (1990), 383-425.

A. Arena, "The jurisprudence of the Sacred Roman Rota: its development and direction after the Second Vatican Council" in *Studia Canonica* 12 (1978), 265-94.

D. Faltin, "The exclusion of the sacramentality of marriage with particular reference to the marriage of baptised non-believers" in *Marriage Studies* IV (ed. J.A. Alesandro), Canon Law Society of America Washington, 1990, 66-104.

N. Picard, "Exclusion de la procréation selon le droit matrimonial ecclésial" in *Studia Canonica* 10 (1976), 37-74.

D. Fellhauer, "The exclusion of indissolubility: old principles and new jurisprudence" in *Studia Canonica* 5 (1975), 105-33.

T. Doyle, "A new look at the *bonum fidei*" in *Studia Canonica* 12 (1978), 5-40.

Conditioned consent

L. Robitaille, "Conditioned consent: natural law and human positive law" in *Studia Canonica* 26 (1992), 75-110.

M. Zurowski, "Le développement de la notion canonique de la célébration conditionelle du mariage" in *Studia Canonica* 11 (1977), 85-114.

L. Wrenn, "A new condition limiting marriage" in *The Jurist* 34 (1974), 292-315.

5

Canonical form of marriage

363 The history of the celebration of marriage shows that even though no particular form of ceremony was required for the validity of the marriage until the Council of Trent, the Church was always anxious to surround the celebration of marriage with some formalities (cf. commentary on Can. 1119). This reflected both the desire of the Church to avoid the dangers associated with clandestine marriages and its sense of the ecclesial dimension of the sacrament of matrimony.

364 During the Middle Ages the Church gradually acquired jurisdiction concerning marriages. Local synods repeatedly condemned secret marriages and reminded the faithful of the penalties attached to them. In practice, clandestine marriage made it possible for people to contract and dissolve their own marriages; not surprisingly, grave abuses arose from the practice.[1] They refrained from declaring clandestine marriages null.

365 In 1563 the Council of Trent issued the *Tametsi* decree which required that, in order to be valid, matrimonial consent must be given in the presence of witnesses, one of whom must be the parish priest of the parish where the marriage was being celebrated. The Council also required parish priests to keep written records of marriages in their parishes.[2]

366 In many regions of Europe *Tametsi* was not promulgated and did not become law. Where this occurred, the expression of consent was subject only to the natural law. The question arose whether cohabitation as man and wife, after an engagement to marry, should be construed as sufficient expression of matrimonial consent. Successive Popes held that it should be so regarded, but in 1892 Pope Leo XIII, by the decree *Consensus mutuus*, revoked this presumption.[3] It was only when the *Ne temere* decree came into force in 1908 that the obligation to marry according to the canonical form was extended to the whole Church.[4]

367 Although many couples today cohabit before marriage, studies show that it "is more likely to be a prelude than an alternative to marriage".[5] Clulow observes that "the frequency with which people still choose to underpin their personal promises with public vows emphasises the social significance with which marriage is imbued".[6] The *Catechism of the Catholic*

---

1 J.A. Brundage, *Law, sex, and Christian society in medieval Europe*, 501. 2 *Decrees of the ecumenical councils* (ed. Tanner), II, 755-6. 3 Cf. T.L. Bouscaren and A.C. Ellis, *Canon law: a text and commentary*, 517. 4 ASS 40 (1907), 525-30. 5 C. Clulow and J. Mattinson, *Marriage inside out*, Penguin, London, 1995, 7. 6 Ibid.

Church states that "the public character of the consent protects the *I do* once given, and helps the spouses remain faithful to it".[7]

Can. 1108 Canonical form

§1 Only those marriages are valid which are contracted in the presence of the local Ordinary or parish priest or of the priest or deacon delegated by either of them, who, in the presence of two witnesses, assists, in accordance however with the rules set out in the following canons, and without prejudice ʌo the exceptions mentioned in Cann. 144, 1112 §1, 1116 and 1127 §§2-3.

§2 Only that person who, being present, asks the contracting parties to manifest their consent and in the name of the Church receives it, is understood to assist at a marriage.

This canon deals with the lawful manifestation of matrimonial consent. It prescribes that consent be exchanged by the parties, in the presence of two witnesses, before one of the following: the local Ordinary, the parish priest, a priest or deacon delegated by the local Ordinary or the parish priest. **368**

The term "local Ordinary" includes to the following: the Roman Pontiff, diocesan Bishops, those who preside over communities that are equivalent to a diocese (Can. 368), Vicars general and episcopal Vicars (Can. 134 §1). The diocesan Administrator, that is, the auxiliary Bishop or priest who governs a diocese when the see is vacant, is also included in this category as he "is bound by the obligations and enjoys the power of a diocesan Bishop, excluding those matters which are excepted by the nature of things or by the law itself" (Can. 427 §1). **369**

Parish priests have ordinary power to officiate at marriages in their parishes (Can. 530, 4°). A number of other priests are equivalent in canonical status to a parish priest. A personal parish priest enjoys the authority of a parish priest in relation to those persons who constitute his personal parish (Can. 1110). A priest who is given charge of a quasi-parish is the proper pastor of this community (Can. 516 §1). A parochial administrator, that is, the priest who is given pastoral charge of a parish when the parish is vacant or when the parish priest is unable to fulfil his duties, has the authority of a parish priest in matrimonial matters (cf. Can. 540 §1). A parochial vicar, that is, a priest who assumes the pastoral care of a parish when the parish priest is absent (Can. 533 §3) or the priest who is responsible for the pastoral care of a parish until a parochial administrator is appointed (Can. 549) similarly have the authority of a parish priest in matrimonial matters. Finally, each of the priests to whom the pastoral care of a parish or several **370**

---

7 n. 1631.

parishes is jointly entrusted has the authority of a parish priest (Can. 517 §1).

371   Although Can. 1108 §1 requires the presence of an ordained minister for the valid exchange of matrimonial consent, the canon refers to one situation where this does not apply. When there are no priests or deacons the local Ordinary can delegate lay persons to act as the official witness of the Church "if the Bishops' Conference has given its prior approval and the permission of the Holy See has been obtained" (Can. 1112 §1).

372   Can. 1108 §1 requires that the parties exchange consent "in the presence of two witnesses". These witnesses are sometimes called "unqualified witnesses" to distinguish them from the official witness; they may be lay or cleric, catholic or non-catholic; there may be one of each sex or both may be of the same sex. They must have reached the use of reason and understand what is taking place.[8]

373   Apart from the instances given above when priests have authority from the law to officiate at marriages, priests and deacons can obtain authority to officiate at marriages in two ways; the Ordinary or parish priest can delegate authority to them (cf. Cann. 137 §1). It is also supplied to them by law in situations of "common error" and "positive and probable doubt" (Can. 144 §2). For these to apply it is not enough for the community to believe that a priest, deacon or lay person has delegation when he or she does not; there must be an objective basis for the belief of the community concerning the status of the minister. In order for the jurisdiction to be supplied, "it is necessary that the one assisting at a marriage … exercises a function, even if it be an auxiliary one, in the parish … which can lead the faithful, at least in appearance, into believing that the person concerned has the necessary faculty".[9] Similarly a priest who resides in a parish but who has not been appointed curate there might be thought to have general delegation for marriages although in fact he has not.[10] In such instances the Church supplies the faculty to the minister for the sake of the common good or to avoid public harm.[11] However a minister who lacks delegation and who is present in a parish only to officiate at a marriage does not acquire delegation by virtue of Can. 144 §2.[12]

---

8 P. Gasparri, *Tractatus canonicus de matrimonio*, n.964: "Pariter esset invalidum matrimonium initum coram testibus, si uterque vel alteruter erat surdus, amens, usu rationis carens, vel, dum nupturientes consensum exprimebant, erat ebrius aut dormiens; ipsi enim incapaces sunt cuiuscumque testificationis" (A marriage would be invalid if contracted before witnesses if one or both were deaf, mad, lacking the use of reason or, while the consent was being given, they were drunk or asleep. Such witnesses are unable to testify that the marriage took place). The inclusion of the "deaf" in this list is based on the presumption that they were present but unaware of what was happening. Clearly a deaf person could be a valid witness if he or she knew that a marriage was being celebrated. **9** Decision c. Stankiewicz, 15 December 1992 in *Studia Canonica* 29 (1995), 523, n. 17. **10** CLD 2, 76-7; CLD 9, 660-672. **11** CLD 8, 170-4. **12** J.M. Huels, *The pastoral companion*, Franciscan Herald Press, Chicago, 1986, 224-5.

The faculty to assist at a marriage is also supplied "in case of positive **374** and probable doubt either of law or of fact" on the part of the Church's minister. This doubt consists in an indeterminate state of mind, or more properly, in a state of indecision as to whether the faculty to assist is supplied by the Church. However the Church supplies the necessary faculty only when there is a serious reason for believing that the minister has the faculty, even though the possibility of error is not excluded. Positive and probable doubt can be either of law or of fact. There is doubt of law when a person is not certain whether he or she has the faculty to assist at a marriage or not. There is doubt of fact when a person is not certain whether, in the concrete case, the fact is verified on which the valid exercise of the faculty to assist depends. In these situations the faculty to assist at a marriage is supplied.[13]

There are two situations when the canonical form does not bind. The **375** extraordinary form of marriage can be used when the person who is competent to assist cannot be approached "without grave inconvenience", for example, when one of the parties is in danger of death; in this case marriage can be celebrated in the presence of witnesses only (Can. 1116).[14] In the case of a mixed marriage, "if there are grave difficulties in the way of observing the canonical form, the local Ordinary of the catholic party has the right to dispense from it in individual cases ..." (Can. 1127 §2).[15]

The canonical form must be observed "if at least one of the parties con- **376** tracting marriage was baptised in the catholic Church or received into it and has not by a formal act defected from it" (Can. 1117).[16] A marriage is invalid due to a defect of form in the following circumstances:

> **a.** when a marriage involving at least one catholic – who has not defected from the Church by a formal act – takes place without a dispensation before a non-catholic minister or in a Registry Office;[17]
> **b.** when a marriage involving at least one catholic – who has not defected from the Church by a formal act – takes place in the catholic Church before a priest or deacon who lacked delegation to assist and the delegation was not supplied by the Church;
> **c.** when there were no witnesses or only one witness;
> **d.** when the assisting minister did not ask for or receive the couple's consent;
> **e.** when the exchange of consent was omitted altogether.

---

13 Cf. decision c. Stankiewicz, *Studia Canonica* 29 (1995), 523-5, nn. 18-20. **14** Cf. fuller commentary below at Can. 1116. **15** Cf. fuller commentary below at Can. 1127. **16** For a comment on defecting from the Church by a formal act, cf. Can. 1086 above. **17** L. Bogdan, "Simple convalidation of marriage in the 1983 Code of Canon Law" in *The Jurist* 46 (1986), 525.

377   If the validity of a marriage is challenged on the grounds that the official witness lacked the faculty to assist, the documentary nullity process is used (cf. Cann. 1686-88). If a person who was bound by the canonical form celebrated marriage in a civil or another religious forum without a dispensation, the pre-nuptial enquiry is sufficient to establish the canonical freedom of the person to marry.[18]

378   The function of the official witness is to "ask the contracting parties to manifest their consent and in the name of the Church receive it" (Can. 1108 §2). The official witness alone carries out this function even though other ministers may be present. He or she must have the use of reason when consent is being exchanged; "in the presence of" means more than physical presence.[19]

Can. 1109   Local Ordinary and parish priest

> Within the limits of their territory, the local Ordinary and the parish priest by virtue of their office validly assist at the marriages not only of their subjects, but also of non-subjects, provided one or other of the parties is of the latin rite. They cannot assist if by sentence or decree they have been excommunicated, placed under interdict or suspended from office, or been declared to be such.

379   By virtue of his office, the local Ordinary can assist, within his diocese, at the marriages of those who live in the diocese and also the marriages of those who happen to be in his diocese but have a domicile elsewhere. A parish priest, and those who are equivalent to him in canon law, have the same authority within their parish – or in the case of the priests mentioned in Can. 517 §1 – within their parishes. Since the jurisdiction of Ordinaries and parish priests is territorial, they require delegation to officiate at marriages outside their respective territories. They can officiate at marriages within their territories "provided one or other of the parties is of the latin rite". They cannot exercise the authority conferred on them by law "if by sentence or decree they have been excommunicated, placed under interdict or suspended from office, or been declared to be such" (cf. Cann. 1331-3); moreover, "the Church cannot supply the faculty in a person who has withdrawn himself from ecclesial communion and presumes to act on his own authority outside of hierarchical communion with the Bishop of the place where the marriage is celebrated".[20]

380   In some jurisdictions the civil law recognises the capacity of a cleric to

---

18 AAS 76 (1984), 747. 19 CLD 8, 820-2. Cf. U. Navarrete, "Sensus verborum *exquirit et recipit manifestationem consensus matrimonialem* (Can. 1108 §2)" in *Periodica* 83 (1994), 611-34. 20 Cf. decision c. Stankiewicz, 15 December 1992 in *Studia Canonica* 29 (1995), 526, n. 22.

perform catholic marriages by virtue of the fact that he is an ordained minister even though he is no longer authorised to act in the name of the catholic Church.[21] This leads to the anomalous situation that a marriage can be recognised in civil law as a catholic marriage whereas the catholic Church does not recognise it as such.

Can. 1110   Personal Ordinaries/parish priests

> A personal Ordinary and a personal parish priest by virtue of their office validly assist, within the confines of their jurisdiction, at the marriages only of those of whom at least one party is their subject.

This canon extends to personal Ordinaries the faculty conferred on Ordinaries   **381** in Can. 1108 §1. It does the same in the case of personal parish priests, for example, emigrant chaplains and military chaplains. The Instruction on the Pastoral Care of Migrants issued by the Congregation for Bishops in 1969 stated:

> A chaplain or missionary on whom a personal parish has been conferred, possesses parochial power together with all the rights and obligations which, according to common law, belong to pastors... A chaplain or missionary to whom a mission with the care of souls has been entrusted, possesses proper power and, with appropriate modifications, is equivalent to a pastor. Power of this kind is personal, that is, it is to be exercised only *vis-à-vis* migrants of the same language and within the confines of the mission. This power, however, by equal right is cumulative with the power of the local pastor. Consequently, every migrant possesses the freedom to go either to the chaplain or missionary or to the local pastor for the celebration of the sacraments, not excepting matrimony.[22]

---

21 A report to the British House of Commons in 1894 outlined the civil law regarding the celebration of catholic marriages in Ireland: "By the law of the Roman Catholic Church, under the decrees of the Council of Trent (which are now received throughout Ireland), the presence of the bishop of the diocese, or priest of the parish (or of some other priest deputed by the priest of the parish) is made indispensable for the solemnization of a marriage recognised as valid by that law; and every Roman Catholic marriage ought, according to the same law (though not under pain of nullity), to be preceded by the publication of banns for three Sundays, unless dispensed with (as in Ireland it usually is) by episcopal licence. Of these matters, however (being requisites of marriage by the internal economy only of the Roman Catholic Church), the law of the land takes no cognizance; and a marriage contracted in the presence of any Roman Catholic priest in Ireland, between two Roman Catholics, although contrary to the law and discipline of their own church, would be legally valid" (report of Mr G. Russell to the House of Commons, Marriage Laws/United Kingdom, 23 August 1894, 13). 22 CLD 7, nn. 38-39 §1-3, 210-1.

382 In 1986 Pope John Paul II promulgated the apostolic constitution *Spirituali militum curae* to regulate the pastoral care of military personnel and their families. The Military Ordinary has the same status as a diocesan Bishop; moreover "in the sphere assigned to them and in regard to the persons committed to their care, priests who are appointed as chaplains in the Ordinariate enjoy the rights and are bound by the duties of parish priests".[23] This includes the right to assist at marriages.

383   A different provision has been made for the pastoral care of "people of the sea". The *motu proprio Stella Maris* which Pope John Paul II promulgated on 31 January 1997 states with regard to the celebration of marriages:

> In order to assist validly and legally at a marriage during the voyage, the chaplain of the Apostleship of the Sea must be delegated by the Ordinary or by the parish priest of the parish in which one or the other of the contracting parties has a domicile or quasi-domicile, or has been staying for at least one month, or, if they are transients, of the harbour parish where they boarded the ship. The chaplain has the obligation to report the details of the celebration to the one delegating him, to be recorded in the marriage registry.[24]

Can. 1111 Delegation

> §1 As long as they validly hold office, the local Ordinary and the parish priest can delegate to priests and deacons the faculty, even the general faculty, to assist at marriages within the confines of their territory.
> §2 In order that the delegation of the faculty to assist at marriages be valid, it must be expressly given to specific persons; if there is question of a special delegation, it is to be given for a specific marriage; if however there is question of a general delegation, it is to be given in writing.

384 The local Ordinary can delegate priests or deacons to officiate at marriages within his diocese; the parish priest can delegate them to officiate at marriages within his parish. Both can give delegation for all cases" (general delegation) or "for an individual case" (special delegation).[25] A curate, or assistant priest, who has received general delegation from his Ordinary or parish priest can subdelegate another priest or deacon to officiate at an individual marriage.

---

23 *Code of Canon Law annotated*, 1161-3, VII. 24 Title III, VII §3, in *Osservatore Romano* (English edition), 19 March 1997, p. 3. 25 General delegation is no longer restricted to assistant priests, or curates (*Comm* 3 (1971), 79).

Can. 1111 §2 specifies how delegation must be given. To be valid, del-   **385**
egation must be given to persons specified either by name or by office (e.g.,
the parish priest of Seapatrick). It must be given "expressly"; it is not sufficient for it to be presumed. Special delegation must identify the specific
marriage: "I hereby delegate/subdelegate Rev ... to officiate at the marriage
of X and Y." General delegation must be given in writing.[26] The cleric who
is delegated or subdelegated must receive it.[27] The delegation-form provides for the acceptance of delegation or subdelegation: "I accept the above
delegation /subdelegation."[28]

If there is positive or probable doubt about the validity of the delegation   **386**
or as to whether it was granted or not, or if there is common error about
these matters, the Church supplies the necessary jurisdiction.[29]

Can. 1112 Lay persons as official witnesses

> §1 Where there are neither priests nor deacons, the diocesan Bishop
> can delegate lay persons to assist at marriages, if the Bishops' Confer-
> ence has given its prior approval and the permission of the Holy See
> has been obtained.
> §2 A suitable lay person is to be selected, capable of giving instruc-
> tion to those who are getting married, and fitted to conduct the mar-
> riage liturgy properly.

In 1974 the Holy See, in response to requests from a number of Bishops that   **387**
lay persons be permitted to assist at marriages, issued the instruction
Sacramentalem indolem.[30] It emphasised several points: the choice of suitable persons and the keeping of proper record of marriages celebrated before a lay person. It stated that lay persons were not competent to dispense
matrimonial impediments.[31]

The Code now incorporates this provision into the general law of the   **388**
Church. The scarcity of clergy refers to a general situation which is likely to
continue for some time, not just an emergency situation envisaged in Can.
1116. Before this provision can be availed of, two steps must be taken: the
Bishops' Conference must have given its approval. Before embarking on
such a course, the Conference must have regard to the civil law regarding
the celebration of marriages. The Canadian Bishops' Conference has issued
such a decree.[32] Secondly, the diocesan Bishop – and he alone – is to del-

---

26 Cf. *Comm* 8 (1976), p.41. Both Chiappetta (n. 3733) and *The Canon Law: letter and spirit* (n. 2238) take the view that general delegation must be given in writing for validity.   **27** L.Chiappetta, *Il codice di diritto canonico*, I, n. 829.   **28** Cf. Appendix I.
29 *The Canon Law: letter and spirit*, n. 2239.   **30** CLD 8, 815-8.   **31** Ibid., 817-7.
32 *The Code of Canon Law annotated*, p. 1328.

egate lay persons to assist at marriages. It should be noted that the 1991 edition of the *Ordo Celebrandi Matrimonium* has a special Rite for the Celebration of Marriage before a Lay Person.[33]

Can. 1113 Freedom established

> Before a special delegation is granted, provision is to be made for all those matters which the law prescribes to establish the freedom to marry.

389 When a minister is delegated to officiate at a marriage ceremony, provision should be made for carrying out the pre-nuptial enquiry before special delegation is granted.

Can. 1114 Duty of official witness

> One who assists at a marriage acts unlawfully unless he has satisfied himself of the parties' freedom to marry in accordance with the law and, whenever he assists by virtue of a general delegation, has satisfied himself of the parish priest's permission, if this is possible.

390 The task of ensuring that nothing stands in the way of the valid and lawful celebration of a marriage falls principally on the parish priest or curate of the parish where each party has a domicile. If another priest is to officiate at the marriage, he must satisfy himself that nothing stands in the way of the valid and lawful celebration of the marriage. A priest who has general delegation to officiate at marriages must have the permission of the parish priest to do so in individual instances. This permission can be presumed.[34] It is needed only for lawfulness.

Can. 1115 Parish where marriage is to be celebrated

> Marriages are to be celebrated in the parish in which either of the contracting parties has a domicile or a quasi-domicile or a month's residence or, if there is question of vagi, in the parish in which they are actually residing. With the permission of the proper Ordinary or the proper parish priest, marriages may be celebrated elsewhere.

391 Marriages may be celebrated in the parish where either party has a domicile

---

33 *Ordo celebrandi matrimonium coram assistente laico*, OCM, nn. 118-51. 34 *The Canon Law: letter and spirit*, n.2245, 627.

or quasi-domicile or a month's residence. The marriage may be celebrated elsewhere with the permission of the proper Ordinary or parish priest. The Irish Bishops' Conference has retained the custom of giving precedence to the parish of the bride or the local Ordinary; hence permission from the bride's parish priest is required when a couple wishes to celebrate their marriage outside that parish.[35]

The marriages of *vagi* are to be celebrated in the parish where they are 392 actually residing. They must be referred to the local Ordinary (Can. 1071 §1, n.1).

Can. 1116 Extraordinary form of marriage

§1 If one who, in accordance with the law, is competent to assist, cannot be present or be approached without grave inconvenience, those who intend to enter a true marriage can validly and lawfully contract in the presence of witnesses only:
1° in danger of death;
2° apart from danger of death, provided it is prudently foreseen that this state of affairs will continue for a month.
§2 In either case, if another priest or deacon is at hand who can be present, he must be called upon and, together with the witnesses, be present at the celebration of the marriage, without prejudice to the validity of the marriage in the presence of only the witnesses.

The law recognises that in certain circumstances it will not be possible or 393 reasonable to insist on the usual canonical form. For example, marriage may be celebrated before witnesses alone if a person competent by law to assist at marriages "cannot be present or be approached without grave inconvenience". The "extraordinary form" of marriage can be used in two circumstances: in danger of death or where it is prudently foreseen that the situation will continue for a month. Canon law does not insist on a civil form of marriage for catholics in these cases. Should it be possible for the marriage to be celebrated civilly, the civil marriage would have full canonical effects, provided the couple intend to enter a true marriage.[36]

A priest or deacon who is at hand in this circumstance must be called 394 upon to be present at the celebration of the marriage. Consent must be expressed in the presence of two witnesses who are aware of what is taking place.

---

35 *Pre-nuptial enquiry* 4. 36 *The Canon Law: letter and spirit*, n. 2249, 628. Cf. J. Hendriks, "Matrimonii forma extraordinaria (Can. 1116)" in *Periodica* 84 (1995), 687-709.

Can. 1117 Those bound by the form

> The form prescribed above is to be observed if at least one of the parties contracting marriage was baptised in the catholic Church or received into it and has not by a formal act defected from it, without prejudice to the provisions of Can. 1127 §2.

395   The requirement to celebrate marriage in the canonical form is of ecclesiastical law only; it binds those "who were baptised in the catholic Church or received into it" (Can. 11). Moreover this canon does not bind those who have "defected from the catholic Church by a formal act". Accordingly the marriages of catholics who have defected from the Church "by a formal act" and have gone through a form of marriage in a different religious or civil ceremony are valid. The meaning of the phrase "defected from the catholic Church by a formal act" has still to be established by ecclesiastical jurisprudence.[37] It would include those who have formally joined another Church or religion.

396   The marriages of those who are not bound by the canonical form are valid in canon law, regardless of where they take place. In the case of mixed marriages, the canonical form can be dispensed "if there are grave difficulties in the way of observing the canonical form" (Can. 1127 §2). This dispensation may be given for the marriage between two catholics only in danger of death.[38]

397   When a marriage takes place between a catholic and a non-catholic of oriental rite, that is, an Orthodox christian, the canonical form obliges only for lawfulness; for validity the presence of a sacred minister is required, as long as the other requirements of law are observed (Can. 1127 §1).

Can. 1118 Place of celebration

> §1 A marriage between catholics, or between a catholic party and a baptised non-catholic, is to be celebrated in the parish church. By permission of the local Ordinary or of the parish priest, it may be celebrated in another church or oratory.
> §2 The local Ordinary can allow a marriage to be celebrated in another suitable place.
> §3 A marriage between a catholic party and an unbaptised party may be celebrated in a church or in another suitable place.

---

37 Cf. commentary on Can.1086 above. Cf. A. Stenson, "The concept and implications of the 'formal act of defection' of Can. 1117" in *CLSGBI Newsletter* 68 (1986), 29-49. **38** *Comm* 17 (1985), 262. The Holy See judges each case on its merits when asked to dispense in these cases (*CLSGBI Newsletter* 78 (1989), 26-28; ibid., 81 (1990), 1-2).

A marriage between catholics or between a catholic and a baptised non-catholic is to be celebrated in the parish church of the catholic party. With the permission of the local Ordinary or parish priest a marriage may be celebrated in another church or oratory.   **398**

An earlier draft of Can. 1118 §2 proposed that the Ordinary could permit the celebration of a marriage in private houses or in another suitable place. The reference to "private houses" was omitted because it was felt that the phrase "in another suitable place" was sufficient.[39] It is no longer forbidden to celebrate marriages in the oratories of seminaries or convents as it was in the 1917 Code (c. 1109 §2).[40]   **399**

A marriage between a catholic and an unbaptised person may take place in a church or in another suitable place. The permission of the local Ordinary is not required. Those arranging such marriages should take account of the provisions of the civil law.   **400**

Time of celebration of marriage

In the late Middle Ages the times of the year when it was permitted to celebrate marriages were strictly laid down: "Church weddings were not normally permitted between the beginning of Advent and 13 January, a period of 6-7 weeks, from Septuagesima Sunday to the first Sunday after Easter (10 weeks), and from the first Rogation Day, the Monday before Ascension Thursday, to the Sunday after Pentecost (3 weeks), making a total of 19-20 weeks in which solemnisation was not possible".[41]   **401**

The 1917 Code stated that, while marriage could be contracted at any time of the year, it was forbidden to give the solemn nuptial blessing from the first Sunday in Advent till Christmas and from Ash Wednesday till Easter Sunday (c. 1108 §2). The *Ordo Celebrandi Matrimonium* (1991) states that the celebration of marriages on Good Friday and Holy Saturday is to be absolutely avoided.[42]   **402**

The celebration of marriage on Sundays and holydays is generally, though not universally, discouraged because of the number of other Masses which take place on those days. The matter may be regulated by particular law.   **403**

The practice of the Church regarding the time of day when marriages are to be celebrated is governed by particular law; for example, the Maynooth Statutes (1956) prescribe that marriages should be celebrated before midday;[43] however celebration at a later time was permitted for a just and reasonable cause.[44] This practice was dictated by the law governing when Mass   **404**

---

39 *Comm* 10 (1978), 103-4. The text of Can. 329 §2 was: "Matrimonium in aedibus privatis vel in alio convenienti loco celebrari Ordinarius loci permittere potest". **40** L. Chiappetta, *Il codice di diritto canonico*, II, n. 3751, 246. **41** A. Cosgrove, "Marriage in medieval Ireland" in A. Cosgrove (ed.), *Marriage in Ireland*, 37. **42** n. 32. **43** n. 195. **44** Ibid.

could be said (c. 821) and the law regarding the Eucharistic fast (c. 808). The law on the eucharistic fast was mitigated by Pope Paul VI in 1964.[45]

Can. 1119 Liturgical form of marriage

> Apart from a case of necessity, in the celebration of marriage those rites are to be observed which are prescribed in the liturgical books approved by the Church, or which are acknowledged by lawful custom.

405   St Paul wrote that Christians should marry "in the Lord" (1 Cor 7:39). The early Church viewed marriage in the light of the teaching of Christ and the apostles. It had however no specifically Christian form of celebration of marriage. It considered that the marriage of Christian spouses celebrated according to the customs of the time was transformed from within by their baptism. Gradually however the Church surrounded the civil and family marriages of the faithful with pastoral care. St Ignatius of Antioch observed that it was fitting for the faithful to contract marriage only "after the Bishop's approval".[46] The purpose of this recommendation was to dissuade Christians from marrying non-Christians. The permission of the Bishop was also required for marriages of the lower clergy and for marriages of orphans entrusted to the Bishop's care. This also applied in the case of marriages not recognised by the civil law, such as that of a patrician woman with a freedman or a slave.[47]

406   It was only in the fourth century that evidence of priestly prayer and blessing is found in connection with marriage. The first evidence of a nuptial Mass with a priestly solemnisation of marriage contracted civilly and in the family dates from the fourth and fifth centuries in the Roman Church.[48] From among all the customs in the marriage ceremony the Church gave liturgical status to the veiling *(velatio)*. Like the virgin who is betrothed to Christ, her only Spouse, a Christian woman who is being joined to a Christian man in marriage received a veil from the hands of the Church as a sign of her new state. The most common form of marriage liturgy in Gaul and the Celtic countries consisted in a blessing of the spouses in the bridal chamber.[49] In the East there was a ceremony of crowning. St John Chrysostom wrote that "crowns are placed on the heads of the spouses as a symbol of their victory, for they have reached the port of marriage unconquered by pleasure".[50]

45 *DOL* 2117.   **46** *Ad Polycarpum,* 5.2.   **47** J. Evenou, "Marriage" in *The Church at prayer*, III, *The sacraments* (ed. Martimort), Geoffrey Chapman, London, new edition 1988, 188.   **48** Ibid. For the history of the liturgical celebration of marriage, cf. K. Stevenson, *Nuptial blessing*, Alcuin Club/SPCK, London, 1982.   **49** Ibid., 191. **50** *Homiliae in 1 Tim 9:2* in *PG* 62:546.

Throughout the Middle Ages, the Church exercised control over the cel- **407**
ebration of Christian marriage. By 1100 it had secured virtual supremacy in
the adjudication of issues relating to the formation of marriage and the separation, divorce, and remarriage of those whose marriages failed.[51] It was
the custom for couples to exchange consent *in facie ecclesiae*, that is, at the
church door.[52]

The Roman Ritual published in 1614 emphasised the role of the priest in **408**
the celebration of marriage rather than the role of the couple. The couple
simply replied "yes" to the question posed by the priest; the latter then said
"ego coniungo vos" (I join you) and sprinkled the couple with holy water;
he blessed a ring which the husband placed on his wife's finger. The wedding Mass followed, with the nuptial blessing after the Our Father.[53]

Vatican II called for the revision of the Marriage Rite "so it will more **409**
clearly signify the grace of the sacrament and will emphasise the spouses'
duties".[54] The first *editio typica* was issued in 1970 and was translated into
many vernacular languages; a revised *editio typica* was issued in 1991 and
vernacular translations are currently being prepared. The revised *Ordo
Celebrandi Matrimonium* has four Rites of Marriage: the Celebration of
Marriage during Mass, the Celebration of Marriage outside Mass, the Celebration of Marriage before a Lay Person,[55] and the Celebration of Marriage between a Catholic and a Catechumen or non-Christian.

Can. 1120 Authority of Bishops' Conferences to draw up marriage rites

> The Bishops' Conference can draw up its own rite of marriage, to be
> reviewed by the Holy See, in keeping with the usages of the place and
> people, adapting these to the christian spirit; however the law must be
> observed which requires that the person assisting at the marriage, be-
> ing present, is to ask for and receive the expression of the contracting
> parties' consent.

Each Bishops' Conference can draw up a rite of marriage for its territory. It **410**
may take account of local customs and traditions, as long as they are in
harmony with christian faith and sensibilities. These rites must be submitted
to the Holy See for approval. The essential element of the Marriage Rite,
asking and receiving the expression of matrimonial consent, must always be
present (Can. 1108 §2).

---

51 J. Brundage, *Law, sex, and Christian society in medieval Europe,* 223. **52** K. Ritzer,
Le mariage dans les églises chrétiennes, Éditions du Cerf, Paris, 1970, 409, note 651.
53 Evenou, 200-1. **54** Fl I, 23, *SC* n. 77. **55** *Ordo celebrandi matrimonium coram
assistente laico.*

Can. 1121 Church requirements

§1 As soon as possible after the celebration of marriage, the parish priest of the place of celebration or whoever takes his place, even if neither has assisted at the marriage, is to record in the marriage register the names of the spouses, of the person who assisted and of the witnesses, and the place and date of the celebration of the marriage; this is to be done in the manner prescribed by the Bishops' Conference or by the diocesan Bishop.

§2 Whenever a marriage is contracted in accordance with Can. 1116, the priest or deacon, if he was present at the celebration, is bound as soon as possible to inform the parish priest or the local Ordinary about the marriage entered into; otherwise the witnesses, jointly with the contracting parties, are so bound.

§3 In regard to a marriage contracted with a dispensation from the canonical form, the local Ordinary who granted the dispensation is to see to it that the dispensation and the celebration are recorded in the marriage register both of the curia, and of the proper parish of the catholic party whose parish priest carried out the inquiries concerning the freedom to marry. The catholic spouse is obliged as soon as possible to notify that same Ordinary and parish priest of the fact that the marriage was celebrated, indicating also the place of celebration and the public form which was observed.

411   The parish priest of the parish where a marriage was celebrated is responsible for recording the marriage in the marriage register of that parish as soon as possible. He should enter the following details: the names of the spouses, the name of the priest or deacon who officiated, the names of the two witnesses, the place and date of the celebration of the marriage.

412   If a marriage took place in accordance with the extraordinary form of marriage, the priest or deacon who attended must inform the parish priest or the local Ordinary about the marriage; if no deacon or priest was present, this responsibility falls on the lay witnesses who were present.

413   When a mixed marriage is celebrated with a dispensation from the canonical form, the local Ordinary of the catholic party who granted the dispensation is to ensure that a record of the dispensation and of the celebration of the marriage is kept in the curia, and that notification of both is sent to the parish where the pre-nuptial enquiry was carried out, i.e., where the catholic party was domiciled. The catholic spouse is obliged to notify both the Ordinary and the parish priest of his or her parish that the marriage took place and where it took place:

When a mixed marriage is celebrated with a dispensation from the canonical form in the church of the party who is not a catholic, the local Ordinary will give advance notice to the parish priest in whose territory the marriage is to take place. It will be the duty of the parish priest to ascertain reliably and exactly all the usual details for entry in the marriage register of his parish together with a note as to the place of marriage and the diocese where the dispensation was granted... He must also send details of the marriage, for entry in the baptismal register, to the place where the catholic party was baptised. He must keep all the papers connected with the marriage in the archives of his parish.[56]

Can. 1122 Marriage entered in baptismal registers

§1 A marriage which has been contracted is to be recorded also in the baptismal registers in which the baptism of the spouses was entered.
§2 If a spouse contracted marriage elsewhere than in the parish of baptism, the parish priest of the place of celebration is to send a notification of the marriage as soon as possible to the parish priest of the place of baptism.

A record of the details of a marriage must be sent to the parish priest of the place of baptism of each party and be entered in the baptism register(s) (Can. 535 §2). The duty to send these notifications, if a marriage took place in a church other than the parish where the parties were baptised, falls on the parish priest of the place of the marriage.   **414**

Can. 1123 Further notifications

Whenever a marriage is validated for the external forum, or declared invalid, or lawfully dissolved other than by death, the parish priest of the place of the celebration of the marriage must be informed, so that an entry may be duly made in the registers of marriage and of baptism.

If a marriage is validated in the external forum or if it is declared null (Can. 1685) or if it is dissolved because of non-consummation (Can. 1142) or in favour of the faith, notification is to be sent to the parishes where the marriage took place and the parish where the parties were baptised.   **415**

---

56 *The directory on mixed marriages*, Veritas, Dublin, 1983, 28-9, n. 15.1.

6

Mixed marriages

416   In current canonical legislation the term "mixed marriage" refers to a marriage between two baptised persons, one of whom was baptised in the catholic Church or was received into it and has not defected from it by a formal act, and the other of whom belongs to a Church or ecclesial community not in full communion with the catholic Church (Can. 1124). A marriage between a catholic and a protestant or a marriage between a catholic and an orthodox christian fall into this category. This is distinguished from a marriage between a catholic and a non-baptised person; in this instance the impediment of disparity of worship arises (Can. 1086). It was only in the Middle Ages that this distinction was clearly defined.

HISTORICAL BACKGROUND

417   The early Church was confronted with the pastoral problem of marriages between christians and non-christians. St Paul instructed the Christian community in Corinth that when a convert to Christianity was married to a person who did not share his or her christian faith, "neither a Christian husband nor a Christian wife should divorce an unbelieving spouse as long as the non-believer was willing to remain married to the Christian" (1 Cor 7:12-16).[1] At the same time he warned the Christian community in Corinth to take great care regarding companions. In he writes: "Do not harness yourselves in an uneven team with unbelievers. Virtue is no companion for crime. Light and darkness have nothing in common. Christ is not the ally of Beliar, nor has a believer anything to share with an unbeliever. The temple of God has no common ground with idols, and that is what we are – the temple of the living God" (2 Cor 6:14-16). The image of being "harnessed" could refer to marriage or to any association with unbelievers.[2] In 1 Peter 3:1-2 Christian wives are addressed as follows: "In the same way, wives should be obedient to their husbands. Then if there are some husbands who have not yet obeyed the word, they may find themselves won over, without a word spoken, by the way their wives behave, when they see how faithful and conscientious they are."

1 R.F. Collins, *Divorce in the New Testament*, 16. **2** F.T. Fallon, *2 Corinthians* (New Testament Message 11), Veritas, Dublin, 1980, 58.

Senior comments on this passage as follows:

> Even though women had a radically subordinate role in society, 1 Peter
> addresses them as free and equal in the christian community, indeed as
> having a demanding role that can serve as example for all the commu-
> nity. Therefore christian wives are to "be submissive to your husbands".
> The proper meaning of the word "submissive" needs to be re-empha-
> sised ... The author is not trying to beat rebellious women back into
> line, nor is he calling for a second-class subordination of women. Even
> though a "mixed marriage" (i.e., between a christian woman and a pa-
> gan husband) presents an extremely difficult challenge to the religious
> convictions of the wife, she is not to flee this situation but to continue
> in it.[3]

In the early centuries of the Church mixed unions were discouraged. Tertullian **419**
(*c.*160-240) distinguished between the union of a person who was baptised
after marriage to a pagan and the union of a person who was baptised before
marriage to a non-Christian. In the former case, the Christian should continue to live with his or her spouse; in the latter case, the marriage had to be
dissolved since it brought with it the possibility of "wounding the true faith".[4]
Such a marriage could lead to disharmony between the couple.[5] The prohibition against mixed marriages referred also to Christian widows. A widow
or widower was allowed to enter into marriage only with another Christian.
Those who marry pagans commit fornication and are to be consequently cut
off completely from communion.[6] Cyprian unequivocally forbade Christians
from entering mixed marriages with unbelievers.[7]

From the late second century until the fourth century, mixed marriages **420**
took place between Christians and pagans, heretics, schismatics and Jews.
The Council of Elvira established formal interdict and sanctions for both the
spouses who contracted a mixed marriage and for the parents who gave their
sons or daughters in marriage to heretics or Jews.[8] Similar legislation was
made at the Council of Nicaea. St Basil stressed that mixed marriages were
defective because they were not based on baptism.[9] St Ambrose held that
marriages with pagans could be accepted only if the unbeliever was dis-

3 D. Senior, *1 & 2 Peter* (New Testament Message 20), Veritas, Dublin, 1980, 54. **4** *Ad uxorem*, II, ch.3: "... De proximo quid sibi voluit ille qui dixit, delictum quidem esse extraneo nubere ... Recenseamus nunc caetera pericula et vulnera, ut dixi, fidei ad Apostolo provisa, non carni tantum, verum etiam ipsi spiritui molestissima." **5** Ibid., II, ch. 8. **6** Ibid., II, ch.3: "Fideles gentilium matrimonio subeuntes sturpri reos constat et arcendos ab omni communicatione fraternitatis." **7** *Testimonium adversus Judaeos II*, 62, *PL* 4, 798. **8** Can. 16: "Haeretici si se transferre noluerint ad Ecclesiam Catholicam, nec ipsis dandas esse puellas; sed neque Judaeis neque haereticis dare placuit, eo quod nulla possit esse societas fideli con infideli; si contra interdictum fecerint parentes, abstineri per quinquennium placet." **9** *PG* 32, 613-715.

posed to embrace Christianity. He felt that in marriage there is only one flesh and one spirit, and that this does not take place in marriage with unbelievers because they are different in faith and there is an infinite gap between the believer and the unbeliever.[10] Ambrose advised Vigilius, the Bishop of Trent: "Teach the people, therefore, to seek ties of marriage not with strangers but from the households of Christians ... There is hardly anything more deadly than being married to one who is a stranger to the faith."[11]

421 The ways in which particular Churches and the Fathers regarded mixed marriage depended on local circumstances and the environment in which Christians found themselves.[12] St John Chrysostom (344-407) tolerated mixed marriage in his community; it was not a source of danger for his flock; on the contrary, many unbelievers entered the Church through marriage with Christians.[13]

422 St Augustine, whose father was pagan, wrote that such unions were no longer to be considered sinful "in our times".[14] He stated that in case of doubt, everything possible should be done to prevent questionable unions and the occurrence of distressing circumstances.[15] The Council of Laodicea (321-81) opposed marriages between Christians and heretics. However it permitted them if the heretical party promised that the children would profess the Christian faith.[16] The Council of Chalcedon (451) forbade Christians to contract marriage with heretics, pagans or Jews except when the **423** latter would solemnly promise to accept the orthodox faith.[17]

During the fifth and sixth centuries the Church strenuously opposed marriage with Jews. Such a marriage "was an affront to the entire ecclesial community because the Christian faith was the connecting link that bound the members of the Church into one body".[18] In the early part of the seventh century marriage to a heretic was commonly regarded as invalid.[19]

424 In the twelfth century canonists began to distinguish between the marriage of a Christian to a baptised person (such as a heretic or schismatic) and the marriage of a Christian to an unbaptised person (such as Jew or a pagan).

---

10 *De Abraham* 1, ch. 8. **11** *Epistola 19*, n. 2-7: "Doce ergo plebem, ut non ex alienigenis, sed ex domibus christianis coniugii quaeratur copula... Sed prope nihil gravius quam copulari alienigenae". **12** A.F.E. Fau, *Mixed marriage: the historical evolution of the impediment of disparity of cult and prohibition of mixed religion up to the legislation of the 1983 Code* (hereafter *Mixed marriage*), Rome, 1993, 36. **13** Ibid. **14** *De fide et operibus*, 19, n. 35.   **15** Ibid.: "Quae autem dubia, omni conandum est ne fiant tales coniunctiones. Quid enim opus est in tantum discrimen ambiguitatis caput mittere." **16** Can. 31: "Quod non oportet cum omni haeretico matrimonium contrahere, vel dare filios aut filias; sed magis accipere, si se Christianos futuros profiteatur." **17** Mansi, VI, Can. 14, p. 1228: "Neque quidem copulari eos nuptiis haeretici, vel Judaei, vel Pagani, nisi forte promiserit se converti in orthodoxam fide".   **18** Fau, *Mixed marriage*, 48. F.J. Schenk has written:"It appears quite reasonable ... to infer that the diriment impediment of Disparity of Cult had its origins in a diriment impediment of the marriage of Christians with Jews" (*The matrimonial impediments of mixed religion and disparity of cult*, Washington, 1939). **19** Ibid., 49.

Gradually the view was accepted that marriages between Christians and unbaptised persons were invalid if entered without dispensation.[20] Huguccio's view that a marriage between two baptised persons, of whom one had been baptised in the catholic Church and the other in a heretical sect was valid later became the accepted teaching.[21] St Thomas Aquinas held that the marriage between a Catholic and a heretic, though sinful, was valid; the contract of two baptised persons could not be broken as it is a sacrament based on their baptism.[22]

Following the Reformation mixed marriages became a point of conflict **425** between the Churches. The Council of Trent decreed that a priest could not assist at a mixed marriage unless the necessary dispensation had been given.[23] Although the first dispensation was granted by Pope Clement VIII in 1603, it was only during the eighteenth century that dispensations were given for marriages with heretics and schismatics. Such dispensations were given on condition that there was no danger of the catholic party losing his or her faith and that the children were brought up in the catholic faith.[24] By the end of the eighteenth century, Bishops in mission countries were given faculties to dispense from the impediment.

The issue of the canonical form in mixed marriages gave rise to contro- **426** versy, particularly in countries where the Reformation had taken hold in a significant way. In 1741 Pope Benedict XIV published a Declaration in which he stated that the canonical form did not bind in the Netherlands in marriages contracted between heretics, or between catholics and heretics.[25]

In the early part of this century the most important legislation was the *Ne* **427** *temere* decree. Its principal provisions were codified in the 1917 Code of Canon Law. The tone of the Code regarding mixed marriages was severe: "The Church everywhere most severely forbids the contracting of marriage between two baptised persons of whom one is a catholic whereas the other is a member of a heretical or schismatical sect; and if there is danger of perversion for the catholic party and the children, the marriage is forbidden also by the divine law itself" (c. 1060).

"Mixed religion" was an impedient impediment, that is; it forbade mar- **428** riage but did not render its celebration null. It could be dispensed when certain conditions were fulfilled (c. 1061 §1):

1° There are just and grave reasons therefor;

---

20 P. Lombardus, *Sent. IV*, 39 in *PL* 192, p. 934: "Non posse contrahi coniugium ab his qui sunt diversae religionis e fidei". **21** Ibid., 67. **22** *IV Sent.*, D.39, q.1 a.1: "Propter hoc, si aliquis fidelis cum haeretica baptizata matrimonium contrahit, verum est matrimonium: quamvis peccet contracto, si sciat eam haereticam: sicut peccaret, si cum excommunicata contraheret: non tamen propter hoc matrimonium dirimetur". **23** *Decrees of the ecumenical councils* (ed. Tanner), II, 756. **24** *CIC Fontes* II, n. 387. **25** *CIC Fontes* V, n. 3527.

2° The non-catholic party shall have given a guarantee to remove all danger of perversion from the catholic party, and both parties shall give written guarantees to baptise and educate all the children in the catholic faith alone;

3° There is moral certainty that the guarantees will be fulfilled. The guarantees are as a rule to be given in writing (c. 1061 §2).

429 With regard to the celebration of these marriages, all sacred rites were forbidden; however if it was foreseen that graver evils would result from this prohibition, "the Ordinary could permit some of the usual ecclesiastical ceremonies, excluding always the celebration of Mass" (c. 1102 §2).

430 Vatican II led to a dramatic change in relationships between the Christian Churches; several significant pieces of legislation regarding mixed marriages were issued: the instruction on mixed marriages, *Matrimonii sacramentum* (18 March 1966),[26] the decree of the Congregation for Oriental Churches on marriages between Roman catholics and Orthodox, *Crescens matrimoniorum* (22 February 1967),[27] and the motu proprio, *Matrimonia mixta* of Paul VI (7 January 1970).[28] This led to extensive dialogue between the Churches regarding marriage: in 1976 the Lutheran World Federation, the World Alliance of Reformed Churches and the Secretariate for Promoting Christian Unity published a *Final Report on the Theology of Marriage and the Problems of Mixed Marriages*;[29] in 1976 the Anglican-Roman Catholic International Commission on the Theology of Marriage and its Application to Mixed Marriages issued a report entitled *Anglican-Roman Catholic Marriage*.[30]

431 The post-Vatican II legislative changes were incorporated in the Latin Code of Canon Law (Cann. 1124-9) and in the Code of Canons of the Eastern Churches. The Church's discipline was refined further in the *Directory for the Application of Principles and Norms on Ecumenism* which was issued by the Pontifical Council for the Promotion of Christian Unity in 1993.[31]

Can. 1124 Permission

Without the express permission of the competent authority, marriage is prohibited between two baptised persons, one of whom was baptised in the catholic Church or received into it after baptism and has not defected from it by a formal act, the other of whom belongs to a Church or ecclesial community not in full communion with the catholic Church.

432 The *Ecumenical directory* outlines the basis of the Church's concern in its

---

26 Fl I, 474-8. **27** Fl I, 481-2. **28** Fl I, 508-14. **29** This was published by the Pontifical Council for the Promotion of Christian Unity in *Information service* 36 (1978), 15-37. **30** Cf. *Infoform* 6 (1976). **31** This will be referred to as *Ecumenical directory*.

ministry to couples entering mixed marriages. In its pastoral care of marriage the main concern of the Church is to uphold "the strength and stability of the indissoluble marital union and the family life that flows from it".[32] Experience shows that it is difficult for couples in mixed marriages and for their children to maintain their Christian faith and commitment and the harmony of family life. For this reason "marriage between persons of the same ecclesial Community remains the ideal to be recommended and encouraged".[33] However the *Ecumenical directory* acknowledges that mixed marriages" contain numerous elements that could well be made good use of and developed both for the intrinsic value [of the parties involved] and for the contribution they can make to the ecumenical movement".[34]

The problems experienced by couples in mixed marriages are a tragic consequence of disunity in the Church. These couples "risk experiencing the tragedy of Christian disunity even in the heart of their own home".[35] Despite this, "differences of confession between the spouses do not constitute an insurmountable obstacle for marriage, when [couples] succeed in placing in common what they have received from their respective communities, and learn from each other the way in which each lives in fidelity to Christ".[36] **433**

"Mixed religion" is no longer an impediment, as in the 1917 Code; in the current law the Church allows the celebration of these marriages only with the express permission of the local Ordinary of the catholic party. Permission differs from dispensation inasmuch as it is "according to the law" and may be presumed when the competent authority cannot be approached.[37] Without this permission the marriage is valid but illicit. Can. 1125 lays down conditions which must be fulfilled before this permission can be given. **434**

Can. 1125 The promises

> The local Ordinary can grant this permission if there is a just and reasonable cause. He is not to grant it unless the following conditions are fulfilled:
>
> 1° the catholic party is to declare that he or she is prepared to remove dangers of defecting from the faith, and is to make a sincere promise to do all in his or her Church;
>
> 2° the other party is to be informed in good time of these promises to be made by the catholic party, so that it is certain that he or she is truly aware of the promise and of the obligation of the catholic party;
>
> 3° both parties are to be instructed about the purposes and essential properties of marriage, which are not to be excluded by either contractant.

32 Ibid., n. 144. 33 Ibid. 34 Ibid., n. 145. 35 *Catechism of the Catholic Church*, n. 1634. 36 *Ecumenical directory*, n. 145. 37 G. Lobo, "The Christian and Canon Law" in J. Hite and D. J. Ward, *Readings, cases, materials in canon law*, 41.

435   In the light of the particular difficulties that arise in mixed marriages, Can. 1125 states that the local Ordinary may permit the celebration of the marriage if there is "a just and reasonable cause". However, he is to ensure that several conditions are fulfilled.

436   The first condition is that the catholic party is to declare that he or she is prepared to remove dangers of defecting from the faith. This is a commitment to "preserve their communion with the Church at all times" (Can. 209 §1) by continuing the practice of their own faith.

437   The second condition is that the catholic party is to make a sincere promise to do all in his or her power to have all the children baptised and brought up in the catholic Church. The obligation to hand on the catholic faith arises from the faith of the catholic party. It arises from the general obligation which all lay members of the faithful have "to strive so that the divine message of salvation may be known and accepted by all people throughout the world" (Can. 211).

438   The duty "to do one's best" is a moral obligation which the catholic party must undertake in good faith.[38] It will be for this person to work out in the particular circumstances of his or her marriage what "doing his or her best" will mean in practice. The Church, in interpreting this obligation, does not require the catholic party to act in a way that would endanger the stability of the marriage. The *Ecumenical directory* makes it clear that in carrying out their duty to hand on the Catholic faith to the children, the Catholic parent is obliged to act "with respect for the religious freedom and conscience of the other parent and with due regard for the unity and permanence of the marriage and for the maintenance of the communion of the family".[39] If, despite the best efforts of the Catholic party, the children are not baptised and brought up in the Catholic Church, the obligation of the Catholic parent to share the Catholic faith with the children does not cease. It could be fulfilled "by playing an active part in contributing to the Christian atmosphere of the home, doing all that is possible by word and example to enable the other members of the family to appreciate the specific values of the Catholic tradition, taking whatever steps are necessary to be well informed about his/her own faith so as to be able to explain and discuss it with them, [and] praying with the family for the grace of Christian unity as the Lord wills it".[40]

439   In order to stress that the obligation of the catholic party applies in all marriages and not only in mixed marriages, the Irish Bishops' Conference requires that the promises be made by all catholics. They are incorporated into the Pre-nuptial Enquiry form issued by that Conference:

6.   Do you accept that marriage has been instituted by God and made a sacrament by Christ?

---

38 L. Örsy, "The religious education of children born from mixed marriages" in *Gregorianum* 46 (1964), 739-60. **39** *Ecumenical directory*, n. 151. **40** Ibid.

7. Are you resolved to remain steadfast in your catholic faith and to practice it regularly?
8. Do you promise to do what you can within the unity of your partnership to have all the children of your marriage baptised and brought up in the catholic faith?[41]

The other party is to be informed before the marriage of the promises **440** made by the catholic party, so that he or she is aware of the promises and the obligation of the catholic party. The fulfilling of this promise will require the understanding of the other spouse. In its consideration of the duties of the Catholic party in a mixed marriage, the *Ecumenical directory* acknowledges that "the non-catholic partner may feel a like obligation because of his/her own Christian commitment".[42] In such a situation, if there is an irreconcilable conflict of conscience between a couple, it would be prudent for them to reflect on the appropriateness of their decision to marry.

The *Ecumenical directory* notes that when the local Ordinary is judging **441** whether there is a "just and reasonable cause" for granting permission for a mixed marriage, he "will take account, among other things, of an explicit refusal on the part of the non-Catholic party" to respect the obligation in conscience of the catholic to fulfil the promises which he or she has made.[43]

The third part of this canon states that both parties "are to be instructed **442** about the purposes and essential properties of marriage, which are not to be excluded by either contractant". The *Ecumenical directory* states that those responsible for the pastoral care of couples entering mixed marriages have a duty to "provide special instruction and support for the Catholic party in living his or her faith as well as for the couples in mixed marriages both in the preparation of the marriage, in its sacramental celebration and for the life together that follows the marriage ceremony".[44] This pastoral care should be adapted to the spiritual condition of each partner, his or her formation and practice of the faith. The *Ecumenical directory* asks that respect be shown for the particular circumstances of each couple's situation, the conscience of each partner and the holiness of the state of sacramental marriage itself.[45] It recommends that the catholic minister should, where possible, cooperate with the minister of the other party. It reminds the catholic minister involved in pre-marriage preparation to stress "the positive aspects of what the couple share together as Christians in the life of grace, in faith, hope and love, along with the other interior gifts of the Spirit".[46] It encourages each person both to remain faithful to his or her own Christian commitment and "to foster all that can lead to unity and harmony, without minimising real differences and while avoiding an attitude of religious indifference".[47] It urges both parties to learn more about each other's religious convictions and beliefs and re-

---

41 Appendix I, Document B. **42** *Ecumenical directory*, n. 150. **43** Ibid. **44** Ibid., n. 146. **45** Ibid. **46** Ibid., n. 148. **47** Ibid.

minds them that prayer together and the reading and study of the Sacred Scriptures are most important ways of living the Christian inheritance they share.[48]

Can. 1126 Form of promises determined by Bishops' Conferences

It is for the Bishops' Conference to prescribe the manner in which these declarations and promises, which are always required, are to be made, and to determine how they are to be established in the external forum, and how the non-catholic party is to be informed of them.

443 Each Bishops' Conference is to prescribe the way in which the promises are to be made. Particular law should specify how they are to be established in the external forum and how the non-catholic party is to be informed.[49]

Can. 1127 Canonical form of mixed marriages

§1 The provisions of Can. 1108 are to be observed in regard to the form to be used in a mixed marriage. If, however, the catholic party contracts marriage with a non-catholic of oriental rite, the canonical form of marriage is to be observed for lawfulness only; for validity, however, the intervention of a sacred minister is required, while observing the other requirements of law.
§2 If there are grave difficulties in the way of observing the canonical form, the local Ordinary of the catholic party has the right to dispense from it in individual cases, having however consulted the Ordinary of the place of the celebration of the marriage; for validity, however, some public form of celebration is required. It is for the Bishops' Conference to establish norms whereby this dispensation may be granted in a uniform manner.
§3 It is forbidden to have, either before or after the canonical celebration in accordance with §1, another religious celebration of the same marriage for the purpose of giving or renewing matrimonial consent. Likewise, there is not to be a religious celebration in which the catholic assistant and non-catholic minister, each performing his own rite, together ask for the consent of the parties.

444 The catholic Church requires that mixed marriages be celebrated in accordance with the canonical form. In the case of a marriage between a Catholic and an Orthodox Christian, the canonical form obliges for lawfulness only;

---

48 Ibid., n. 149. **49** For examples of particular law promulgated by Bishops' Conferences, cf. *Code of Canon Law annotated*, appendix III, 1309-1434.

for validity however the presence of a sacred minister is required while observing the other requirements of law (Can. 1127 §1). In other words, if the marriage takes place in the presence of a "sacred minister" of the Orthodox Church, it is regarded as valid by the catholic Church.

If there are grave difficulties in the way of observing the canonical form **445** in other mixed marriages, for example, marriages involving Catholics and Protestants, the local Ordinary of the catholic party can dispense from it in individual cases. It is a matter for the pastoral judgement of the local Ordinary to determine which reasons would justify the granting of a dispensation from the canonical form. The Irish Bishops' Conference, for example, stated that while "a dispensation will not be granted simply on request, ... where serious pastoral reasons seem to warrant it, a request for a dispensation will be sympathetically considered".[50] The *Ecumenical directory* gives examples of reasons that would justify the granting of the dispensation from canonical form: "the maintaining of family harmony, obtaining parental consent to the marriage, the recognition of the particular religious commitment of the non-catholic partner or his/ her blood relationship with a minister of another Church or ecclesial Community".[51] If the marriage is to take place outside his diocese the Bishop should consult the Ordinary of the place of marriage.

It is not permitted to have a religious ceremony in which a catholic offi- **446** cial witness and the non-catholic minister jointly ask for the consent of the parties. Moreover it is forbidden to have, either before or after the canonical celebration, another religious celebration of the same marriage for the purpose of giving or renewing matrimonial consent. The Catholic Bishops of England and Wales recommend a second service of blessing and thanksgiving in the church of the other party, provided it does not include the giving or renewing of consent.[52] They do so as this "provides the other party with the opportunity to give witness to his or her responsibilities before the Christian community to which that person belongs".[53] It is important to make it clear that this second ceremony does not involve a marriage-ceremony or a renewal of consent.

The liturgical form of mixed marriages

The 1917 Code forbade the celebration of marriages between catholics and **447** non-catholics in a catholic church. It added that if the diocesan Bishop judged that this rule could not be insisted upon without causing other greater evils he might allow the marriage to take place in the church but without Mass (c. 1109). These prohibitions were abrogated in 1966.[54] The new law permitted

---

50 *Directory on mixed marriages* 12.4. **51** Ibid., n. 154. **52** *Mixed marriages*, London, 1990, 28. **53** Ibid. **54** *Matrimonii sacramentum*, Fl I, 477, IV.

the celebration of mixed marriages "with sacred rites and with the customary blessings and sermon".[55] The Roman Missal issued in 1969 included three rites for the celebration of marriage: the celebration of marriage during Mass, the celebration of marriage outside Mass and the celebration of marriage between a Catholic and an unbaptised person. *Matrimonia mixta* stated with regard to the choice of rite:

> With regard to the liturgical form of the celebration of a mixed marriage, if it is to be taken from the Roman Ritual, use must be made of the ceremonies in the rite of celebration of marriage promulgated by our authority, whether it is a question of a marriage between a Catholic and a baptised non-Catholic (nn. 39-55) [the celebration of marriage outside Mass] or of a marriage between a Catholic and an unbaptised person (nn. 55-66). If, however, the circumstances justify it, a marriage between a Catholic and a baptised non-Catholic can be celebrated, subject to the local Ordinary's consent, according to the rites for the celebration of marriage within Mass (nn. 19-38).[56]

448　　The *Ecumenical directory* states that "because of problems concerning Eucharistic sharing which may arise from the presence of non-catholic witnesses and guests, a mixed marriage celebrated according to the Catholic form ordinarily takes place outside the Eucharistic liturgy".[57] The Archdiocese of Dublin advises its clergy not to refuse the request for a nuptial Mass in these circumstances without first consulting the Chancery.[58]

449　　When a marriage is celebrated in the catholic Church, the minister of the non-catholic party should be invited to attend. The visiting minister may be seated in a place of honour in the sanctuary and may wear appropriate liturgical dress. The catholic priest should invite this minister to participate in the ceremony by words of greeting or exhortation and by additional prayers and blessings at the close of the actual marriage ceremony itself. If the marriage is celebrated apart from Mass, the minister may be invited to read a lesson from Scripture, give a brief exhortation and bless the couple.[59] The *Ecumenical directory* states that while the reading of Scripture during Mass is to be done by members of the Church, the diocesan Bishop may permit this to be done by the member of another Church of ecclesial community "on exceptional occasions and for a just cause".[60] The celebration of a mixed marriage would constitute such a "just cause".

450　　If the marriage is celebrated in another Church with a dispensation from canonical form, a catholic priest or deacon may, at the invitation of the minister of the other Church or ecclesial community, offer other appropriate

---

55 Ibid. **56** Fl I, 513, n. 11. **57** *Ecumenical directory*, n. 159. **58** Unpublished memo, "Mixed marriages and related questions", q. 20. **59** *Ecumenical directory*, n. 158. **60** Ibid., n. 133.

prayers, read from the Scriptures, give a brief exhortation and bless the couple.[61] He should wear choral dress.

A catholic priest may not celebrate marriage according to the rites of **451** another Church. He may, however, take part in a service of blessing and thanksgiving in the Church of the other denomination following a marriage in the catholic Church. There should not however be anything which could be understood as a second marriage rite (Can. 1127 §3). Catholics may act as witnesses at marriages in other christian churches and vice versa.[62]

The Celebration of Marriage between a Catholic and an Unbaptised Per- **452** son is comprised of the following elements: an introductory rite, a liturgy of the Word, a liturgy of marriage, and a concluding rite.

Are there circumstances in which the marriage between a catholic and an **453** unbaptised person may be celebrated within Mass? Although *Matrimonia mixta* does not explicitly envisage the celebration of such marriages within Mass,[63] a diocesan Bishop could, in my opinion, permit this in individual cases if he considered it appropriate.

Can. 1128 Pastoral care for mixed marriages

Local Ordinaries and other pastors of souls are to see to it that the catholic spouse and the children born of a mixed marriage are not without the spiritual help needed to fulfil their obligations; they are also to assist the spouses to foster the unity of conjugal and family life.

Couples in mixed marriages have special difficulties. It is the pastoral re- **454** sponsibility of the local Ordinary and the parish priest to ensure that the catholic party and the children of the marriage have the spiritual help needed to fulfil their obligations. The *Catechism of the Catholic Church* notes that "through ecumenical dialogue Christian communities in many regions have been able to put into effect a common pastoral practice for mixed marriages".[64]

Can. 1129 Disparity of cult

The provisions of Cann. 1127 and 1128 are to be applied also to marriages which are impeded by the impediment of disparity of worship mentioned in Can. 1086 §1.

---

61 Ibid., n. 157. **62** Fl I, 498. **63** Fl I, 513, n. 11. **64** n. 1636. A common approach was agreed in 1986 between the Church of Ireland and the Catholic Bishop of Ferns (cf. *The diocese of Ferns: interchurch marriage* (two reports).

457 The provisions of Cann. 1127-8 apply also to marriages between a catholic and a person who is not baptised.

456   Mixed marriages create special difficulties for the couples themselves and their families. At the same time, when approached with maturity and in good faith, they can witness in a unique way to the unity which is Christ's desire for his Church (Jn 17:21). They pose a challenge to ministers of all the Churches and call for a unique expression of pastoral charity. Experience has made the Churches wary of mixed marriages, especially since in some instances children of mixed marriages grow up with a weak or confused sense of Christian identity. Despite their unease, the Churches should not lose sight of the positive opportunities which mixed marriages create if couples prepare well and receive helpful support from their families and from their respective faith traditions. After all, as one writer has put it, "it must be remembered that the marriages of the early Christians were mixed marriages and ... out of them an entire Christian civilisation grew".[65]

---

65 G. A. Kelly, "Mixed marriage" in *The new Catholic encyclopedia*, vol. 9, 292.

7

The secret celebration of marriage

Can. 1130 Permission to celebrate secret marriage

> For a grave and urgent reason, the local Ordinary may permit that a marriage be celebrated in secret.

Marriage is by its nature a social and ecclesial reality which has important **457** consequences for the spouses and their children. Marriages involving a catholic are governed by civil law as well as by canon law (Can. 1059). It is the wish of the Church that marriages be conducted in accordance with the formalities laid down by both jurisdictions; it is reluctant to permit the celebration of marriages which "cannot be celebrated by the civil law or be recognised by it" (Can. 1071 §1, 2°). The stability of marriage is enhanced when it is upheld by both the civil law and canon law. However "for a grave and urgent reason, the local Ordinary may permit that a marriage be celebrated in secret" (Can. 1130). The law has been relaxed; the previous law required a "very urgent and very grave cause" for what was then called "a marriage of conscience" (c. 1104). The reasons which traditionally were considered sufficient to justify a secret marriage included the following: the state of secret concubinage of two people who are publicly considered to be man and wife, the disparity of social status of the spouses, the unreasonable opposition from family members, certain conditions imposed by civil laws. In this regard, Örsy refers to the civil law in some jurisdictions that outlaw interracial marriages. He adds that "in such a case, the value the law intends to protect is the right of the faithful to marry".[1]

Can. 1131 What is involved in secret marriage

> Permission to celebrate a marriage in secret involves:
> 1° that the investigations to be made before the marriage are carried out in secret;
> 2° that the secret in regard to the marriage which has been celebrated is observed by the local Ordinary, by whoever assists, by the witnesses and by the spouses.

---

1 *Marriage in canon law*, 197.

458   When a local Ordinary gives permission for the celebration of a secret marriage, several things are involved: firstly, the investigation to establish the canonical freedom of the couple is carried out in secret (1°); secondly, the local Ordinary who gave permission for the marriage, the officiating minister, the witnesses and the spouses themselves are obliged to observe secrecy in regard to the marriage (2°).

Can. 1132 Cessation of the obligation of secrecy

> The obligation of observing the secret mentioned in Can. 1131, 2° ceases for the local Ordinary if from its observance a threat arises of grave scandal or of grave harm to the sanctity of marriage. This fact is to be made known to the parties before the celebration of the marriage.

459   Should a danger of grave scandal or grave harm to the sanctity of marriage arise because of the secrecy of the marriage, the local Ordinary is not obliged to observe the secret. This is the case since the local Ordinary is responsible for the common good of his diocese and especially the avoidance of scandal in the celebration of the sacraments or the state of christian marriage (Can.392 §2). The couple should be informed of this before the celebration of the marriage.

Can. 1133 Registration in the secret archive

> A marriage celebrated in secret is to be recorded only in a special register which is to be kept in the secret archive of the curia.

460   A marriage which was celebrated in secret must be registered in the secret archive in the diocesan curia.

8

The effects of marriage

Can. 1134 Permanent and exclusive bond

From a valid marriage there arises between the spouses a bond which of its own nature is permanent and exclusive. Moreover, in christian marriage the spouses are by a special sacrament strengthened and, as it were, consecrated for the duties and the dignity of their state.

Can. 1134 is the foundational canon in this section. It is based on c. 1110 of **461** the 1917 Code and the teaching of Vatican II.[1] The Council taught that the marriage-bond is rooted in the irrevocable personal consent of the spouses; it arises "from the human act by which they surrender themselves to each other".[2] The Church regards even the natural bond of marriage – as celebrated by those who are not baptised – as intrinsically permanent and exclusive.

Marriage between the baptised has been raised by Christ the Lord to the **462** dignity of a sacrament (Can. 1055 §1). The natural qualities of permanence and unity "acquire a distinctive firmness by reason of the sacrament" (Can. 1056). Provided they are in the state of grace, the spouses receive the grace to be faithful and to endure in their commitment to each other. Grelot writes:

[Christian doctrine] therefore sets forth firmly as a fundamental principle, that man would not by his own powers be capable of fully attaining the ideal of marriage ... : the miracle of redemptive grace is needed. Only this grace can create a new man by totally renewing his whole being (Eph 4:22-24; Ps 50:12). By remedying in this way the natural injury which befell man's sexuality like the other aspects of his being, it makes possible the sanctification of the couple.[3]

By the sacrament of matrimony, "the spouses are fortified and, as it were, **463** consecrated for the duties and dignity of their state".[4] Vatican II continues: "Fulfilling their conjugal and family role by virtue of this sacrament, spouses are penetrated with the spirit of Christ and their whole life is suffused by faith, hope and charity; thus they increasingly further their own perfection and their mutual sanctification, and together they render glory to God".[5]

1 Fl I, 399, *LG* n. 41e; Fl I, 950-1, *GS* n. 48. 2 Fl I, 950, *GS* n. 48. 3 *Man and wife in scripture*, 101. 4 Fl I, 951, *GS* n. 48b. 5 Ibid.

464   Christ abides with the couple "so that their love [will] increasingly re-
semble his own love for the Church [and] so that it will truly become mutual
dedication in absolutely faithful love".[6]

465   By virtue of the sacrament of matrimony, parents share in the sanctify-
ing office of the Church. As Can. 835 §4 states, "parents have a special
share in this [sanctifying] office when they live their married lives in a
christian spirit and provide for the christian education of their children".
The specific mission of married couples in the Church is "to transmit human life and to educate their children"; in this way "they are ... cooperating
with the love of God the Creator and are, in a certain sense, its interpret-
ers".[7]

Can. 1135 Equality of spouses

> Each spouse has an equal obligation and right to whatever pertains to
> the partnership of conjugal life.

466   This canon affirms that in christian marriage husband and wife enjoy a genuine equality in their relationship with each other and in the responsibilities
which they carry out together. Pope John Paul II has commented on Eph
5:22-23 ["Wives, be subject to your husbands, as to the Lord. For the husband is the head of the wife"], a text which has a "patriarchal" ring for many
people today. He writes:

> The author knows that this way of speaking, so profoundly rooted in
> the customs and religious tradition of that time, is to be understood
> and carried out in a new way: as a "mutual subjection out of reverence
> for Christ" (cf. Eph 5:21). This is especially true because the husband
> is called the "head" of the wife as Christ is the head of the Church; he
> is so in order to give "himself up for her" (Eph 5:25), and giving him-
> self up for her means giving up even his own life. However, whereas
> in the relationship between Christ and the Church the subjection is
> only on the part of the Church, the "subjection" in the relationship
> between husband and wife is not one-sided but mutual.[8]

467   The roles of husband and wife in marriage are complementary and equal
in dignity.

Can. 1136 Obligation and right of parents

> Parents have the most serious obligation and the primary right to do

---

6 Vorgrimler, *Commentary on the documents of Vatican II*, V, 235. 7 Fl I, 953, *GS* n.
50b. 8 *The dignity of women (Mulieris dignitatem)*, n. 24.

all in their power to ensure their children's physical, social, cultural, moral and religious upbringing.

The obligation of parents "to ensure their children's physical, social, cultural, moral and religious upbringing" of their children is an inalienable personal duty. The comprehensive way in which this canon is framed makes the point that the religious upbringing of children must be integrated into the holistic growth of each individual. The catholic school supports parents in fulfilling their role. Gospel values are communicated not only in religion classes but in the overall ethos of the school. Ethos can be understood as follows: "The concept of ethos refers to the fundamental purpose of the school, its ultimate meaning and reference point. When we speak about ethos, we are describing the core beliefs of the school community, its covenant and charter. Ethos is a kind of map which helps us on our educational journey without becoming lost or disoriented. Ethos refers to the credo of the school community".[9]   **468**

Both the Church and the State have a role to play in the education of children, but they cannot, and should not try to take over the irreplaceable role and rights of parents. Only in exceptional circumstances, such as when parents are clearly incapable of fulfilling their role, should another agency take over the role of rearing the children.   **469**

Can. 1137 Children of valid or putative marriage are legitimate

> Children who are conceived or born of a valid or of a putative marriage are legitimate.

Despite considerable pressure to remove this canon, the Code Commission retained it for two reasons: firstly, because it might have consequences in particular law, and secondly, in order to highlight the sanctity of marriage.[10] A marriage is valid if consent was expressed legitimately by two parties who were capable of marriage (Can. 1057 §1); it is putative "if it has been celebrated in good faith by at least one party" (Can. 1061 §3). A child born or conceived during either category of marriage is regarded in canon law as legitimate.   **470**

Can. 1138 Presumptions regarding paternity and legitimacy

> §1 The father is he who is identified by a lawful marriage, unless by clear arguments the contrary is proven.

9 K. Treston, *Transforming Catholic schools. Visions and practices for renewal*, Creation Enterprises, 1992, cited in Council for Catholic Maintained Schools, *Life to the full*, Veritas, Dublin, 1996, 9. **10** *Comm* 10 (1978), 106; ibid., 15 (1983), 240.

§2 Children are presumed legitimate who are born at least 180 days after the date the marriage was celebrated, or within 300 days from the date of the dissolution of conjugal life.

471 The law presumes that the husband of a woman who has a child is the father of the child. The presumption however gives way to contrary proof.

472 A child born within 180 days of the contracting of a marriage is presumed to be legitimate; a child born within 300 days of the termination of conjugal life is also presumed to be legitimate.

Can. 1139 How children are legitimated

Illegitimate children are legitimated by the subsequent marriage of their parents, whether valid or putative, or by a rescript of the Holy See.

473 Children born of a couple who are not married can become legitimate in two ways: firstly, by the marriage of their parents or if their existing union is validated; secondly, by a rescript granted by the Holy See. This might be granted, for example, if one of the parents died before the marriage could take place.

Can. 1140 No distinction between legitimate and illegitimate children

As far as canonical effects are concerned, legitimated children are equivalent to legitimate children in all respects, unless it is otherwise expressly provided by the law.

474 Legitimacy no longer has any practical effects in the general law of the Church . The phrase "unless otherwise expressly provided by the law" allows particular law to make a distinction if it is judged appropriate.

9

The validation of marriage

The validation of marriage is a "legal mechanism for transforming an exist- **475** ing union, created and sustained by marital affection but having no juridical status into a canonically valid marriage".[1] It presupposes that the consent of the parties, though canonically invalid, continues to exist. This can be done either by simple validation (Cann. 1156-60) or retroactive validation (Cann. 1161-65).

ART.1: SIMPLE VALIDATION

Can. 1156 Invalid due to an impediment

> §1 To validate a marriage which is invalid because of a diriment impediment, it is required that the impediment cease or be dispensed, and that at least the party aware of the impediment renews consent.
> §2 This renewal is required by ecclesiastical law for the validity of the validation, even if at the beginning both parties had given consent and had not afterwards withdrawn it.

Simple validation is "an act by which an invalid marriage becomes valid **476** through renewal of consent, after the renewing party knows or suspects the marriage in question is null".[2] It presupposes that matrimonial consent was given in a recognised ecclesiastical or civil ceremony; it cannot be used when the parties have lived together in a "common law" union. A marriage which is invalid because an impediment was present at the time of consent can be validated if the impediment ceases or if it is dispensed. For example, the impediment of an existing marriage bond ceases on the death of the previous spouse. Impediments of purely ecclesiastical law can be dispensed (cf. Cann. 1078-80).

The law presumes that matrimonial consent once given perseveres until **477** its withdrawal is established (Can. 1107). However for reasons of prudence canon law requires – for the validity of the validation – that at least the person who is aware of the impediment should renew their consent.[3] The

1 L. Örsy, *Marriage and canon law*, 240. **2** L. Bogdan, "Simple convalidation of marriage in the 1983 Code of Canon Law" in *The Jurist* 46 (1986), 511. **3** L. Chiappetta, *Il codice di diritto canonico*, II, 284, n. 3866.

renewal of consent is more than a simple re-affirmation of a formerly elicited inefficacious consent:

> Renewed consent implies a new decision to marry (vs. a decision to remain married) made absolutely or conditionally by the renewing party, after that person has called into question the validity of the marriage.[4]

478 In the commentary on Can. 1159 (cf. par. 116 above), I accepted Örsy's view that non-catholics who marry catholics are bound by the canons on marriage. It follows therefore that the obligation to renew consent binds both parties in a mixed marriage.[5] It does not apply to the validation of the following marriages: a) a marriage between two non-baptised parties; b) a marriage between a non-baptised person and a baptised non-catholic; c) a marriage between a person who was never a catholic and a doubtfully baptised person; d) a marriage between two certainly baptised non-catholics. Bogdan writes:

> All that would be required for a convalidation between persons in the above categories would be the perduring naturally sufficient consent of both parties and the cessation of the cause(s) of nullity. For example, once a diriment impediment binding such persons in the above-mentioned categories ceases (e.g., cessation of *ligamen* by the death of a previous spouse), and the previously given naturally sufficient consent perdures, marriage is convalidated by natural law without any further formalities on the part of the couple, provided no obstacles of natural law stand in the way. Furthermore, it would follow that neither party would have had to know or suspect that the marriage in question was previously invalid.[6]

Can. 1157 New act of the will

> The renewal of consent must be a new act of will consenting to a marriage which the renewing party knows or thinks was invalid from the beginning.

479 The renewal of consent must be a new act of the will.[7] By this act the renewing party consents to a marriage which he or she knows or thinks was invalid from the beginning; it is not simply the repetition of consent already

---

4 Bogdan, 513. **5** L. Örsy, *Marriage in canon law*, 243-4. This view is disputed. For the opposite view, cf. *The Canon Law: letter and spirit*, 654, n.2334. The advice given by this commentator is sound: "In the case of the validation of a mixed marriage, should the non-catholic party have difficulty with the idea of renewing consent, perhaps the best solution to the situation, provided there is reason to believe that the consent of the other party perseveres, is a retroactive validation without any renewal of consent (see Cann. 1161-1165)". **6** Ibid., 517. **7** *Comm* 5 (1973), 89.

given. If a person believes that the marriage was valid from the beginning, any renewal of consent will be invalid on the grounds of simulation because the person is only going through the motions of renewing consent which he or she believes is already valid.[8]

Can. 1158 Invalid due to an impediment

> §1 If the impediment is public, consent is to be renewed by both parties in the canonical form, without prejudice to the provision of Can. 1127 §2.
> §2 If the impediment cannot be proved, it is sufficient that consent be renewed privately and in secret, specifically by the party who is aware of the impediment provided the other party persists in the consent given, or by both parties if the impediment is known to both.

If the impediment is widely known, the renewal of consent must be carried **480** out in the canonical form.[9] If it is occult, consent can be renewed privately and in secret, specifically by the party who is aware of the impediment, provided that the other party persists in the consent given. If both parties are aware of an occult impediment, consent must be renewed privately and in secret by both parties.

It is important to take account of the law on convalidation when the **481** impediment of existing marriage bond (*ligamen*) arises. For example, if a divorced Protestant (A) married an unmarried Protestant (B), the marriage would be invalid due to *ligamen*. If A's former spouse later died, the cause of nullity would cease; the invalid marriage is convalidated according to the natural law provided the consent of both parties perdures and there is no other obstacle to the validity of the marriage. If this second marriage breaks down and either party wishes to marry a catholic, it would have to be determined whether the impediment of *ligamen* remained during the entire period of the second marriage (A+B). Bogdan writes:

> Since the effective date of the new code it is not sufficient to ascertain the presence of ligamen only at the time of the attempted second marriage (A+B) ... If ligamen ceased by the death of a former spouse while both parties remained in an invalid union, currently such a union would be automatically convalidated at the time of the cessation of the im-

---

[8] J.J. O'Rourke writes: "It is far different to say 'Although I do not think it necessary I am repeating my marriage vows' than to say 'Because I do not think it necessary I do not now intend to marry'. Even if the party believes himself or herself already married to the other party, that party by exchanging vows for the second time would be expressing his or her prevailing will about being married to the other party" ("Considerations on the convalidation of marriage" in *The Jurist* 43 (1983), 390). Such an act of "repeating my marriage vows" does not, in my view, amount to a "new act of will".   [9] Cf . *Comm* 10 (1978), 122.

pediment provided the naturally efficient consent of both parties continued.[10]

Can. 1159 Invalid due to defect of consent

§1 A marriage invalid because of a defect of consent is validated if the party who did not consent, now does consent, provided the consent given by the other party persists.
§2 If the defect of the consent cannot be proven, it is sufficient that the party who did not consent, gives consent privately and in secret.
§3 If the defect of consent can be proven, it is necessary that consent be given in the canonical form.

482   A marriage invalid because of a defect of consent is validated if the person who did not consent now does so, provided that the consent given by the other party still persists. The following paragraphs specify how this is to be done.

483   If the defect cannot be proven in the external forum, it is enough for the party who did not consent to do so privately and in secret. A person might, for example, exclude the right to intercourse that is open to procreation; later, having become aware that this had invalidated the consent invalid, and having abandoned this intention, he or she could renew consent privately and in secret.

484   If the defect of consent can be proven or is publicly known, the party whose consent was defective is required to renew consent in the canonical form.

Can. 1160 Invalid due to defect of form

For a marriage which is invalid because of defect of form to become valid, it must be contracted anew in the canonical form, without prejudice to the provisions of Can. 1127 §2.

485   A defect of form is of its nature public and is subject to proof in the external forum. The validation of a marriage which is invalid due to a defect of form requires that consent be given anew in the canonical form.[11]

486   This difficulty often arises in the context of mixed marriages. As a rule, the canonical procedures for the simple validation of a mixed marriage do not differ from those that apply to the simple validation of marriages between two catholics. The renewal of consent in the canonical form can be

---

10 Bogdan, 529. **11** For a list of those situations where a marriage is invalid due to defect of form, cf. commentary on Can. 1108 above.

dispensed "if there are grave difficulties in the way of observing the canonical form" (Can.1127§2); consent however must be renewed in some public form.[12]

ART.2: RETROACTIVE VALIDATION

Can. 1161 Outline of procedure

> §1 The retroactive validation of an invalid marriage is its validation without the renewal of consent, granted by the competent authority. It involves a dispensation from an impediment if there is one, and from the canonical form if it had not been observed, as well as a referral back to the past of the canonical effects.
> §2 The validation takes place from the moment the favour is granted; the referral back, however, is understood to have been made to the moment the marriage was celebrated, unless it is otherwise expressly provided.
> §3 A retroactive validation is not to be granted unless it is probable that the parties intend to persevere in conjugal life.

The "radical sanation" or "healing" of a marriage is an act of the competent **487** authority which renders valid consent which was invalid from the beginning.[13] There is no requirement to renew consent; also, any impediment of ecclesiastical law is dispensed as is the canonical form. The principal effect of this form of validation is that its effects are retroactive; in other words, the marriage is validated from the time the invalid consent was given. This retroactive validation is not to be granted unless it is probable that the parties intend to persevere in their married life. Therefore enquiries should be made as to the stability of the marriage.

Can. 1162 In case of defective consent

> §1 If consent is lacking in either or both of the parties, a marriage cannot be rectified by a retroactive validation, whether consent was absent from the beginning or, though given at the beginning, was subsequently revoked.
> §2 If the consent was indeed absent from the beginning but was subsequently given, a retroactive validation can be granted from the moment the consent was given.

---

12 *The Canon Law: letter and spirit*, 656, n. 2343. 13 The terms "radical sanation" or "healing" of a marriage are another way of describing what is meant by the term "retroactive validation".

488 If consent is lacking in either or both parties, a marriage cannot be rectified by a retroactive validation. This is the case when consent was absent from the beginning or although given then was later revoked. If consent was absent at the beginning but was later given, the marriage can be validated retroactive to the time when the consent was given (Can. 1162 §2).

Can. 1163 In case of a diriment impediment/defect of form

§1 A marriage which is invalid because of an impediment or because of defect of the legal form, can be validated retroactively, provided the consent of both parties persists.
§2 A marriage which is invalid because of an impediment of the natural law or of the divine positive law, can be validated retroactively only after the impediment has ceased.

489 A marriage which is invalid because of an impediment or because of a defect of canonical form can be validated retroactively provided the consent of both parties persists. If the impediment is of natural law or of the divine positive law, the marriage can be validated retroactively only after the impediment has ceased (Can. 1163 §2).[14]

Can. 1164 Awareness of parties

A retroactive validation may validly be granted even if one or both of the parties is unaware of it; it is not, however, to be granted except for a grave reason.

490 A retroactive validation may validly be granted even if one or both of the parties is unaware of it. It should not be granted except for a grave reason.[15]

Can. 1165 Competent authority

§1 Retroactive validation can be granted by the Apostolic See.
§2 It can be granted by the diocesan Bishop in individual cases, even if a number of reasons for nullity occur together in the same marriage, assuming that for a retroactive validation of a mixed marriage the conditions of Can. 1125 will have been fulfilled. It cannot, however, be granted by him if there is an impediment whose dispensation is reserved to the Apostolic See in accordance with Can. 1078 §2 or if

14 The laws regarding the dispensation of impediments (Cann. 1078-80) do not apply to impediments of natural law or of divine positive law. **15** *Comm* 10 (1978), 124.

there is question of an impediment of the natural law or of the divine positive law which has now ceased.

Retroactive validation can be granted by the Apostolic See either in an individual case or for a number of marriages. The Apostolic See alone is competent to act in cases involving a reserved impediment (e.g., the impediment of orders arising from priesthood) or the cases of mixed marriages where the promises to be made by the catholic party to a mixed marriage have not been met. The Apostolic See alone grants sanations in cases involving natural or divine positive law impediments when the impediment has ceased to exist. These are the impediments of sacred orders, public vow of perpetual chastity in a religious institute, crime and prior bond. It does not sanate marriages which are invalid because of the impediment of consanguinity in the direct line or second degree of the collateral line, nor in cases of impotence. **491**

The diocesan Bishop – and those equivalent to him (cf. Cann. 368/381 §2) – is competent to validate marriages retroactively in individual cases if the cause of nullity was a defect of form, a defect of consent or an undispensed impediment. In the case of a mixed marriage or a marriage involving the impediment of disparity of cult, the diocesan Bishop can only validate the marriage as long as the promises have been made. He cannot grant a retroactive validation if the dispensation of an impediment is reserved to the Apostolic See (Can. 1078 §2) or there is an impediment of the natural law or of the divine positive law which has not ceased. **492**

The diocesan Bishop – and those equivalent to him – can delegate his faculty to retroactively convalidate marriages to priests and deacons (Can. 137 §1). **493**

When a marriage is validated in the external forum the parish priest of the place of validation must enter the details in the marriage register of the place of validation. The parish(es) where both parties were baptised should be notified (Can. 1123). **494**

495

BIBLIOGRAPHY

J.B. Mullan, "Nullity and convalidation of marriage" in *CLSGBI Newsletter* 50 (1981), 34-40.

G. Sheehy, "Nullity and convalidation of marriage" (some comments on Canon Mullan's article) in *CLSGBI Newsletter* 52 (1982), 12-5.

W. Gasche, "The law concerning invalid convalidations" in *CLSGBI Newsletter* 52 (1982), 16-8.

F.J. Courtney, ""The plea of invalid convalidation in defect of form cases" in *CLSGBI Newsletter* 52 (1982), 19-24.

J.J. O'Rourke, "Considerations on the convalidation of marriage" in *The Jurist* 43 (1983), 387-91.

L.A. Bogdan, "Simple convalidation of marriage in the 1983 Code of Canon Law" in *The Jurist* 46 (1986), 511-31.

K. Matthews, "Validations or convalidations? That is the question" in *Unico ecclesiae servitio* (edd. Thériault and Thorn), Faculty of Canon Law, Saint Paul University, Ottawa 1991, 133-47.

10

Procedural law of marriage

Church procedures are outlined in Book VII of the Code of Canon Law. **496**
Parts I-II deal with general concepts and procedures; part III deals with Certain Special Procedures, among which cases concerning the declaration of nullity of marriage are particularly important. [1]

The Church's jurisdiction in matrimonial cases

The marriages of the baptised are sacramental and come under the jurisdic- **497**
tion of the Church (Cann. 1401, 1°/1671). This includes the definition of marriage, the celebration of marriage, the pastoral care of marriage, and determining the validity of marriage and the status of the persons involved when doubt is raised about the matter. Judicial power, that is, the authority to settle disputes and to give judgement on issues, is vested in the diocesan Bishop. The diocesan Bishop may exercise this power personally, but he normally does so through a judicial Vicar and judges (Can. 391 §2).

Competent forum

"Competence" in canon law refers to the ability of an ecclesiastical court or **498**
judge to hear and make a decision about a case. The general norms of canon law regarding competence are stated in Cann. 1404-16. The observance of these norms promotes the orderly administration of justice and the protection of rights in the Church.[2] The failure to observe them has the effect of rendering the proceedings "irremediably null" (Can. 1620, 1°).

The Roman Pontiff reserves some cases to himself; these include cases **499**
involving Heads of State (Can. 1405 §1, 1°) and other cases which he may decide to reserve to himself (ibid., 4°). Can. 1673 determines which Church tribunal is competent in canon law to judge marriage nullity cases.

> The following tribunals are competent in cases concerning the nullity
> of marriage which are not reserved to the Apostolic See:
> 1° the tribunal of the place where the marriage was celebrated;

---

1 This section does not deal in detail with procedural law; it focuses on the main elements of the nullity procedure – and other procedures – which concern those engaged in parish ministry. 2 P. Branchereau, "La competence dans les causes matrimoniales" in *Dilexit iustitiam*, 316.

2° the tribunal of the place where the respondent has a domicile or quasi-domicile;

3° the tribunal of the place where the plaintiff has a domicile, provided that both parties live within the territory of the same Bishops' Conference, and that the judicial Vicar of the domicile of the respondent, after consultation with the respondent, gives consent;

4° the tribunal of the place in which in fact most of the proofs are to be collected, provided that consent is given by the judicial Vicar of the domicile of the respondent, who must first ask the respondent whether he or she has any objection to raise.

500   Firstly, the tribunal of the place where the marriage took place is competent. Regional marriage tribunals enjoy competence to judge marriages that took place in the constituent dioceses of the region.

501   Secondly, the tribunal of the place where the respondent has a domicile or quasi-domicile is competent.[3] This is based on the maxim *actor sequitur forum rei* (the plaintiff follows the tribunal of the respondent). This means that the respondent is given whatever advantages accrue to having a home venue. These could be financial, through not having to travel to a different place.

502   Thirdly, "the tribunal of the place where the petitioner has a domicile [is competent] provided that both parties live within the territory of the same Bishops' Conference, and that the judicial Vicar of the domicile of the respondent, after consultation with the respondent, gives consent". The forum where the petitioner has a domicile is competent if two conditions are fulfilled. The first is that both parties reside within the territory of the same Bishops' Conference. The second is that the consent of the judicial Vicar of the respondent's domicile must be obtained. This cannot be presumed.[4] The judicial Vicar who must give consent is the judicial Vicar of the diocese where the respondent has a domicile, not the judicial Vicar of the regional tribunal; if there is no diocesan judicial Vicar, the consent of the diocesan Bishop must be obtained.[5]

503   Fourthly, "the tribunal of the place in which in fact most of the evidence is to be collected [is competent], provided that consent is given by the judicial Vicar of the respondent, who must first ask the respondent whether he or she has any objection to raise". If he or she has no objections to this forum, the judicial Vicar may give consent; if the respondent does object, the judicial Vicar should withhold consent unless he judges that the objection is unreasonable. In judging where "most of the evidence" is, the criterion is the weight to be attributed to each of the proofs, not just the number

3 The person who brings the case to the tribunal is known as "the petitioner"; the other party is known as "the respondent". **4** Cf. *Roman replies and CLSA advisory opinions* 1989, 45-8. **5** *AAS* 78 (1986), 1323.

of witnesses.[6] The Apostolic Signatura[7] has stated that this forum can be used if the respondent's place of residence is unknown.[8]

Can. 1674 deals with the question: who may challenge the validity of a mar- **504**
riage?

> The following are capable of impugning the validity of a marriage:
> 1° the spouses themselves;
> 2° the promotor of justice, when the nullity of the marriage has already been made public, and the marriage cannot be validated or it is not expedient to do so.

Either of the parties to a marriage may challenge its validity, even the one **505**
who was responsible for the nullity of the marriage. The promotor of justice can also impugn the validity of a marriage when the nullity of the marriage has already been made public and it is not possible or expedient to validate it (Can. 1674, 2°).[9]

FORMAL NULLITY PROCESS

The nullity procedure can be divided into four main parts: petition, instruc- **506**
tion, discussion and decision. The petition is the formal plea to the tribunal; it may be accepted or refused, according to law. The instruction is the name given to the gathering of evidence. The discussion phase involves the study of the case by the advocate(s) and the defender of the bond. The decision is given in accordance with the law by a duly constituted college of judges. The detailed steps of this procedure are outlined below.

Petition

Drawing up a petition The Church is anxious to avoid disputes and trials **507**
except as a last resort. In matrimonial cases an ecclesiastical tribunal should ensure before accepting a case that all reasonable pastoral means have been used to bring about a reconciliation and validation (Can. 1676). To accept a case too quickly or to suggest recourse to the tribunal too precipitately could

---

6 *AAS* 81 (1989), 892-4; *The Jurist* 50 (1990), 307-9. 7 "The Apostolic Signatura functions as the supreme tribunal [of the catholic Church] and also ensures that justice in the Church is correctly administered" (*Pastor bonus*, art. 121). 8 *Periodica* 62 (1973), 590-1. Cf. F. Daneels, "The forum of most of the proofs" in *The Jurist* 50 (1990), 305. 9 The promotor of justice is "the official guardian of the public good, that is, the good of the Church, of its rights and laws, and the general good of the community" (*The Canon law: letter and spirit*, 830, n. 2889).

destroy the possibility of solving a marital difficulty. For this reasons, some tribunals, in order to ensure that every possibility of reconciliation has been exhausted, require that a couple be separated for a specified period before a petition will be accepted.

508   A judge cannot investigate any case unless a plea, drawn up in accordance with canon law, is submitted by one of the parties or by the promotor of justice (Can. 1674). In the case of a marriage nullity petition, the person wishing to submit a plea may obtain the assistance of a canonist who can draw up the plea in the proper manner.[10] More often, the initial request to a tribunal comes in the form of an informal letter outlining the basis of the plea or by way of an application form which includes the relevant information.

509   **Can. 1504** outlines the elements which must be included in a petition:

> The petition by which a suit is introduced must:
>
> 1° state the judge before whom the case is being introduced, what is being sought and from whom it is being sought;
> 2° indicate on what right the plaintiff bases the case and, at least in general terms, the facts and proofs to be evinced in support of the allegations made;
> 3° be signed by the plaintiff or the plaintiff's procurator, and bear the day, the month and the year, as well as the address at which the plaintiff or the procurator resides, or at which they say they reside for the purpose of receiving the acts;
> 4° indicate the domicile or quasi-domicile of the respondent.

510   The judge to whom the plea is addressed must enjoy competence to accept it (cf. Cann. 1502/1673).

511   A petition is a request addressed to the competent judicial authority by a person seeking a decision. It must state the tribunal before whom the case is being introduced, and what is being sought; it must indicate the grounds on which the petitioner bases his or her case, and, at least in general terms, the facts and evidence to be submitted in support of the petition; it must be signed by the petitioner or his or her representative (procurator), and bear the date on which it was made and the address of the petitioner; it must also indicate the domicile or quasi-domicile of the respondent (Can. 1504). Failure to observe the main provisions of Can. 1504 could lead to the rejection of the petition (Can. 1505 §3).

---

10 G. Sheehy, "Introducing a case of nullity of marriage: the new Code and the practice of local tribunals" in *Dilexit justitiam*, 344.

Acceptance of the petition When he has satisfied himself that the matter is **512** within his competence and the petitioner has a right to stand before the Court, the presiding judge must by decree either admit or reject the petition (Can. 1505 §1). The petition can be rejected if, for example, "if it is certainly clear from the petition that the plea lacks any foundation, and that there is no possibility that a foundation will emerge from a process" (Can. 1505 §2, 4°). The decree of rejection must give the reasons for the decision, at least summarily, both in law and in fact; it must also indicate the means by which it can be challenged.[11] The law provides for the possibility of an appeal:

> A party is always entitled, within ten canonical days, to have recourse, based upon stated reasons, against the rejection of a petition. This recourse is to be made either to the tribunal of appeal or, if the petition was rejected by the presiding judge, to the collegiate tribunal. A question of rejection is to be determined with maximum expedition (Can. 1505 §4).

If the recourse is successful, the case is returned to the tribunal which re- **513** jected it.[12]

"If within one month of the presentation of a petition, the judge has not **514** issued a decree admitting or rejecting it in accordance with Can.1505, the interested party can insist that the judge perform his duty. If, notwithstanding this, the judge does not respond, then after ten days from the party's request the petition is to be taken as having been admitted" (Can. 1506).

Citation of the respondent In the same decree by which the petition was **515** accepted, the judge is obliged to summon the other party. This summons (or citation) informs the respondent of the plaintiff's plea and allows him or her the opportunity of defence. If the summons is not lawfully communicated to the respondent, the acts of the case are null and the judgement of the tribunal is irremediably null due to the denial of the right to defence. Failure to communicate the summons to the respondent is one example of a denial of this right (Can. 1620, 7°). The petition – which has just been accepted – is to be attached to the summons unless, for grave reasons, the judge considers that it is not to be communicated to the other party before he or she gives evidence (Can. 1508 §2).

---

11 P. Churchill, *The admission and rejection of the libellus in the canonical tradition and especially according to the 1983 Code of Canon Law*, Rome, 1993, 133. **12** *Comm* 11 (1979), 85.

Can. 1677 The joinder of the issue

> §1 When the petition has been accepted, the presiding judge or the ponens is to proceed to the notification of the decree of summons, in accordance with Can. 1508.
>
> §2 On the expiry of fifteen days from the notification, the presiding judge or the ponens shall, unless one or other party requests a session for the joinder of the issue, within ten days by his decree determine ex officio the formulation of the doubt or doubts and notify the parties.
>
> §3 The formulation of the doubt is not only to ask whether the nullity of the particular marriage is proven, but also to determine the ground or grounds upon which the validity of the marriage is being challenged.
>
> §4 After ten days from the notification of the decree, if the parties have not lodged any objection, the presiding judge or the ponens is by a new decree to arrange for the instruction of the case.

516   Can. 1677 §2 provides that "on the expiry of fifteen days from the notification [of the summons], the presiding judge or the *ponens* shall, unless one or other party requests a session for the joinder of the issue, within ten days by his decree determine *ex officio* the formulation of the doubt or doubts and notify the parties". The *dubium* (doubt) is usually phrased as follows: "Whether the nullity of the marriage is proved on the grounds that, for example, the respondent simulated his consent". If the parties do not object to this decree within ten days of being notified, the presiding judge or *ponens* is, by a new decree, to arrange for the hearing of the case (Can. 1677 §4). Once the doubt is agreed and communicated to the parties, it cannot validly be altered except by a new decree, issued for a grave reason, at the request of the party, and after the other party has been consulted and his or her observations considered (Can. 1514). The emergence of new facts which substantially change the nature of the case would constitute a grave reason.

Instruction

517   *The trial of the issue*   The instruction of a case begins with the declarations of the parties. Each party separately makes a sworn deposition (Can. 1532). Each party may nominate witnesses (Can. 1547). Can. 1558 stipulates that they are to be examined at the office of the tribunal unless the judge deems otherwise. Frequently witnesses are interviewed in the parish where they live. As a matter of practice, however, witnesses should not be interviewed in their own homes unless, for reasons of health, it is not possible to meet them elsewhere.

518   The defender of the bond and the legal representatives of the parties have a right to attend the interviews with the parties and the witnesses (Can. 1678 §1, 1°). In his Address to the Roman Rota in 1988 Pope John Paul II

reminded defenders of the bond "to ensure that the questions are put to experts in a clear and relevant manner, that their competence be respected and that answers are not expected from them on canonical matters".[13] The parties and witnesses are examined (that is, interviewed) by the judge. This task can be delegated, even to lay auditors (interviewers); frequently the defender of the bond and the parties' representatives are not present.

In marriage nullity cases the declarations of the parties, while not having the force of full proof, are particularly important since they alone have first-hand knowledge of what has happened. One way of corroborating the evidence of the parties is to obtain the evidence of character witnesses (Can. 1679).

519

In cases involving impotence or defects of consent arising from mental illness, the judge is to obtain the evidence of experts, "unless from the circumstances this would obviously serve no purpose" (Can. 1680).[14] Given the predominance of cases involving psychological grounds, it is important that the role of expert evidence be properly understood. The judge has discretion to decide if the evidence of an expert is required in a case;[15] it is for him or her to decide if "expert information could complete or explain something which does not enjoy sufficient clarity".[16] For example, the services of an expert witness will be sought in cases which involve psychopathology or mental disorder when such illness did not manifest itself at the time of the marriage.[17] Judges most commonly seek the assistance of experts in psychiatry or psychology. Breitenbeck explains the help which such a witness can give:

520

> [The expert's report should contain] a description of the allegedly incapacitating factor from the perspective of the expert's discipline, utilising concrete details reflective of the party' (partys') relational behaviour, activity and capacity; indications of the destructive or disruptive consequences of the factors concerning which clarification is being sought, and the consequential effects on a person's faculty to evaluate critically, to understand, to will, to effect, to be responsible for actions; should a diagnosis be given, the expert ought to explain precisely the nature and degree of the illness, the consequences this particular dysfunction has, had or continues to have on a person's ability to function interpersonally in a marriage relationship; trace the chronology of the incapacitating factor: pre-marital, marital, post-marital

13 *Papal allocutions to the Roman Rota*, 202. **14** M. Breitenbeck, "The use of experts in marriage nullity cases" in CLSA, *Proceedings of the fifty-first annual convention 1989*, 30-47; A. Mendonça, "The role of experts in 'incapacity to contract' cases (Can. 1095)" in *Studia Canonica* 25 (1991), 417-50; M.F. Pompedda, "Dialogue et collaboration entre les juges et les experts dans les causes de nullité de mariage" in *L'Année Canonique* 37 (1995-6), 183-96. **15** Cf. *Comm* 11 (1979), 264. **16** F. Gil de las Heras, "Organización judicial de la Iglesia en el nuevo Código" in *Ius Canonicum* 24 (1984), 184, cited in M. Breitenbeck, 33. **17** Breitenbeck, ibid., 33.

history, its latency or dormancy, and the transitory or permanent nature of such factor; indications of manner unique to particular discipline according to which the expert discharged the function specified by judicial decree and drew conclusions about the person under consideration.[18]

521   The judge retains the responsibility to weigh carefully the conclusions of the expert in the light of all other evidence and to reach a judgement accordingly. In his Address to the Roman Rota in 1987, Pope John Paul II drew attention to the dangers inherent in the use of experts. Anthropological theories which are at odds with the Christian view of the human person and attitudes towards marriage which are opposed to Christian teaching can colour the judgement of an expert. The Pope stated that "dialogue and constructive communication between the judge and the psychiatrist or psychologist are easier if the starting point for both is within the horizon of a common anthropology, in such a way that the vision of one remains open to that of the other, yet within their differences of method, interest and purpose".[19]

522   Can. 1680 states that in cases involving defect of consent by reason of mental illness, the judge is to use the services of one or more experts, "unless from the circumstances this would obviously serve no purpose..." One writer has commented that "provided there is sufficient evidence to place the gravity and effects of the [psychological] disturbance at the time of the marriage beyond doubt, then the services of an expert would clearly be superfluous and a possible source of unnecessary expense and delay"; however he warns that the judges must not "play at being amateur psychologists".[20] What however is to be done in the situation, which is by no means rare, when a respondent refuses to co-operate with the Tribunal? In this situation "the possibility of having an expert study the acts of the case remains".[21]

Can. 1598 Publication of the acts

§ When the evidence has been assembled, the judge must, under pain of nullity, by a decree permit the parties and their advocates to inspect at the tribunal office those acts which are not yet known to them. Indeed if the advocates so request, a copy of the acts can be given to them. In cases which concern the public good, however, the judge can decide that, in order to avoid very serious dangers, a given act is not to

18 Ibid., 39-40. **19** *Papal allocutions to the Roman Rota*, 192, n. 3. For other material on this topic, cf. A. McGrath, "At the service of the truth: psychological sciences to the Canon Law of Marriage" in *Studia Canonica* 27 (1993), 379-400; A. Mendonça, "The role of experts in 'incapacity to contract' cases" in *Studia Canonica* 25 (1991), 417-50. **20** McGrath, 396. **21** Ibid.

be shown to anyone. He must take care, however, that the right of defence always remains intact.

§2 To complete the proofs, the parties can propose others to the judge. When these have been assembled, the occasion arises anew for the decree mentioned in §1, if the judge considers it necessary.

In his Address to the Roman Rota in 1989, Pope John Paul II stated: **523**

> The right of defense demands of its very nature the concrete possibility of knowing the proofs adduced by the opposing party and *ex officio*. Can. 1598 §1 therefore lays down that when the evidence has been assembled, the judge must, under the pain of nullity, permit the parties and their advocates to inspect at the tribunal acts which are not yet known to them. This is a right of the parties and their advocates. The same canon provides for a possible exception. In cases that concern the public good, the judge can decide that, so as to avoid very serious dangers, some of the acts are not to be shown to anyone; he must take care, however, that the right of defense always remains completely intact.[22]

The Revision Commission was aware of the difficulties to which this **524** canon could give rise.[23] A recent commentator has written à propos of this canon: "It is a proven fact that the understanding of confidentiality before the ecclesiastical marriage-nullity courts is a significant fact in enabling those courts to secure a more accurate picture of the truth than is the case before many corresponding civil courts, especially those in which the so-called "adversarial procedure" is the norm".[24] Daneels, commenting on the Pope John Paul II's 1989 Address, noted that "whatever the difficulties which could occur, the right of defense is to be given great importance in matrimonial cases in which there is a question of the personal status of the parties themselves as well as of the sacred bond of matrimony, which is not at the disposition of the parties".[25]

Discussion

Advocate's pleadings   When the case has been concluded, the judge is to **525** determine a suitable period of time for the presentation of pleadings and

---

22 *Papal allocutions to the Roman Rota*, 206. **23** *Comm* 11 (1979), 134-5; *Congregatio plenaria*, 469-79. **24** *The Canon Law: letter and spirit*, 900, footnote 1. **25** F. Daneels, "The right of defense" in *Studia Canonica* 27 (1993), 92-3. For further material on this topic, cf. E. Dillon, "Confidentiality of testimony – an implementation of Can. 1598" in *The Jurist* 45 (1985), 289-96; J. G. Johnson, "Publish and be damned: the dilemma of implementing the canons on publishing the acts and the sentence" in *The Jurist* 49 (1989), 210-40; D. Nau, "Publish and be damned: one practitioner's experience" in *The Jurist* 51 (1991), 442-50.

observations (Can. 1601). The conclusion of the case marks the end of the gathering of proofs. "Pleadings" take the form of a written submission prepared by an advocate on behalf of the petitioner (or respondent) in which the merits of the case are presented.

526 *Observations of defender of the bond* "Observations" are made in written form by the defender of the bond, an official of the tribunal who is required "to present and expound all that can reasonably be argued" against the nullity of the marriage (Can. 1432). In his Address to the Roman Rota in 1988, Pope John Paul II, referring to cases involving psychic incapacity, spoke of the duty of the defender of the bond to assist in the correct interpretation and use of expert evidence.[26]

Decision

527 *The judgement* Marriage nullity cases are reserved by law to a collegiate tribunal of three judges (Can. 1425 §1, 1°). Bishops' Conferences can however permit the Bishop to entrust first instance cases to a sole clerical judge "if ... it is impossible to constitute a college of judges" (Can. 1425 §4). The Irish Bishops' Conference issued a decree permitting this:

> In accordance with the prescription of Can. 1425 §4 and in respect of cases of nullity at first instance, if it is not possible, because of the scarcity of judges, to constitute a College of Judges for each case without causing undue delay in determining the cases before the court, the Irish Bishops' Conference hereby decrees that the Bishop-Moderator of each Regional Marriage Tribunal may entrust cases to a sole clerical judge of proven knowledge and experience who, where possible, shall associate with himself an assessor and an auditor. This decree is to be reviewed after five years.[27]

528 The Irish Bishops' Conference also decreed that "in accordance with Can. 1421 §2 ... lay persons, duly qualified and experienced, may be appointed judges in ecclesiastical tribunals in this country".[28] This has not led to a substantial change in practice as few lay persons are sufficiently qualified in canon law to act as judges.

---

26 *Papal allocutions to the Roman Rota*, 198-203. **27** Decree n. 19 in *Intercom* 18 (1987/8), supplement, 14. Similar decrees were made by the Bishop's Conference of Canada (*Code of Canon Law annotated*, 1333) and by the Bishop's Conference of India (ibid., 1356). **28** Decree n. 18, ibid., 13. Similar decrees were made by the Canadian Bishops' Conference (cf. *Code of Canon Law annotated*, 1333), the Bishops' Conference of England and Wales (ibid., 1341), the Bishops' Conference of India (ibid., 1356), and the Bishops' Conference of Nigeria (ibid., 1390).

When the pleadings and observations have been submitted, a date is set   **529**
for the hearing of the case (Can. 1609 §1). The judges are required to bring
to the meeting of the tribunal their written conclusions on the merits of the
case, with the reasons in law and in fact for reaching their conclusions (Can.
1609 §2). Can. 1609 §§3-5 specifies how the meeting of the tribunal is to be
conducted:

> Having invoked the divine Name, [the judges] are to offer their con-
> clusions in order, beginning always with the ponens or relator in the
> case, and then in order of precedence. Under the chairmanship of the
> presiding judge, they are to hold their discussion principally with a
> view to establishing what is to be stated in the dispositive part of the
> judgement.
>
> In the discussion, each one is permitted to depart from an original
> conclusion. A judge who does not wish to accede to the decision of the
> others can demand that, if there is an appeal, his or her conclusions be
> forwarded to the higher tribunal.
>
> If the judges do not wish, or are unable, to reach a decision in the
> first discussion, they can defer their decision to another meeting, but
> not beyond one week, unless the instruction of the case has to be com-
> pleted in accordance with Can. 1600.

Marriage enjoys the favour of the law (Can. 1060); in order to return a   **530**
decision of *Constat de nullitate* (that the nullity of the marriage is proven)
the judges who form a collegiate tribunal must reach their decision with
moral certitude which must be derived from the acts and the proofs (Can.
1608). In the absence of such certitude that a marriage has been shown to be
null, the presumption of validity will hold. A decision may be arrived at
either unanimously or by majority vote. When the decision has been reached,
one of the judges – the *ponens* – must draw up a sentence outlining the
reasons for the decision of the tribunal. This judgement must be submitted to
the individual judges for their approval (Can. 1610 §2). The judgement is to
be issued not later than one month from the day on which the case was decided, unless in a collegiate tribunal the judges have for grave reasons stipulated a longer time (Can. 1610 §3).

Publication of the judgement   Can. 1614 requires that the tribunal publish   **531**
the judgement as soon as possible by communicating it to the parties; it
must also indicate to the parties how they can appeal against the judgement.
This canon states that until the judgement is published "it has no effect". In
his above-mentioned Address to the Roman Rota in 1989, Pope John Paul
II wrote:

In relation to the right of defense, it cannot be a matter of surprise to speak also of the necessity of publishing the judgement. How could one of the parties defend himself or herself in the court of appeal against the judgement of the lower tribunal if [he or she is] deprived of the right to know the reasons, both in law and in fact, supporting it?[29]

532   This provision causes the same difficulties for tribunals as Can. 1598. There is a tension between, on the one hand, the desire of many parties and witnesses for confidentiality and, on the other, the right of defence of the parties. The present law gives priority to the right of defence and a denial of this renders a judgement null (Can. 1620, 7°).[30]

Can. 1682 The appeal

§1 The judgement which has first declared the nullity of a marriage, together with the appeals, if there are any, and the other judicial acts, are to be sent ex officio to the appeal tribunal within twenty days of the publication of the judgement.
§2 If the judgement in favour of the nullity of the marriage was given in first instance, the appeal tribunal, after weighing the observations of the defender of the bond and, if there are any, of the parties, is by its decree either to ratify the decision without delay, or to admit the case to ordinary examination in the new instance.

533   If the decision at first instance is negative, that is, if it upholds the validity of the marriage, the parties can appeal to the appeal tribunal; if the decision is positive, that is, if it declared the marriage null, a party who feels aggrieved can appeal to the appeal tribunal. In the event of the appeal tribunal overturning the judgement of first instance, the case can be heard at a third instance. This will normally be the Roman Rota (Can. 1444 §1, 2°).

534   When a decree of nullity is issued, the judicial Vicar must notify the Ordinary of the place where the marriage was celebrated. The latter must ensure that a record of the decree of nullity and of any *vetitum* imposed is entered in the registers of marriage and baptism as soon as possible (Can. 1685).[31]

535   In his Address to the Roman Rota in 1965, Pope Paul VI called on tribunals to avoid every delay not demanded by the particular nature of special circumstances of the individual case. He stated that "... every culpable delay ... in the administration and execution of justice is already in itself an

---

29 *Papal allocutions to the Roman Rota*, 206. 30 For material on this topic, cf. the bibliography given above in the comment on Can. 1598. 31 A *vetitum* is a clause prohibiting marriage; a court may attach such clause to its judgement if it considers that precautions should be taken before one or both parties enter another relationship (cf. Can. 1684 §1).

injustice, which each member of ecclesiastical tribunals must meticulously strive to avoid".[32]

In the above-mentioned Address, Pope Paul VI stated "that it is in itself **536** an injustice which is unacceptable within the Church that a person could not think of obtaining justice without great expense".[33] He added that "since they are most generous in granting free legal aid, ecclesiastical tribunals are far removed from this reproach".[34] Can. 1649 §1, 3° stipulates that "the Bishop who is responsible for governing the tribunal is to establish norms concerning ... the granting of free legal aid and the reduction of expenses".

Can. 1686 The documentary (nullity) process

> On receiving a petition in accordance with Can. 1677, the judicial Vicar or a judge designated by him, can omit the formalities of the ordinary process and, having summoned the parties, and with the intervention of the defender of the bond, declare the nullity of the marriage by a judgement, if from a document which is not open to any contradiction or exception there is certain proof of the existence of a diriment impediment or a defect of form, which it is equally certain has not been dispensed from, or of the lack of a valid proxy mandate.

The process outlined above is the formal procedure for the nullity of mar- **537** riage. In some instances however a marriage can be shown to be invalid on the basis of a document which proves the existence of diriment impediment, a defect of form or the lack of a valid proxy mandate (Can. 1686).[35] The person seeking a declaration of nullity using this procedure must draw up a petition alluding to the existence of a document or documents which establish the existence of an impediment or a defect of form. On receipt of the petition, the judicial Vicar or a judge designated by him, can summon the parties; the defender of the bond should intervene, making appropriate observations; finally the judge is to issue a judgement, stating the reasons in law and in fact for the decision.

If a judge is unable to reach an affirmative decision on the basis of the **538** documentary process, the case should be remitted to the ordinary process.

If the defender of the bond judges that the defects mentioned in Can.1686, **539** or the lack of dispensation, are not certain he must appeal to the judge of second instance (Can. 1687 §1). The acts are to be sent to the appeal judge; the latter must be informed in writing that the decision has been reached by way of the documentary process. The parties also have the right of appeal (Can. 1687 §2).

In the event of an appeal, the judge of second instance is to decide the **540**

---

32 *Papal allocutions to the Roman Rota*, 81. 33 Ibid. 34 Ibid. 35 *Comm* 11 (1979), 269.

case, having consulted the parties and having heard the defender of the bond, in the same way as in Can. 1686. He may decide to ratify the first instance decision, or he may decide that the case should be heard according to the ordinary full process, in which event he is to send it back to the tribunal of first instance for full hearing. As with the first instance judge, he does not return a negative decision.

11

The separation of the spouses

ART. I: THE DISSOLUTION OF THE BOND

There are a number of canonical procedures which dissolve the bond of marriage. They must be distinguished from marriage nullity procedures. [1]   **541**

Dissolution of a non-consummated marriage

Can. 1141 states the theological-canonical principle that "a marriage which is ratified and consummated cannot be dissolved by any human power or by any cause other than death". This is the synthesis that emerged from the medieval dispute between the schools of Paris and Bologna concerning the formation of the bond of marriage. Hence a valid marriage contracted between two baptised christians and which is subsequently consummated by an act of sexual intercourse performed "in a human manner" cannot be dissolved by the will of the couple or by any external authority, civil or ecclesiastical.   **542**

Can. 1142 states that "a non-consummated marriage between baptised persons or between a baptised person and an unbaptised person can be dissolved by the Roman Pontiff for a just reason, at the request of both parties or of either party, even if the other is unwilling". This is a valid marriage; as such it is intrinsically indissoluble, that is, it cannot be dissolved by the couple. It can be dissolved by the Pope by virtue of a power which is described as "ministerial" or "vicarious". Woestman cites Capello's explanation of the nature of this power: **543**

> The power by which the Roman Pontiff dissolves a [non-consummated] ratified marriage, is not proper jurisdictional power ... It is completely special, extraordinary, indeed ministerial and instrumental insofar as it is exercised by the authority of and in the name of Christ himself;

---

1 Cf. W.H. Woestman, *Special marriage cases*. The revised edition of this work was published by the Faculty of Canon Law, Saint Paul University, Ottawa, in 1992.

wherefore it is properly vicarious power, and in the true and strict sense divine power.[2]

544 Given the nature of this power, the Pope can validly act only if there is a just cause. Therefore when requesting the dissolution of a marriage that is ratified but not consummated, it is necessary to establish not only the fact of non-consummation but also that there is a just cause and that the Church will not be harmed by scandal through the granting of the dissolution.

545 The marriage may be dissolved, even if the other is unwilling (Cann. 1141/1697).

546 The authority to give judgement on the fact of the non-consummation of marriage and on the existence of the just reason for granting the dispensation lies with the Apostolic See alone (Can. 1698). During the process of drafting the Code, it was suggested that the faculty of giving this dispensation be accorded to Bishops. The Commission held that it was opportune to reserve it to the Apostolic See.[3] These cases are dealt with by the Congregation for Divine Worship and the Discipline of the Sacraments.[4] The Pope, acting on advice given him personally, gives the dispensation (Can. 1698 §2).

547 The procedure by which the non-consummation of a marriage is investigated is administrative in nature, not judicial. Hence the complex rules of competence which apply in nullity cases (Can. 1673) do not apply. The diocesan Bishop of the place of domicile or quasi-domicile of the petitioner may accept the petition seeking the dispensation (Can. 1699 §1).[5]

548 Detailed norms for this procedure were issued by the Congregation for the Sacraments in 1986.[6] The purpose of the procedure is to ascertain whether the marriage has been consummated. This non-consummation can be shown in three ways: by the physical argument, that is, showing with the assistance of medical experts that the woman is still a virgin or that, given the state of the sexual organs of either party or both, sexual intercourse could not have taken place; by the moral argument, that is, using the sworn testimony of the parties and of witnesses who knew of the fact of non-consummation at a non-suspect time, as well as witnesses to the credibility of the parties, documents and other indications to arrive at a moral certitude concerning the non-consummation; by circumstantial evidence, that is by proving from evidence beyond dispute that the parties did not have the opportunity to engage in sexual intercourse.[7] Evidence must also be given of the presence of a "just cause" for the granting of the dispensation.

549 If the diocesan Bishop who accepted the petition judges it to be well-

---

2 Ibid., 8-9. **3** *Comm* 11 (1979), 275. **4** *Pastor bonus*, n.67. **5** Those who are equiparated in law to diocesan Bishops may also institute these proceedings (AAS 64 (1972), 245). **6** For an English translation, cf. Woestman, *Special marriage cases*, 119-26. **7** *The Canon Law: letter and spirit*, 643, n. 2300.

founded, he must arrange for the instruction of the case. He can either refer it to his marriage tribunal or that of another diocese. Alternatively, he may refer it to a suitable priest (Can. 1700 §1). If a case has special difficulties, the diocesan Bishop is to consult the Holy See (Can. 1699 §2).[8] Recourse to the Holy See is available if a Bishop rejects a petition for dispensation (Can. 1699 §3).

A diocesan Bishop may assign the instruction of these processes in a   **550**
stable manner or case by case to his own tribunal, to that of another diocese or to suitable priest. If however evidence of non-consummation arises in a case that is being instructed as a nullity case, "the tribunal can, with the consent of the parties, suspend the nullity case and complete the instruction of a case for a dispensation from a non-consummated marriage" (Can. 1681).

In attempting to establish the truth of the situation, the instructor will   **551**
hear both parties. Witnesses and experts may be called to give evidence. While an advocate is not assigned to the parties, "a legal expert can aid the parties in introducing the case, collecting the proofs and, in the case of a negative decision, in presenting the case again".[9] When the evidence has been gathered, there is no publication of the acts (Can. 1703 §1).

At this stage, the instructor must write a report which will include a   **552**
summary of the whole process. The acts must be submitted to the defender of the bond who is required "to present and expound all that can be reasonably be argued against the ... dissolution" (Can. 1432). Finally, the Bishop is to write a *votum* (opinion). The 1986 norms specify how this should be drawn up:

> The Bishop will consider the fact of non-consummation and the just cause for granting the dispensation. Moved by pastoral motives he will consider the opportuneness of the favour, the absence of scandal, bewilderment of the faithful and harm of any kind that could arise from the granting of the favour. He will also consider the consequences of the requested grant in relation to the good of souls, restoration of peace of conscience, and will refer explicitly to all of this in his votum.[10]

The Bishop is to send all the acts to the Apostolic See, together with his   **553**
votum and the observations of the defender of the bond (Can. 1705 §1). This is usually done through the Papal Legate of the country.

If the Apostolic See judges that further evidence is required, it will no-   **554**
tify the Bishop, specifying the points on which clarification is sought (Can. 1705 §2).

If the Apostolic See judges that the non-consummation is not proven,   **555**
the legal expert referred to in Can. 1701 §2 can inspect the acts of the case – though not the *votum* of the Bishop (Can. 1705 §3) – in the tribunal office

---

8 For examples, cf. Woestman, *Special marriage cases*, 121. **9** 1986 instruction, in Woestman, 121-2, n. 6. **10** Ibid., 125, n. 23c.

in order to decide whether anything further of importance can be brought forward to justify another submission of the petition (Can. 1705 §3).

556   If the rescript of dispensation is granted it is sent by the Apostolic See to the Bishop. He will notify the parties and direct the parish priests of the place where the marriage took place and the place(s) where the parties were baptised, to enter a note in the appropriate register (Can. 1706). It should be noted that there is a strong possibility of a *vetitum* in non-consummation cases.

The pauline privilege

557   The procedure known as the "pauline privilege" traces its origins to 1 Corinthians 7:12-15. By virtue of it, a marriage celebrated between two unbaptised parties is dissolved if, after one has received baptism, the other "departs" or leaves the marriage. The marriage is dissolved by the fact that a new marriage has been contracted by the baptised party; it is dissolved in favour of the faith of that person. The validity of the subsequent marriage depends on the fulfilment of the conditions laid down in Cann. 1143-7.

> Can. 1143 §1 In virtue of the pauline privilege, a marriage entered into by two unbaptised persons is dissolved in favour of the faith of the party who received baptism, by the very fact that a new marriage is contracted by that same party, provided the unbaptised party departs. §2 The unbaptised party is considered to depart if he or she is unwilling to live with the baptised party, or to live peacefully without offence to the Creator, unless the baptised party has, after the reception of baptism, given the other just cause to depart.

558   Can. 1143 §2 outlines what "depart" means. If, as a consequence of his or her partner's baptism, the unbaptised person can no longer live with the baptised spouse, he or she is considered to have departed from the marriage. This is also the case if, as a result of the baptism, the unbaptised person is unwilling "to live peacefully without offence to the Creator"; this means that his or her conduct makes it impossible for the baptised person to fulfil the obligations arising from his or her faith. If however the baptised person were to give his or her spouse "just cause to depart", for example, by being unfaithful, the pauline privilege cannot be invoked.

559   For the valid use of the pauline privilege three conditions are necessary: a) there is a valid marriage; b) one of the spouses is validly baptised; c) the unbaptised spouse refuses either to physically cohabit, or to peacefully cohabit with the baptised spouse. With regard to b) it is not necessary that the baptism be conferred within the catholic Church.[11] Woestman emphasises

11 Reply of the Congregation of the Doctrine of the Faith on 30 August 1976, in *CLD* 8, 837-40; reply of 6 May 1959, in *CLD* 5, 534-5.

the faith dimension of this privilege: "St Paul saw the necessity of coming to the aid of the newly baptised when their Jewish or pagan consorts refused to cohabit, or to cohabit peacefully. Something had to be done in favour of the faith of the converts. Although our world differs greatly from that of St Paul, the use of this privilege still today favours the faith of converts, so that they can more easily live their faith"[12]

Before the baptised party can invoke the pauline privilege, the unbaptised spouse must be interpellated, that is, questioned, in order to verify that the essential conditions for using the privilege are present. Cann. 1144-7 state how this is to be done. **560**

Can. 1144 The interpellations

> §1 For the baptised person validly to contract a new marriage, the unbaptised party must always be interpellated whether:
> 1° he or she also wishes to receive baptism;
> 2° he or she at least is willing to live peacefully with the baptised party without offence to the Creator.
> §2 This interpellation is to be done after baptism. However, the local Ordinary can for a grave reason permit that the interpellation be done before baptism; indeed he can dispense from it, either before or after baptism, provided it is established, by at least a summary and extra-judicial procedure, that it cannot be made or that it would be useless.

The purpose of the interpellation is to discover the disposition of the unbaptised party. Two issues must be clarified: firstly, if he or she wishes to receive baptism, and secondly, if he or she is willing to live peacefully with the baptised party. If the answer to both questions is negative, the unbaptised person is deemed to have "departed" from the marriage. If the unbaptised party wishes to be baptised, but does not wish to return to his or her spouse, the former's sincerity is to be considered doubtful. The baptised party is to be allowed to enter a second marriage.[13] **561**

If the baptised party responds affirmatively to both questions, several possibilities arise: **562**

> Their marital life may be continued with no possibility of a second marriage; or, depending on the circumstances, the baptised party may be allowed to separate with no possibility of a second marriage using the privilege. In this case, if the local Ordinary is informed that the non-baptised party may well indicate a willingness to live in peace but is not sincere, he may dispense with the second question regarding

12 Woestman, 38. 13 T. Doyle, *The Code of Canon Law: a text and commentary*, 815.

peaceful cohabitation and ask only the first question concerning baptism.[14]

563   The interpellation is usually done after baptism; however the local Ordinary may for a grave reason permit it to be done before baptism. He can also dispense from it entirely, provided it is established that it cannot be made or that it would be futile. Even in these circumstances, the local Ordinary must still establish that the parties were not baptised at the time of their marriage, that the unbaptised party has not received baptism and the unbaptised party is not willing to live in peace with the baptised party.

Can. 1145 How the interpellations are to be done

§1 As a rule, the interpellation is to be done on the authority of the local Ordinary of the converted party. A period of time for reply is to be allowed by this Ordinary to the other spouse, if indeed he or she asks for it, warning the person however that if the period passes without any reply, silence will be taken as a negative response.

§2 Even an interpellation made privately by the converted party is valid, and indeed it is lawful if the form prescribed above cannot be observed.

§3 In both cases there must be lawful proof in the external forum of the interpellation having been done and of its outcome.

564 Interpellations must be done formally, but they can be done privately if the formal procedure cannot be observed (Can. 1145 §3). In the former situation, it is carried out by the Ordinary of the converted party or his delegate; the unbaptised party is questioned and a specified period of time is left for his or her response. If he or she fails to respond within the allotted time, the Ordinary may interpret this silence as a negative answer; he must have warned the unbaptised party of this in advance. When the interpellation is carried out privately, it must be done in writing or in the presence of witnesses. Whichever form of the interpellations is used, the law requires that the fact of the interpellation and its outcome must admit of proof in the external forum (Can. 1145 §3).

Can. 1146 The second marriage

The baptised party has the right to contract a new marriage with a catholic:

14 Ibid.

1° if the other party has replied in the negative to the interpellation, or if the interpellation has been lawfully omitted;

2° if the unbaptised person, whether already interpellated or not, who at first persevered in peaceful cohabitation without offence to the Creator, has subsequently departed without just cause, without prejudice to the provisions of Cann. 1144 and 1145.

The baptised party has the right enter marriage with a catholic if the **565** unbaptised party responded negatively to the interpellations or failed to respond within the period specified, or if the interpellations were lawfully dispensed and the fact of departure has been clearly established. If, after baptism, the unbaptised party lived in peace with the converted party but subsequently departed, it must be established that the latter has departed and also that the converted party did not give him or her a "just cause" for departing (Can. 1146).

Can. 1147 Entering a mixed marriage

However, the local Ordinary can for a grave reason allow the baptised party, using the pauline privilege, to contract marriage with a non-catholic party, whether baptised or non-baptised; in this case, the provisions of the canons on mixed marriages must also be observed.

The local Ordinary may "for a grave reason" permit the converted party to **566** enter a new marriage with a baptised non-catholic or even with an unbaptised person. In this instance he is to see to it that the norms regarding mixed marriages are observed (Can. 1147).

Polygamous marriage

Can. 1148 Polygamous marriage

§1 When an unbaptised man who simultaneously has a number of unbaptised wives, has received baptism in the catholic Church, if it would be a hardship for him to remain with the first of the wives, he may retain one of them, having dismissed the others. The same applies to an unbaptised woman who simultaneously has a number of unbaptised husbands.

§2 In the cases mentioned in §1, when baptism has been received, the marriage is to be contracted in the legal form, with due observance, if need be, of the provisions concerning mixed marriages and of other provisions of law.

§3 In the light of the moral, social and economic circumstances of place and person, the local Ordinary is to ensure that adequate provision is made, in accordance with the norms of justice, christian charity and natural equity, for the needs of the first wife and of the others who have been dismissed.

567   The situation envisaged in Can. 1148 is that of a man who, prior to baptism, was married at the same time to several unbaptised wives. The canon provides that he may, if it would be difficult for him to remain with the first of the wives, retain one of them, having dismissed the others. The same applies to an unbaptised woman who had several unbaptised husbands.

568   In this situation, when baptism has been received, the marriage is to take place in the legal form. All the requirements of law are to be observed: pre-marital instruction, dispensation of the impediment of disparity of cult, the pre-marital promises and assurances that the faith of the convert will not be endangered.[15]

569   The phrase "having dismissed the others" was debated in the Revision Commission.[16] Can.1148§3 emphasises the requirements of natural justice: "In the light of the moral, social and economic circumstances of place and person, the local Ordinary is to ensure that adequate provision is made, in accordance with the norms of justice, christian charity and natural equity, for the needs of the first wife and of the others who have been dismissed".

Separation due to captivity or persecution

Can. 1149 Separation due to captivity or persecution

> An unbaptised person who, having received baptism in the catholic Church, cannot re-establish cohabitation with his or her unbaptised spouse by reason of captivity or persecution, can contract another marriage, even if the other party has in the meantime received baptism, without prejudice to the provisions of Can. 1141.

570   During the transportation of slaves in the 16th century married couples were often separated and had little chance of ever meeting again. In the constitution *Apostolis* Pope Gregory XIII gave Ordinaries, parish priests and confessors the faculty to dispense from their earlier marriages those who, after baptism, wished to marry catholics. Can. 1149 permits the remarriage of those who were married before their baptism as catholics and whose conjugal life cannot be restored because of captivity or persecution. The new marriage dissolves the prior natural bond. This applies even if the other party has in the meantime also been baptised, provided that the couple have

---

15 Woestman, 51. **16** *Comm* 10 (1978), 114.

not established marital life even briefly and engaged in sexual intercourse. Were this to occur after the baptism of both, the marriage would be "ratified and consummated" and as such be indissoluble (Can. 1141).[17]

Can. 1150 Favour of the law

> In a doubtful matter the privilege of the faith enjoys the favour of the law.

Can. 1150 states that "in a doubtful matter the privilege of the faith enjoys **571** the favour of the law". This does not mean that non-sacramental marriages are presumed to be invalid – which would be in conflict with Can. 1060; rather it establishes a practical principle that if, during the process for the dissolution of such a marriage, a doubt arises with regard to certain facts, the law gives the benefit of the doubt to the faith of the baptised party. If the doubt concerns the baptism of one or other of the parties, this principle cannot be invoked since the norms of Cann. 1143-9 cannot be applied in such cases.

Other Privilege of the Faith cases

There is another form of dissolution of natural-bond marriages, namely, the **572** dissolution of marriages where one of the parties was baptised at the time of the marriage. This developed only in this century when the 1917 Code restricted the impediment of disparity of cult to marriages in which one party was baptised in the catholic Church (c. 1071 §1).[18] Since the promulgation of the 1917 Code a body of jurisprudence has developed. In 1924 the Holy Office dissolved in favour of the faith the marriage of a baptised non-Catholic woman to a Jew; they were divorced and the woman was permitted to marry a Catholic.[19] In that same year, it dissolved in favour of the faith the marriage of an unbaptised man to a baptised Anglican who, after a divorce, sought to become a Catholic and marry a Catholic woman.[20] In 1950 the Holy Office dissolved a marriage contracted before the Church with a dispensation from the impediment of disparity of cult; after a divorce, the Catholic husband wished to marry an unbaptised woman.[21] In 1959 a non-sacramental marriage was dissolved to permit a baptised non-catholic – who did not intend to become a Catholic – to marry a Catholic.[22] In the same year the marriage of an unbaptised man was dissolved to allow him, without his being baptised, to marry a Catholic.[23] In 1964 the Holy Office

---

17 *Comm* 10 (1978), 115-6.   18 Previously a marriage between an unbaptised person and a person baptised in another Church was regarded as invalid (cf. "Other Privilege of the Faith cases" in *The Canon Law: letter and spirit*, 649, n. 2320).   19 *CLD* 1, 551-2. 20 *CLD* 1, 553-4. 21 *CLD* 3, 486-8. 22 *CLD* 5, 540-1. 23 *CLD* 5, 542-4.

directed the diocese of Fresno to instruct a case involving a Catholic man who had married an unbaptised woman with a dispensation from disparity of cult and who, after a divorce, civilly married a Catholic woman.[24] In the early 1970s there was a change of policy at the Congregation for the Doctrine of the Faith and the conversion of the non-Catholic party was required for a dissolution to be granted.[25] This practice changed with the instruction *Ut notum est* which was issued by the Congregation for the Doctrine of the Faith on 6 December 1973.[26] In 1976 a reply was given in which conversion was not required.[27] In 1982 the favour was granted to a catholic who had entered marriage with a dispensation from the impediment of disparity of cult and who, after separation, wished to enter religious life.[28] The common feature of these cases is that one of the spouses was not baptised; for this reason, they are often described as non-baptism cases.

573   The Revision Commission prepared draft canons in this area but they were not incorporated in the Code.[29] The Code of Canons of the Eastern Churches however explicitly states that "in order to obtain the dissolution of a ... marriage bond in favour of the faith, the special norms issued by the Apostolic See are to be followed" (Can. 1384).

ART. 2: SEPARATION WHILE THE BOND REMAINS

574   It was suggested to the Revision Commission that all the material in this section be removed from the Code and the matter be left to Bishops' Conferences.[30] It has no practical application in English-speaking countries as couples who wish to obtain a legal separation have recourse to the civil courts. It will suffice here to note two basic principles. Spouses have the obligation and the right to maintain their common conjugal life; they have a moral obligation to live in harmony and in a way that promotes the unity of their marriage. Spouses also have a right to maintain a common conjugal life. Often social pressures have a destructive influence on the "common conjugal life" of couples; for example, emigration, unemployment, and antisocial working hours give spouses little time together; prison policies also make it difficult for wives to keep in touch with husbands who are incarcerated. The *Charter for the Rights of the Family* states: "Families have a right to a social and economic order in which the organisation of work permits the members to live together, and does not hinder the unity, well-being, health and the stability of the family, while offering also the possibility of wholesome recreation".[31]

575   The second principle is that a person whose spouse has committed adul-

24 *CLD* 6, 648. 25 For example, cf. *CLD* 7, 771-6; *CLD* 8, 840-1. 26 *CLD* 8, 1177-84. Cf. Woestman, 127-37. 27 *CLD* 8, 845. 28 *CLD* 10, 184-5. 29 *Comm* 5 (1973), 86; ibid., 9 (1977), 177; ibid., 15 (1983), 240-1. 30 *Comm* 10 (1978), 118. 31 Art 10.

tery has under certain conditions "the right to sever the common conjugal life" (Can. 1152 §1). This right also arises when "a spouse ... occasions grave danger of soul or body to the other or to the children, or otherwise makes the common life unduly difficult" (Can. 1153 §1).

Can. 1707 Presumed death of spouse

§1 Whenever the death of a spouse cannot be proven by an authentic ecclesiastical or civil document, the other spouse is not regarded as free from the bond of marriage until the diocesan Bishop has issued a declaration that death is presumed.

§2 The diocesan Bishop can give the declaration mentioned in §1 only if, after making suitable investigations, he has reached moral certainty concerning the death of the spouse from the depositions of witnesses, from hearsay and from other indications. The mere absence of the spouse, no matter for how long a period, is not sufficient.

§3 In uncertain and involved cases, the Bishop is to consult the Apostolic See.

When a spouse is believed or alleged to be dead, before the surviving spouse **576** is regarded as free to marry, the death must be proved by an authentic death certificate, ecclesiastical or civil, or the diocesan Bishop of the surviving spouse must issue a declaration presuming that the death has taken place.

Before issuing the declaration mentioned above, the diocesan Bishop **577** must reach moral certitude about the fact of death. He will do this by an appropriate investigation which will involve hearing from witnesses, weighing up rumour and hearsay and other indications. The intervention of the defender of the bond is not mandatory in these cases, but in certain cases the diocesan Bishop may consider it useful.

If after the appropriate investigation the Bishop is still uncertain, or if **578** the case is particularly difficult, he is to consult the Apostolic See (the Congregation for Divine Worship and the Discipline of the Sacraments).[32]

---

32 Cf. Woestman, 105-10.

12

Elements of family law

579 There are many norms in the post-Vatican II legislation and in the Code of Canon Law that deal with the family and the rights and obligations of parents and children. However they are scattered throughout the Code in an unsystematic way.[1] Corecco has observed that the status of the family as the *ecclesia quasi domestica* (domestic Church) "does not appear in the context of the sacrament of marriage as the outcome of that sacrament".[2] In this section I will outline the theology of the family as it has been expounded in recent documents of the Magisterium[3] as well as the principal elements of family law.

ECCLESIAL VOCATION OF THE FAMILY

580 In matrimonial consent a man and a woman "mutually give and accept one another for the purpose of establishing a marriage" (Can. 1057 §2). The relationship which they establish with each other is a continuing expression of that mutual self-gift. The Church relates the love of husband and wife to the communion of love between God and his chosen people: "their bond of love becomes the image and the symbol of the covenant that unites God and his people".[4] Conjugal love leads the spouses to express their love in a way that "makes them capable of the greatest possible gift, the gift by which they become co-operators with God for giving life to a new human person".[5] In marriage and in the family "a complex of interpersonal relationships is set up ... through which each human person is introduced into the human family and into the family of God which is the Church".[6]

581 The members of a family have a mission and vocation in society and in the wider Church not just as individuals, but precisely as a family. The essence and role of the family is "to guard, reveal and communicate love".[7]

---

1 Cardinal Felici, in an address to the Synod of Bishops in 1980 on Family Law in the draft Code of Canon Law ("De iure familiae in schemate C.I.C."), stated that the proposed new Code did not have an organic treatment of family law as the structure of the Code did not permit this (*Comm* 12 (1980), 225-6). **2** E. Corecco, "Theological justifications of the codification of the Latin Canon Law" in *The new Code of Canon Law* (edd. Thériault-Thorn), Ottawa, 1986, vol. 1, 75. **3** The teaching of Pope John Paul II includes the following: *Familiaris consortio* (1981), the Charter of the Rights of the Family (1983), Letter to Families from Pope John Paul II (1994), Letter of the Pope to Children in the Year of the Family (1994). **4** Fl II, 823, *FC* n. 12. **5** Ibid. **6** Ibid., 826, n. 15.

Familiaris consortio identifies four ways in which the family fulfils this role: forming a community of persons, serving life, participating in the development of society and sharing in the life and mission of the Church.

The love that unites the members of a family is an expression of ecclesial **582** communion.[8] The first dimension of that communion is that which develops between husband and wife: "by virtue of the covenant of married life, the man and woman are no longer two but one flesh and they are called to grow continually in their communion through day-to-day fidelity to their marriage promise of total mutual self-giving".[9] The relationship between husband and wife is the "foundation on which is build the broader communion of the family, of parents and children, of brothers and sisters with each other, or relatives and other members of the household".[10] This communion is based on ties of flesh and blood, but it is also a participation in the life of grace:

> The Holy Spirit, who is poured forth in the celebration of the sacraments, is the living source and inexhaustible sustenance of the supernatural communion that gathers believers and links them with Christ and with each other in the unity of the Church of God. The Christian family constitutes a specific revelation and realisation of ecclesial communion, and for this reason too it can and should be called the domestic Church.[11]

Selfishness, disagreement, tension and conflict can inflict serious harm on **583** family relationships. For this reason *Familiaris consortio* reminds families that "participation in the sacrament of reconciliation and in the banquet of the one Body of Christ offers the Christian family the grace and the responsibility of overcoming every division and of moving towards the fullness of communion willed by God, responding in this way to the ardent desire of the Lord: that they may be one".[12]

The second task of the Christian family is to transmit and to nurture life. **584** God "calls [spouses] to a special sharing in his love and in his power as Creator and Father, through their free and responsible cooperation in transmitting the gift of human life".[13] Parents have the task of nurturing the children they procreate: "by begetting in love and for love a new person who has within himself or herself a new vocation to growth and development, parents by that very fact take on the task of helping that person effectively to live a fully human life".[14]

The third task of the Christian family is to share in the development of **585** society. *Familiaris consortio* states that "the experience of communion and

---

7 Ibid., 828, n. 17. **8** C. Van der Poel, "Marriage and family as expressions of communio in the Church" in J. Provost (ed.), *The Church as Communion* (Canon Law Society of America, Permanent Seminar Studies 1), Washington, 1984, 59-88. **9** Fl II, 829, *FC* n. 19. **10** Ibid., 831, n. 21. **11** Ibid. **12** Ibid. **13** Ibid., 837, n. 28. **14** Ibid., 845, n. 36.

sharing that should characterise the family's daily life represents its first and fundamental contribution to society".[15] No family however is an island; it has a duty to reach out in compassion and in charity to other families.[16]

586   The fourth task of the Christian family is to share in the life and mission of the Church. The Church is a communion and the Christian family plays its part in the life of the Church above all by living its own domestic communion as well as it can. It is "in the love between husband and wife and between the members of the family – a love lived out in all its extraordinary richness of values and demands, totality, oneness, fidelity and fruitfulness – that the Christian family's participation in the prophetic, priestly and kingly mission of Jesus Christ and of his Church finds expression and realisation".[17]

A CANONICAL PERSPECTIVE ON THE FAMILY

587   In this section I will indicate how parents and children are perceived in canon law under three headings: the sacraments, catechesis and pastoral care. I will also consider a number of issues which have been the subject of judicial and legislative action by the Church in recent years.

588   The status of married couples or parents is stated in the Charter of Rights in Book II of the Code of Canon Law: "those who are married are bound by the special obligation, in accordance with their own vocation, to strive for the building up of the people of God through their marriage and family" (Can. 226 §1). Contemporary Church teaching stresses the secular vocation of the laity, a vocation which takes the form of "engaging in temporal affairs and by ordering them according to the plan of God".[18] Corecco comments: "In the lay person, thanks to matrimony above all else, in which the natural sphere is elevated by the sacrament to the supernatural level, the Church finds her point of insertion in history, which permits her to establish a structural connection between the economy of Creation and that of Redemption".[19]

The Sacraments

589   Can. 835 §4 states that "parents have a special share in the [sanctifying] office [of the Church] when they live their married lives in a christian spirit and provide for the christian education of their children". They have special

---

15 Ibid., 851, n. 43. 16 Ibid., 852, n. 44. 17 Ibid., 857, n. 50. The document distinguishes three aspects of the Christian family's role in the Church: its role as a believing and evangelising community (nn. 51-4), its role as a community in dialogue with God (nn. 55-62) and its role as a community at the service of man (nn. 63-4). 18 *The vocation and mission of the laity (Christifideles laici)*, n. 15i. Cf. Ibid., n. 40. 19 E. Corecco, "Theological justifications of the codification of the Latin Canon Law" in *The new Code of Canon Law* (edd. Thorn-Thériault), 88.

duties regarding the celebration of baptism, and their children's reception of confirmation, first communion and first confession.

Baptism[20]   At the baptism of a child parents accept the responsibility of training their child in the practice of the faith.[21] The Church is concerned that parents "be suitably instructed on the meaning of this sacrament and the obligations attaching to it" (Can. 851, 2°). It is the role of the parish priest "to see to it that either he or others duly prepare the parents, by means of pastoral advice and indeed by prayer together". Can. 851, 2° adds that "a number of families might be brought together for this purpose and, where possible, each family visited". As a condition for the lawful baptism of a child, the Church has stipulated that there be a "well-founded hope that [the child] will be brought up in the catholic religion" (Can. 868 §1, 2°). This condition is usually fulfilled by the fact that the parents, or the catholic parent in a mixed marriage, are practising the catholic faith. In accordance with catholic tradition, a child is given a sponsor at baptism. The sponsor's task is to support the parents in the catholic rearing of the child (Can. 872). The preface to *The Rite of Infant Baptism* states however that "it is of the very order of creation that the parents have a more important ministry and role in the baptism of children than have godparents".[22]   **590**

Confirmation   "Parents and pastors of souls ... are to see that the faithful are properly instructed to receive the sacrament and come to it at the opportune time" (Can.890). The introduction to the *Rite of confirmation* states: "The initiation of children into the sacramental life is for the most part the responsibility of christian parents. They are to form and gradually develop a spirit of faith in the children and, with the help of catechetical institutions, prepare them for the fruitful reception of the sacraments of confirmation and the Eucharist".[23]   **591**

By the reception of confirmation the faithful continue their path of christian initiation. The Church requires that they be "properly instructed". Children with developmental disabilities – including the profoundly retarded – who are baptised have a canonical right to receive the sacrament of confirmation whether or not they are capable of participating in any kind of catechetical programme.[24] Such children should however receive catechetical formation appropriate to their ability (Can. 777, 4°).   **592**

The Blessed Eucharist   By virtue of baptism children are entitled to exercise the rights attributed to all Christ's faithful, for example, the right to hear   **593**

20 M. Quinlan, "Parental rights and admission of children to the sacraments of initiation" in *Studia Canonica* 25 (1991), 385-402. **21** OBP 2nd ed. 1973, n. 77. **22** Fl II, 30, n. 5. **23** DOL 2512. **24** J. Huels, "Canonical right to the sacraments" in E. Foley (ed.), *Developmental disabilities and sacramental access*, Liturgical Press, Collegeville, Minn., 1994, 103.

the Word of God and receive the sacraments (Can. 213). In this context it is important to note the provisions made in the *Directory on Children's Masses* (1973):

> The Church, which baptises infants and entrusts them with the gifts conferred by this sacrament, should make sure that they grow in communion with Christ and with the Christian community. The sign and pledge of this communion is to share in the Eucharistic table, and these children are either being prepared for this, or are being led to an ever deeper understanding of what it means.[25]

594 The Church has produced special *Eucharistic Prayers for Children's Masses* to make it easier for children to take part in the celebration of Mass.[26] The *Directory on Children's Masses* makes provision for younger children:

> Infants who are unable or unwilling to take part in the Mass can be left in a separate room in the charge of parish helpers, for example, and brought in at the end of Mass for the blessing with the community. However, in Masses of this kind care must be taken that the children do not feel neglected because of their inability to participate in and understand what is being done and proclaimed in the celebration. At the very least some account must be taken of their presence, for example, by saying a special word to them at the beginning ...[27]

595 When they reach the use of reason, children should receive first communion (Can. 913 §1). If they are in danger of death before that age, they should be confirmed (Can. 889 §2) and, if they can distinguish the Body of Christ from ordinary food and receive holy communion with reverence, "the blessed Eucharist may be ... administered to [them]" (Can. 913 §2).

596 With regard to first communion, Can. 914 states that "it is primarily the duty of parents, ... as it is the duty of the parish priest, to ensure that children who have reached the use of reason are properly prepared and ... are nourished by this divine food as soon as possible".

597 *Penance* All the faithful who have reached the age of discretion are bound faithfully to confess their grave sins at least once a year (Can. 989). Parents have a responsibility to help their children, especially with regard to the celebration of first confession. The Irish Bishops' Conference, for example, stated:

> ... It is the responsibility of the parents to bring the children to the

---

25 Fl I, 256, n. 8. **26** Fl II, 53-7. **27** Fl I, 259-60, nn. 16-7 (note different translation).

church. Therefore, the sacrament should be celebrated at a time which is convenient to parents. Parents are encouraged to receive the sacrament of reconciliation along with their children. This witness is important for the children's developing awareness of the need for reconciliation ... It is the responsibility of the parents to bring the children to the celebration of the sacrament of reconciliation, just as it is the parents' responsibility to bring their children to the Sunday celebration of the Eucharist.[28]

Persons with learning disabilities are not capable of committing mortal sin. **598** Nevertheless they are able to recognise when they have done wrong and "if they are minimally capable of acknowledging their faults, feeling some sense of contrition for them, and making satisfaction for them ... , they may validly receive sacramental absolution.[29]

The role of Christian parents in nurturing vocations   Pope John Paul II has **599** reminded married couples of their obligation to give a good example to their children: "By your way of life, you witness to the vocation of marriage. The daily example of united couples fosters in the young the desire to imitate them. Young people, by receiving in their families a witness to the love of God, will be led to discover its depths".[30] The Pope then added that "it is often in families of radiant faith that vocations to the priesthood and religious life are born".[31] Vatican II had taught: "The duty of fostering vocations falls on the whole Christian community... The greatest contribution is made by families which are animated by a spirit of faith, charity and piety and which provide, as it were, a first seminary, and by parishes in whose abundant life the young people themselves take an active part".[32]

Duties of children in the Church[33]   By virtue of their baptism and confir- **600** mation, children are called to exercise the mission which God entrusted to the Church to fulfil in the world (Can. 204 §1). As they grow older their obligations as members of the Church increase in accordance with their ability to understand and assume them. For example, the obligation to observe the law on abstinence begins to bind those who reach the age of fourteen (Can. 1252).

---

28 Norms issued in 1993.   **29** Huels, 108.   **30** To families at St-Anne-d'Auray, 20 September 1996, in *Osservatore Romano* (English edition), 2 October 1996, 4. **31** Ibid. This has been a constant theme in the teaching of Pope John Paul II: in *Pastores dabo vobis* he speaks of the duty of parents to encourage vocations (n.41e), the role of the parents of seminarians in the formation of their sons (n. 68h). Cf. also Pope John Paul II's Letter to Priests on Holy Thursday 1994. **32** Fl I, 708, *OT* n. 2. **33** R. Coppola, "La posizione e la tutela del minore dopo il nuovo Codice di diritto canonico" in *The New Code of Canon Law* (Acts of the 5th International Congress of Canon Law, Ottawa, 19-25 August 1986), I, 345-53.

Catechesis (handing on the faith)

601   Can. 226 §2 states that "because they gave life to their children, parents have the most serious obligation and the right to educate them. It is therefore primarily the responsibility of christian parents to ensure the christian education of their children in accordance with the teaching of the Church" (cf. Can. 1136). Catholic education is the responsibility of the whole catholic community and is delivered initially through the influence of three key partners, the home, the school and the parish community.[34] The parish priest is charged with the responsibility of ensuring that the resources of the Church are at the disposal of the Church's mission of handing on the faith to each generation. He is specifically required "to promote and to foster the role of parents in the family catechesis mentioned in Can. 774 §2".

602   This primary role of parents is stated further in Can. 793 §1:

> Parents, and those who take their place, have both the obligation and the right to educate their children. Catholic parents have also the duty and the right to choose those means and institutes which, in their local circumstances, can best promote the catholic education of their children.

603   Pastors of souls have the right and duty to make all possible arrangements so that all the faithful may avail themselves of a catholic education (Can. 794 §1). Where it is possible, the catholic Church fulfils this responsibility by setting up catholic schools. Parents, in turn, have an obligation to send their children to schools which will provide for the catholic education of their children and, if they cannot do this, they are bound "to ensure the proper catholic education of their children outside the school" (Can. 798).

604   In catholic schools there should be close cooperation between parents and the teachers to whom they entrust their children to be educated. In fulfilling their task, teachers are to collaborate closely with the parents and willingly listen to them (Can. 796 §2).

Pastoral care of the family

605   The diocesan Bishop is responsible for the pastoral care of the flock committed to his care. He is "to be solicitous for all Christ's faithful entrusted to his care, whatever their age, condition, or nationality" (Can. 383 §1).

606   The pastoral care of the family includes the preparation of children for the celebration of the sacraments and the involvement of parents in that preparation. It also includes the catechetical formation of children and young adults

---

34 Council for Catholic Maintained Schools (N. Ireland), *Life to the Full*, 1996, 6. Cf. A.P. Purnell, *Our Faith story*, Collins, London, 1985.

and the involvement of their parents in that process. The "care of souls" includes, in addition, the support of families and individuals in difficult situations. Can. 528 §1, which outlines the duties of a parish priest, states that "he is to have a special care for the catholic education of children and young people". He is "to be especially diligent in seeking out the poor, the suffering, the lonely, those who are exiled from their homeland, and those burdened with special difficulties" (Can. 529 §1). The Code explicitly mentions "the mentally and physically handicapped" (Can. 777, 4°).

Much of what today is done under the heading of "family ministry" is **607** carried out by the lay faithful and often in special movements or associations which were set up to support families with special needs. Many who carry out this ministry have personal and family experience of dealing with special needs, such as deafness, blindness, cerebral palsy and similar conditions. Parish priests are required "to ensure that the faithful are concerned for the community of the parish ... and that they take part in and sustain works which promote this community" (Can. 529 §2).

Duty of the Church to promote the welfare of children

Child sexual abuse   The Church has traditionally striven to uphold the dig- **608** nity and rights of children in many practical ways. The provision of hospitals and orphanages for abandoned children is but one example.[35] In recent years many dioceses throughout the world have taken various legislative initiatives in order to promote the welfare of children, particularly in response to sexual abuse. In 1994 the Irish Bishops' Conference established an Advisory Committee to consider the response of the Church.[36] In 1996 it issued a report entitled *Child Sexual Abuse: Framework for a Church Response*. It describes sexual abuse as follows:

> The sexual abuse of children is a grave violation of their right to bodily integrity and an invasion of their right to physical and emotional privacy. It represents an interference with their right to enjoy physical and mental health and with their right to grow and develop in an environment which recognises their inherent dignity and worth and which is conducive to the realisation of their full potential. [It] is a betrayal of a trust given to those who have a responsibility to safeguard the well-being of the children with whom they are in contact, however temporary that contact may be.[37]

---

35 Cf. C. M. Rousseau, "Innocent III, defender of the innocents and the law: children and papal policy" in *Archivium Historiae Pontificiae* 32 (1994), 31-42. **36** Bishops in many other countries have taken similar action. **37** *Child Sexual Abuse: Framework for a Church Response*, Veritas, Dublin, 1996, 11.

609 This Report states that "the safety and welfare of children should be the first and paramount consideration following an allegation of child sexual abuse.[38] It outlines procedures which are to be followed when complaints of child sexual abuse are made against clergy or religious. Victims of child abuse are entitled to all the support the community can reasonably offer.[39]

610 It should be noted that in canon law sexual offences against minors by clerics "may be punished with just penalties, not excluding dismissal from the clerical state if the case so warrants"(Can. 1395 §2). The prevention of abuse is preferable and various dioceses have issued guidelines for appropriate behaviour towards minors. For example, in March 1995 the Bishop of Lafayette (U.S.A.) approved a set of protocols for the interaction of priests and minors.[40]

611 *Protection of young people in religious groups or movements* Diocesan Bishops have a duty of vigilance in their diocese; they must ensure that "abuses do not creep into ecclesiastical discipline" (Can. 392 §2). They have a duty to exercise vigilance in regard to groups or movements, especially if there are allegations that they are alienating spouses from one another or attempting to isolate young people from their parents. Most of these groups have no connection with the catholic Church and are in no way subject to the vigilance of the Bishops; if however they operate within the catholic Church, diocesan Bishops have a duty of vigilance regarding their activities and should exercise it to protect families.

Protection of the Family

612 In 1983 the Holy See issued a *Charter of the Rights of the Family*. It was addressed primarily to the governments of the world and called on them to "protect the family through measures of a political, economic, social and juridical character which aim at consolidating the unity and stability of the family so that it can exercise its specific function".[41] This call has been taken up by Bishops in many countries who have identified social attitudes and policies that are hostile and harmful to family life.[42]

613 In many countries today efforts are being made to give legal recognition to "marriage" between homosexuals. An Italian jurist has argued that this "would immediately have an inevitable social effect, i.e., the weakening of the family in general and in particular of a legal institution such as lawful

---

38 Ibid., 3.3, 23. **39** Bishop Matthew Clark, "Pastoral reflections on child sexual abuse in the Church" in S. Rossetti (ed.), *Slayer of the soul*, Twentythird publications, 1991, 182. **40** Cf. *Origins* 25 (1995), 21-2. **41** Preamble I. **42** For example, in their Pastoral Letter *Love is for life* (1985) the Irish Bishops identified poverty, poor housing and unemployment as factors which put most strain on families (nn. 214-9).

marriage".[43] He holds that the two schools of thought which favour this development – he labels them "liberationist" and "liberal" – are opposed to the idea that "there are objective, or ... natural modes of interpersonal communication, modes that the law is called on to formalise, regulate and guarantee".[44] He argues as follows:

> The status that marriage establishes, that of husband and wife, can be assigned only after the demonstration of a formal and public intention to that end by the spouses; however, it is not precisely their desire that established the status, but rather the public recognition that this union has a human and social meaning that transcends the subjectivity of the spouses. The insight that marriage is the foundation of the family, that is, of the basic cell of society ... is based on the ... perception that marriage has its own structural purpose, that is, the regulation of sexual activity in order to guarantee the order of generations, and that this purpose is not culturally conditioned, nor did it emerge in the course of history only at a particular stage of humanity's economic development, but is a principle that essentially characterises the human being.[45]

614 Since this issue is one that affects the status of the family which is based on the covenant relationship of husband and wife (cf. Can. 1055 §1), the Church must reflect carefully on the implications of legislative initiatives that would put same-sex unions on the same footing as marriage.

Proclaiming "the Gospel of life"

615 In *Veritatis splendor* (1993) John Paul II called on the Pastors of the Church to exercise their prophetic (or teaching) ministry by proclaiming the moral teaching of the Church particularly in those areas that touch the family most intimately, the transmission of life and respect for unborn life.[46] They must proclaim what the Pope has called "the Gospel of Life".

PASTORAL CARE OF THOSE WHOSE MARRIAGES HAVE BROKEN DOWN

616 One of the sad facts of modern life is the high incidence of marital breakdown. The reasons for this are many and complex, but they are undoubtedly related to social changes. Three German Bishops, Lehmann, Saier and Kasper issued a document entitled "Pastoral ministry: the divorced and remarried"

---

43 F. D'Agostino, "Should the law recognize homosexual unions?" in *Osservatore Romano* (English edition), 21 May 1997, 9. **44** Ibid., 10. **45** Ibid. **46** n. 114.

in 1993. They list the most important social changes which affect marriage today: the separation between family and the world of work and the resulting tension between family and profession, new understandings of the roles of men and women, the increased length of a marriage, the dissolution of the traditional extended family and isolation of the nuclear family, and the insufficient support given marriage and family life in this social climate.[47] They add to these social factors personal factors: unreasonable expectations of happiness that will necessarily be disappointed, human immaturity and personal failure in daily life, mutual misunderstanding and insufficient dedication to the point of infidelity and culpable destruction of the marital community or even physical abuse in the marriage.[48] Regardless of the causes of marital breakdown, the personal consequences are usually disappointment, sadness, personal injury, self-doubt and feelings of guilt. Experience shows that in the event of marital breakdown "[the wife] is likely to find herself in poverty and [the husband] is likely to find himself without family".[49]

617   It is the mission of the Church to reach out in pastoral charity to accompany, support and encourage those struggling with such traumas, and to make its resources available to help them. "Family ministries" have developed to help the couples concerned and their children; the provision of counselling services, for example, reflect the concern of the Church that everything possible be done to prevent the breakdown of marriages.

618   The Church also reaches out to minister to those whose marriages have broken down or ended with the death of a spouse. The Beginning Experience is a valuable help to these people. It is an especially-designed week-end retreat which helps separated and widowed persons make a new beginning in life. It is a ministry to the lonely carried out by a trained team of volunteers. Participants are encouraged to share their needs and to deal with the natural process of grief and loneliness. The team-leaders share their own experiences through the week-end sessions; this is followed by individual reflection and small group discussion.

The divorced and remarried

619   *Pastoral care*   Many of those whose marriages have failed seek happiness in a second union. While this places them in an irregular position *vis-à-vis* the Church, they still belong to the Church and to the parish community in which they live. Pope John Paul II has written:

> However, let these men and women know that the Church loves them, that she is not far from them and suffers because of their situation. The divorced and remarried are and remain her members because they have

---

47 *Origins* 23 (1994), 671. **48** Ibid. **49** C. Clulow and J. Mattinson, *Marriage inside out*, 17.

received baptism and retain their Christian faith. Of course, a new union after divorce is a moral disorder which is opposed to precise requirements deriving from the faith, but this must not preclude a commitment to prayer and to the active witness of charity.[50]

The divorced and remarried are not excluded from the pastoral care of the Church. Pope John Paul II called on pastors, especially parish priests, "with an open heart to guide and support these men and women, making them understand that even when they have broken the marriage bond they must not despair of the grace of God, who watches over their way".[51]　　**620**

The sacraments　　The Church teaches that "of its very nature, celebration of the Eucharist signifies the fullness of the profession of faith and fullness of ecclesial communion".[52] In the life of the Church, ruptures of ecclesial communion have been marked by exclusion from eucharistic communion. This exclusion may be temporary or permanent, depending on the seriousness of the breach involved. The breach may be in the area of faith or morals. In the history of the Church, the exclusion from holy communion of those who have remarried during the life-time of their spouses is long and consistent.[53] It is reflected in Can. 915.　　**621**

The teaching and discipline of the Church are rooted in the New Testament (Mk 10:11-12; 1 Cor 7:10-11). The Catechism of the catholic Church says that divorce "does an injury against the covenant of salvation, of which sacramental marriage is the sign".[54] Contracting a new union, even if it is recognised by the civil law, adds to the gravity of the rupture: "the remarried spouse is then in a situation of public and permanent adultery".[55]　　**622**

The discipline of the Church in this area is closely linked to its theological understanding of the sacraments has been outlined in a number of documents of the Magisterium. In *Familiaris consortio* Pope John Paul II reaffirmed the discipline of the Church with regard to the divorced who have remarried: they cannot be admitted to holy communion because "their state and condition of life objectively contradict that union of love between Christ and the Church which is signified and effected by the Eucharist".[56] He added that "if [they] were admitted to the Eucharist, the faithful would be led into error and confusion regarding the Church's teaching about the indissolubility of marriage".[57] Reconciliation in the sacrament of penance "can only be granted to those who, repenting of having broken the sign of the Covenant　　**623**

---

50 *Origins* 26 (1997), 584.　　**51** Ibid.　　**52** *"In quibus rerum circumstantiis"*, Fl I, 557. **53** It can be found in the earliest Church councils: Elvira (306), Arles (314), Angers (314), Vannes (315). Cf. H. Crouzel, *L'église primitive face au divorce*, 312-6. **54** n. 2384. **55** Ibid. The Catechism points out that the sexual act must take place exclusively within marriage: "outside of marriage it always constitutes a grave sin and excludes one from sacramental communion" (n. 2390). **56** Fl II, 889, n. 84d. **57** Ibid., n. 84d.

and of fidelity to Christ, are sincerely ready to undertake a way of life that is no longer in contradiction to the indissolubility of marriage".[58] In other words, if they are unable to separate they "take on themselves the duty to live in complete continence, that is, by abstinence from the acts proper to married couples".[59]

624   In the Post-Synodal Apostolic Exhortation *Reconciliatio et paenitentia* (1984), Pope John Paul II referred to "certain situations, not infrequent today, affecting Christians who wish to continue their sacramental religious practice but who are prevented from doing so by their personal condition, which is not in harmony with the commitments freely undertaken before God and the Church".[60] He pointed to two "equally important principles" which must be kept in mind in regard to these situations. The first is that of compassion and mercy "whereby the Church, as the continuer in history of Christ's presence and work ... ever seeks to offer, as far as possible, the path of return to God and of reconciliation with him".[61] The second principle is that of truth and consistency "whereby the Church does not agree to call good evil and evil good". The Pope concludes:

> Basing herself on these two complimentary principles, the Church can only invite her children who find themselves in these painful situations to approach the divine mercy by other ways, not however through the sacraments of penance and the Eucharist, until such time as they have attained the required dispositions.[62]

625   In 1994 the Congregation for the Doctrine of the Faith reaffirmed this teaching.[63] It pointed out that the exclusion of the divorced and remarried from the Eucharist was not "a punishment or a discrimination ... but rather expresses an objective situation that of itself renders impossible the reception of holy communion".[64] It states that "communion with Christ the Head [in holy communion] can never be separated from communion with his members, that is, with the Church". It then adds:

> Receiving Eucharistic communion contrary to the norms of ecclesial communion is therefore a contradiction. Sacramental communion with Christ includes and presupposes the observance, even if at times difficult, of the order of ecclesial communion, and it cannot be right and fruitful if a member of the faithful, wishing to approach Christ directly, does not respect this order.[65]

58 Ibid.   **59** Ibid.   **60** Published by Catholic Truth Society, London, 1984, 134, n. 34a. **61** Ibid., 135, n. 34b. **62** Ibid. **63** Letter to the Bishops of the Catholic Church concerning the Reception of Holy Communion by Divorced and Remarried Members of the Faithful. Cf. *Origins* 24 (1994), 337-41. **64** Ibid., 339, n. 4. **65** Ibid., 340, n. 9.

One of the pastoral tasks of the Church is to accompany those who are in this **626** difficult situation. The fact that they are unable to receive holy communion does not imply that they are in personal bad faith; it is an acknowledgement that the situation in which they find themselves creates an objective obstacle between them and full communion in the Church. Their situation is irregular and will remain so as long as the obstacle remains.

The solution for some couples in irregular unions is for the person who **637** was previously married to seek a declaration of nullity of the first marriage. If this is granted, the civil union can be validated and the couple can again be admitted to holy communion. In many cases, however, the first marriage will not be declared null because there are no grounds of nullity; the marriage was clearly valid.

There are however occasionally marriages which are almost certainly **628** null but whose nullity cannot, for various reasons, be established in the external forum. Some have proposed an "internal forum" or "pastoral solution" which would allow those concerned to receive holy communion on the basis of their personal conviction that the first marriage was invalid. Cardinal Ratzinger has made it quite clear that the magisterium has not sanctioned the use of the "internal forum" solution.[66] In the Letter to the Bishops of the Catholic Church concerning the Reception of Holy Communion by Divorced and Remarried Members of the faithful he writes:

> It is certainly true that a judgement about one's own dispositions for the reception of holy communion must be made by a properly formed moral conscience. But it is equally true that the consent that is the foundation of marriage is not simply a private decision since it creates a specifically ecclesial and social situation for the spouses, both individually and as a couple. Thus the judgement of conscience of one's own marital situation does not regard only the immediate relationship between man and God, as if one could prescind from the Church's mediation that also includes canonical laws binding in conscience. Not to recognise this essential aspect would mean in fact to deny that marriage is a reality of the Church, that is to say, a sacrament.[67]

If the question of access to the Eucharist and the implications that this has **629** for a person's status within the ecclesial community is left to individual clergy, there is a danger of serious scandal. Take the case of a man who, after many years of marriage, abandons his wife and goes off with another woman, taking no responsibility, financial or otherwise, for his wife and children. Some time later, a parish minister hears a version of the story from this man or his new partner, and judging that she and the man have been "hard done by"

66 *The Tablet* 245 (1991), 1311. **67** *Origins* 24 (1994), 340, n. 8.

decides to re-admit them to the eucharist. What of the rights of the deserted spouse, who in order to raise her family in accordance with the teaching of the Church, has remained faithful to her marriage vows? Not surprisingly, Cardinal Ratzinger observed that "the numerous abuses committed in some countries attest to the unworkability of the internal forum solution".[68]

530   Cardinal Ratzinger accepts that there are some rare cases where appeal to the Church's canonical practice has not availed and where a matter of conscience is at stake; in these instances, the parties can have recourse to the Sacred Penitentiary.[69] In these instances, the Sacred Penitentiary may issue a document of freedom (*documentum libertatis*).[70]

631   Cardinal Ratzinger stresses that the discipline of the Church in this matter does not derive from a purely disciplinary law. He quotes from a report of the International Theological Commission:

> Faithful to the radicalism of the Gospel, the Church cannot refrain from stating with St Paul the apostle: "To those now married, however, I give this command (though it is not mine; it is the Lord's): a wife must not separate from her husband. If she does separate, she must either remain single or become reconciled to him again. Similarly, a husband must not divorce his wife" (1 Cor 7: 10-11). It follows from this that new unions following divorce cannot be considered regular or legitimate.[71]

632   The discipline of the Church is a judgement pronounced by Jesus himself (Mk 10:6ff). Understood in this way, "this harsh norm is a prophetic witness to the irreversible fidelity which binds Christ to his Church. It shows also that the spouses' love is incorporated into the very love of Christ (Eph 5:23-32)".[72]

633   The situation of the divorced and remarried is often painful, but the Church, faithful to her understanding of her own nature as communion and of the implications of both the Eucharist and the sacrament of matrimony, is unable to compromise on fundamental principles. She is bound to witness to the enduring character of a sacramental marriage because the relationship of baptised husband and wife has been transformed into a sign of the enduring, faithful love of Christ for his body, the Church. The Church is also bound to respect the nature of the Eucharist as the "sacrament of unity". Whatever ruptures ecclesial communion in the domestic Church will be reflected in a rupture of eucharistic communion; in the judgement of the Church divorce

---

68 Ibid. **69** *The Tablet* 245 (1991), 1311. **70** Cf. U. Navarrete, "Conflictus inter forum internum et externum in matrimonio" in *Investigationes theologico-canonicae*, Università Gregoriana Editrice, Rome, 1978, 333-46. **71** "Propositions on the doctrine of Christian marriage" in *International Theological Commission: texts and documents 1969-1985* (ed. M. Sharkey), 175, n. 5.1. **72** Ibid., n. 5.2.

and remarriage does so. If the link between ecclesial communion and eucharistic communion is broken, the reception of holy communion becomes a
purely personal, even a private matter. On the other hand, the Church – following the example of Christ – is anxious not "to break the bruised reed or to
quench the dimly burning wick". It will accompany and encourage those
who find themselves in difficulty and will help them to avail of other sources
of grace until such time as they are able to receive holy communion. In this
way, the Church attempts to be faithful both to its own teaching and to its
task of embodying Christ who reaches out to heal the broken-hearted.[73]

---

73 Cf. J. McAreavey, "Divorce, re-marriage and the Eucharist: a further view" in *Doctrine and Life* 45 (1995), 171-7; "Eucharistic communion and belonging to the Church"
in *CLSGBI Annual Conference* (1995), 22-30; I. Fuček, "Possono i divorziati civilmente
risposati accostarsi alla santa comunione?" in *Periodica* 85 (1996), 35-58.

Documents

634 *Documents of the Holy See*

Vatican II, Pastoral constitution on the Church in the Modern World, *Gaudium et spes* nn. 47-52 (1965), Fl I, 949-57.

Paul VI, Encyclical letter *Humanae vitae* (1968).

Sacred Congregation for the Doctrine of the Faith, Declaration on Certain Problems of Sexual Ethics (*Personae humanae*) (1975), Fl I, 486-99.

John Paul II, Apostolic exhortation *Familiaris consortio* (1981), Fl II, 815-98.

Code of Canon Law (1983).

John Paul II, *Charter of the Rights of the Family* (1983).

John Paul II, Apostolic exhortation *Reconciliatio et paenitentia* (1984).

John Paul II, *The dignity of women*, Apostolic letter *Mulieris dignitatem* (1988).

Code of Canons of the Eastern Churches (1990).

John Paul II, *Veritatis splendor* (1993).

Congregation for the Doctrine of the Faith, Letter to the Bishops of the Catholic Church concerning the reception of Holy Communion by divorced and remarried members of the faithful in *Origins* 24 (1994), 337-41.

Catechism of the Catholic Church (1994).

John Paul II, *Letter to Families* in *Origins* 24 (1994), 637-59.

John Paul II, Encyclical letter *Evangelium vitae* (1995).

Pontifical Council for Promoting Christian Unity, *Directory for the application of principles and norms on ecumenism* (1993).

Pontifical Council for the Family, *The truth and meaning of human sexuality: guidelines for education within the family*, Mediaspaul, 1996.

Congregation for Catholic Education, *Directives on the formation of seminarians concerning problems related to marriage and the family* in *Origins* 25 (1995), 161-7.

Pontifical Council for the Family, *Preparation for the sacrament of marriage* in *Origins* 26 (1996), 98-109.

Pontifical Council for the Family, *Morality of conjugal life* (Handbook for Confessors), Catholic Truth Society, 1997.

Documents of International Theological Commission　　　　**635**

"Propositions on the doctrine of christian marriage" in *International Theological Commission: texts and documents 1969-85*, ed. M. Sharkey, Ignatius Press, San Francisco, 1989, 163-74.
"Christological theses on the sacrament of marriage" in *International Theological Commission: texts and documents 1969-85*, ed. M. Sharkey, Ignatius Press, San Francisco, 1989, 175-83.

Inter-Church documents　　　　**636**

The Theology of Marriage and the Problems of Mixed Marriages: Dialogue between the Lutheran World Federation, the World Alliance of Reformed Churches, the secretariate for Promoting Christian Unity-Roman Catholic Church 1971-1977: Final Report, Venice 1976, published by the Pontifical Council for the Promotion of Christian Unity in *Information Service* 36 (1978/1), 16-36.
Anglican-Roman Catholic Mariage: the report of the Anglican-Roman Catholic International Commission on the Theology of Marriage and its Application to Mixed Marriages, published by Church Information Office and Catholic Information Office in *Infoform* 6/20 (1976), 1-31.

Appendices

APPENDIX 1: PRE-NUPTIAL ENQUIRY FORM ISSUED BY IRISH BISHOPS' CONFERENCE

637 Following extensive consultation the Irish Bishops' Conference issued a *Pre-nuptial enquiry form* in 1991.[1] It also issued an accompanying booklet, *Pre-nuptial enquiry: pastoral guidelines*, for the guidance of those using it. With regard to marriage banns the Irish Bishops' Conference stated:

> In accordance with the prescription of Can. 1067, and by reason of the issue (dated 22 April 1984)[2] by the Bishops' Conference of the new Pre-nuptial Enquiry Form with its accompanying explanatory document, the Irish Bishops' Conference hereby decrees that the publication of marriage banns be required no longer.[3]

Completion of the Pre-nuptial Enquiry

638 The Pre-nuptial Enquiry is carried out in the parish where the person has a domicile or quasi-domicile. In the case of a mixed marriage, the forms of the baptised non-catholic or non-baptised person should be completed in the parish of the catholic party.[4]

639 The Pre-nuptial Enquiry is completed by the parish priest or curate of the parish where the person has a domicile or quasi-domicile. In practice, if there are a number of priests in a parish, the introductory part of the form and document A are filled out by the priest on duty. It is preferable however that document B be filled out by the priest who is officiating at the marriage (if he is a priest of the parish). In the case of a mixed marriage, the pre-nuptial enquiry is carried out by the parish priest of the catholic party.

640 When an Irish couple resident in England wishes to get married in Ireland, these pre-nuptial papers should be prepared in the parish where each party lives and not in their native parishes when, for example, they are on

---

1 Cf. pp. 226-32 below. 2 This form was later replaced in 1991. 3 *Intercom* 18 (1987-8), supplement, decree 13, 10. 4 This topic will be considered in more detail in the section dealing with mixed marriages.

holidays. This procedure will allow their parish clergy in England to assist the couple with the necessary marriage preparation. If this is not done, there is a danger that the couple will arrive home for their marriage without any pre-marriage preparation or instruction. A priest attached to the Irish Emigrant Chaplaincy has been appointed to collect and disseminate information concerning pre-marriage preparation for the many Irish people living in South-East England.

641 The Pre-nuptial Enquiry is usually carried out in the form of a personal interview between the person and the priest, using the given form. It should not be done in the presence of both parties. The Pre-nuptial Enquiry form has four parts: the front cover, parts A, B and C.[5] For pastoral reasons, it should be filled out in two stages: the front cover (giving name, address, proposed date and place of marriage etc.) and document A can be filled out when the person wishing to marry makes their initial contact with a priest of their own parish. This initial contact must be made at least three months before the date of the proposed marriage since the Irish Bishops' Conference requires that couples give this notice of marriage.[6]

642 Document A deals with personal data: name and address, date of birth, religion, place of baptism and confirmation, occupation, details regarding parents. Some of this information is obtained so that the marriage can be registered civilly.

643 It also deals with matrimonial impediments. In order to check if a person was not married before, it is normally not necessary to obtain letters of freedom. If the person can provide a recent baptismal certificate, that is, one issued in the last six months, this is sufficient to show that he or she has not been previously married. However in some instances further information may be necessary:

> If further evidence is needed in the case of someone who after the canonical age for a valid marriage has had an unbroken stay (or stays) of six months or more in a parish (or parishes) other than his/her *parochia propria* [own parish] written confirmation of freedom to marry should be obtained from one or more competent sources or persons. Such written confirmation is, in practice, the normal way of establishing the freedom of the non-Catholic party in a mixed marriage.[7]

644 Document B should be filled in when the couple have completed a pre-marriage course or some other form of preparation. A note at the start of this section of the form states that "the priest should interview each candidate separately and alone". This should apply to the whole form. It is of the ut-

---

5 Guidance on the use of the forms is provided in *Pre-nuptial enquiry: pastoral guidelines* which was issued by the Irish Bishops' Conference in 1991. **6** This came into effect at Easter 1981. **7** *Pre-nuptial enquiry*, Veritas, Dublin, 1991, 9.

most importance that the priest meet the person proposing to marry. If both parties are from the same parish, they will often come together to get their "papers". While it will be appropriate for the priest to talk to them as a couple about their future plans, to encourage them to attend a pre-marriage course and to give them details about courses that would be convenient for them, the filling of the Pre-nuptial Enquiry form should always be done with each person individually. This is to ensure that if either person has any worries or fears about the proposed marriage he or she will have the opportunity to express them to the priest. This is particularly important if there are pressures arising, for example, from a pregnancy.

645   Document C is addressed to the priest. He should be satisfied that the person is capable of contracting marriage, is free from impediments and is marrying freely. Having gone through the preparation or having been in a position to oversee it, the priest is required to state that, as far as he is aware, nothing stands in the way of the lawful and valid celebration of the marriage.

646   Each Pre-nuptial Enquiry form should be accompanied by evidence of baptism and confirmation. A baptismal certificate should be obtained, one issued not more than six months prior to the date of marriage. Where one of the parties to the marriage is adopted the baptismal certificate should be obtained by the priest from the Diocesan Central Register of Baptism for Adopted Children.[8] Notification of marriage is sent there afterwards.

647   Once the completion of a Pre-nuptial Enquiry form has begun, it should be kept in the parish archive. Given the nature of the information it contains, a Pre-nuptial Enquiry form "should be regarded as [a] confidential document [and] be stored in a safe place".[9]

Gathering and forwarding the Pre-nuptial Enquiry forms

648   If both parties live in the same parish and are going to be married in that parish, the form is put in a special envelope along with the baptism and confirmation certificates. When the marriage has taken place, the sealed envelope containing both Pre-nuptial Enquiry forms and the relevant certificates is put in the parish archive.

649   If the parties live in different parishes, each should have the Pre-nuptial Enquiry form completed by his or her parish priest. The parish priest of the groom will send the latter's form to the parish priest of the bride.[10] This parish priest will keep them in his own parish if the marriage is to take place there. If the marriage is to take place elsewhere, it is the responsibility of the

---

8 Ibid., 6. Most dioceses in Ireland have set up a Central Register; however dioceses in N.Ireland were not required to do so. The relevant information is in the parish where the adopted child was baptised. For further information, contact Catholic Family Care Society (N.I.), 164 Bishop St., Derry or 511 Ormeau Rd., Belfast. 9 Ibid., 4. 10 Under no circumstances should the man's form be given to the man to deliver to the parish priest of the woman or vice versa.

parish priest of the bride to send them to the place of marriage. If the bride lives in parish A, and the groom lives in parish B, and the marriage is scheduled to take place in parish C, the procedure is as follows: the parish priest of the groom will send the groom's form to the parish priest of the bride; the parish priest of the bride will forward both forms to parish C where the marriage is to take place.

If a marriage is to take place outside Ireland, the parish priest of the bride **650** must send the completed forms and other documents to the office of his Bishop. The Bishop will issue testimonial letters and send the papers to the office of the Bishop of the diocese where the marriage is to take place. This Bishop will grant a *nihil obstat* if he is satisfied that the papers are in order and then forward the papers to the parish where the marriage is to take place.[11]

In the case of a mixed marriage, the parish priest of the catholic party **651** must satisfy himself that both parties are free to marry. He will complete the pre-nuptial enquiry form for the catholic party. With regard to the party who belongs to another Church or ecclesial communion, the Archdiocese of Dublin issues the following advice:

> A careful use of the Pre-Nuptial Enquiry form can be envisaged for the other party provided it covers only data relevant to them and is primarily for record purposes. Obviously they will *not* be asked questions 7 and 8 [document B]; *nor are they obliged to sign the form* lest they be under the mistaken impression that they are making or signing Catholic Promises. It is required that they provide proof of freedom to marry (letter from parents etc).[12]

Storing the Pre-nuptial Enquiry forms

Parish priests are required to retain pre-nuptial enquiry forms so that they **652** can be inspected by the Bishop when he visits the parish.[13] They should therefore be stored in the parish where the marriage was celebrated.

There is one exception to this norm: when a mixed marriage takes place **653** with a dispensation from the canonical form, the Pre-nuptial Enquiry forms are completed in the parish of the catholic party and are stored there (Can. 1121 §3).

---

11 A *nihil obstat* means that nothing stands in the way of the valid celebration of the marriage.   **12** Memorandum issued to clergy in March 1996.   **13** Maynooth Statutes, n. 196 §3.

CONFIDENTIAL

PRE-NUPTIAL ENQUIRY

Date of notice of marriage ....

Name ....

Parish .... Diocese ....

Proposed partner ....

Parish .... Diocese ....

Witnesses .... Address ....

....

Witnesses .... Address ....

....

Date of marriage .... Place of marriage ....

Diocese ....

Priest or deacon officiating ....

Person to whom papers are to be sent

Name ....

Address ....

....

DOCUMENT A: BACKGROUND INFORMATION

To establish canonical freedom to marry, this document should be completed as soon as can be arranged after notice of the proposed marriage has been given and not later than two months before the proposed date of marriage.

(The priest should interview each candidate separately and alone.)

1. Surname ....

   Christian names ....

   Present address ....

   .... (telephone) ....

   Date of birth ....

   Religion ....

   Place of Baptism .... Date ....

   Place of Confirmation .... Date ....

   Occupation ....

2. Father's name ....

   Address ....

   State if deceased (*N. Ireland* only) ....

   Father's occupation (*N. Ireland* only) ....

   Mother's maiden name ....

   Address ....

3. Proposed address after marriage ....

4. (a) Are you related to your proposed partner by blood or marriage or adoption? ....

    If yes, to what degree? ....

    (b) Is your proposed partner baptised? ....

    If yes, in what Christian denomination? ....

    (c) (*if the person is a minor in civil law at the proposed date of the marriage*)
    Have you the written consent of your parents/guardians/judiciary? ....

    (d) Are you bound by religious vows/promises of celibacy? ....

    (e) Have you ever contracted a religious or civil marriage? ....

    If yes
    Name of spouse ....

    Date and place of marriage ....

    Cause and date of cessation of bond ....

    Is your partner aware of your previous marriage(s)? ....

    (f) Have you any obligations arising from a previous union? ....

    If yes, please specify ....

    Is your partner aware of these obligations? ....

5. Have you been resident for six months or more in a parish other than your present one since reaching the canonical age for marriage? ....

    (a) If yes, where? ....

    ....

    ....

    ....

    (b) Who can establish your freedom to marry? ....
    (*If in doubt, written confirmation should be obtained.*)

    ....

DOCUMENT B: QUESTIONS TO BE ANSWERED BY THE CANDIDATE FOLLOWING APPROPRIATE COURSE OF INSTRUCTION

(The priest should interview each candidate separately and alone.)

1. What marriage preparation have you undertaken? ....
    ....

2. (a) For how long have you known your partner? ....

    (b) When did the courtship begin? ....

3. Are you entering marriage free from any kind of pressure from parents, fiancé(e) or anyone else? ....

4. (a) Do you intend to enter a permanent marriage that can be dissolved only by death? ....

    (b) Do you accept that marriage involves a lifelong responsibility to love and support each other? ....

    (c) Do you accept that being married means being faithful to each other for life? ....

    (d) Do you understand and accept the rights and duties of marriage in relation to having and rearing children? ....

    (e) Are you quite sure that you are giving full consent to this marriage without reservation? ....

5. Have you and your partner discussed future married life seriously? ....

    (The following questions are to be asked of all Catholics.)

6. Do you accept that marriage has been instituted by God and made a sacrament by Christ? ....

7. Are you resolved to remain steadfast in your Catholic faith and to practise it regularly? ....

8. Do you promise to do what you can within the unity of your partnership to have all the children of your marriage baptised and brought up in the Catholic faith? ....

        Signature of party ....

        Declared orally (and signed) by the party in my presence.

SEAL

        Signature of priest.................................. Date ....

SUPPLEMENTARY OATH

I hereby confirm the above declaration on oath

        Signature of party ....

SEAL

        Signature of priest................................... Date ....

DOCUMENT C: TO BE FILLED IN BY PRIEST

1. (a) Are you satisfied that this person understands and accepts the meaning and implications of Christian marriage? ....

   ....

   (b) Are you satisfied that this person is free from all impediments to marriage? ....

   ....

   (c) Are you satisfied that this person is entering marriage of his/her own free will? ....

   ....

2. (*if a mixed marriage*)
   Is the party aware of the nature and content of the promises made by the Catholic party?..

   ....

3. Further comments or reservations ....

   ....

   ....

Signature of priest .... Date ....

PERMISSION TO MARRY OUTSIDE THE PARISH

Parish .... Diocese ....

Marriage of ....

.... and

....

I hereby give permission for the above marriage to take place outside this parish.

Signature of priest........................... Date ....

DELEGATION

Parish ....Diocese ....

I hereby delegate/sub-delegate ....

to officiate at the marriage of ....

to ....

Signature .... Date ....

SEAL

Parish Priest/Curate

I accept the above delegation/sub-delegation

Signature.. Date ....

Appendices

PERMISSION FOR A MIXED MARRIAGE

I hereby grant permission to ....

a baptised Catholic to contract marriage with ....

a baptised .... in virtue of Canon 1125 and in compliance with the conditions stated therein.

Furthermore, if the circumstances require it, a Dispensation from the Impediment of Disparity of Cult is granted.

Date .... Signature ....

SEAL

Diocese ....

TESTIMONIAL LETTER

Having seen the attached documents, I testify that ....
.... are free to contract marriage, provided that a Nihil Obstat is granted by the diocese in which the marriage is to be contracted.

Date .... Signature ....

SEAL

Diocese ....

NIHIL OBSTAT

The documents submitted to this Curia have been examined and there is nothing to prevent the above marriage from being contracted in accordance with the requirements of the law.

Date .... Signature ....

SEAL

Diocese ....

NOTIFICATION OF MARRIAGE

Church .... Diocese ....

Please enter in the baptismal register of the parish of ....

the marriage of .... son/daughter of ....

and .... who was baptised on .... and who

on .... was married in this Church to ....

Please sign the acknowledgement and return this form to:

Name ....

Address ....

....

I have made the above entry of marriage in the baptismal register of this parish.

Signature .... Date ....

NOTIFICATION OF FUTURE RESIDENCE

Parish .... Diocese ....

.... and....................................

married in this parish on the ....

are due to take up residence at ....

....

I commend them to your welcome and care.

Signature of priest .... Date ....

REGISTER OF PRE-NUPTIAL ENQUIRY (*to be retained*)

Groom ....

Address ....

Bride ....

Address ....

Date of marriage .... Place ....

Priest to whom papers were sent

Name ....

Address ....

....

Signature of priest .... Date ....

APPENDIX 2: CIVIL REGISTRATION OF CATHOLIC MARRIAGES IN IRELAND

In Ireland clergy act solely as official witnesses of the Church. However when the Registrar of Marriages is notified about a marriage and is satisfied that everything is in order the marriage will be registered civilly. The couple will then be regarded as married before the civil law with all the consequent rights and obligations. **654**

The civil registration is done by sending the statutory form to the Registrar. Although in civil law it is the responsibility of the groom to notify the Registrar, in practice this is done by the parish priest, or curate, of the parish where the marriage took place. **655**

When the details are being entered on the statutory form, great care should be taken: the bride's maiden name should be given; the names of both parties should be given as on their birth certificates and should be spelt exactly as they are spelt there. "Marital condition" should be given accurately: bachelor/spinster, widow/widower, divorced. The occupation of the parties should also be given accurately. A person may not be described as "unemployed"; it is necessary to give an occupation, e.g., unemployed labourer. In the Republic of Ireland the maiden surname of each party's mother should be given; in the North of Ireland the father's name is required. The names of parents are required, not the names of godparents. **656**

This form must be signed by parties, the witnesses and the officiating priest or deacon. The civil form should be filled out in good time before the marriage using the information given in the pre-nuptial enquiry form and be checked with the couple. In the event of mistakes being made, it is difficult to amend the records and the civil registration of the marriage may be delayed, causing inconvenience to the couple.[14] The civil form is usually signed immediately after the nuptial Mass or marriage rite.[15] **657**

In some cases there may be a doubt as to whether a Church marriage can be registered civilly. When, for example, one of the parties has obtained a foreign divorce there may be some doubt as to whether it will be recognised in Irish law. In such cases the relevant divorce papers should be submitted to the Registrar's Office in good time before the marriage is planned; three weeks should be allowed for the study of the documents. As a matter of pastoral practice, the date for the marriage should not be set until the doubt has been resolved. **658**

In the Republic of Ireland when two parties wish to marry one of whom has received a Church annulment, the subsequent marriage will not be recognised in civil law unless the party who was previously married has also obtained a civil decree of nullity or has obtained a decree of divorce. **659**

14 Letter of M. Mulkerrins (General Register Office) in *Intercom* 20 (1990), 25; cf. also letter of S. Hall (General Register Office) in *Intercom* 27 (1997), 18. **15** The Church disapproves of the practice of signing the register on the altar (cf. Can. 1239 §1).

APPENDIX 3: MARRIAGES OF IRISH CITIZENS CELEBRATED IN ROME

660 A considerable number of Irish couples choose to celebrate their marriages in Rome. They should make the same kind of pastoral preparation as couples who marry in Ireland. It is important that their marriages are celebrated in such a way that they will be recognised in the civil law; special care is needed as the civil formalities are more complex than in normal circumstances.[16]

Church documents

661 Responsibility for gathering the Church documents rests as usual with the parish priest of the bride; he will send them to his Bishop; the latter will send them to the church in Rome where the marriage is to take place. The documents should arrive at least one month before the marriage. As a precaution they should be sent by registered mail. The documents are as follows: a) baptism and confirmation certificates; b) some written confirmation of freedom, if it is necessary; c) pre-nuptial enquiry forms; d) a letter from the bride's parish priest permitting the celebration of the marriage outside the parish; e) consent forms signed by parents/guardians when one or both parties are under age; f) documents showing the cessation of a previous bond or the dispensation of an impediment.

Civil documents: Irish passport holders

662 Irish passport holders must apply to the Department of Foreign Affairs for the *nulla osta* document.[17] The following documents are required: a) the statutory declaration form completed in the presence of, and witnessed by, either a notary public or a commissioner for oaths; b) civil birth certificate (original only); c) parental consent form, if the person is under twentyone years of age; d) death certificate of a previous spouse, if widowed; e) final decree, if divorced.

663   The statutory forms must be completed not more than twelve weeks before the proposed date of marriage and be returned to the Department of Foreign Affairs eight to ten weeks before the proposed date of marriage. The name of the priest who will officiate at the marriage and the place of the marriage must be given on the statutory form. The place of marriage is very important as the *nulla osta* will be sent by the Department of Foreign Affairs

---

16 Similar procedures obtain in other foreign jurisdictions. Couples should always seek information from the Embassy or Consul of the country concerned. Some African and Caribbean countries now offer a "marriage package holiday" as part of their tourism strategy. **17** *Nulla osta* is the Italian form of *nihil obstat*; it is a declaration that nothing stands in the way of the valid celebration of the marriage.

via the Irish Embassy in Rome to the church where the marriage is to take place. The fee to be sent with the forms is IR£18. It is important to ensure that there are no differences between names and other details on Church and civil documents. If there is any difference – for example, in the forms of name – the persons concerned should get in touch with the Consular Section. A sworn affidavit may be required to explain differences to the satisfaction of the Italian authorities.

After the marriage has taken place the usual notifications will be sent to **664** the parish(es) of the bride and groom. A Church certificate will be issued after the ceremony. The marriage will be registered by the Italian state and the couple should arrange – for example, through the priest who officiated at the marriage – to get a civil certificate of marriage from the Italian authorities. This will be important as the Church certificate of marriage may not be acceptable in Ireland for certain purposes such as taking out a mortgage or selling a house. The Italian civil authorities will issue a civil marriage certificate after several months. When this has been obtained it should be kept in a safe place as it is expensive and difficult to replace. For this reason couples should have certified copies made by a notary public or a commissioner for oaths.[18]

Civil documents: British passport holders

A person resident in Ireland who holds a British passport and who wishes to **665** marry outside the British Isles must go to the District Registrar in his or her area and give notice of the proposed marriage. Each party is required to give notice in his or her own area. The notice will be forwarded to the General Register Office, Belfast. Twenty-one clear days after the notice was given a *Certificate of No Impediment* will be issued to the person through his or her local registrar. On arrival in Rome, this certificate should be brought to the British Embassy. The British Embassy will issue a *nulla osta* indicating that there is no civil obstacle to the celebration of the marriage. The Italian civil authorities will issue a civil marriage certificate after the marriage has taken place. On their return home couples may deposit the marriage certificate with the General Register Office, Belfast. In the event of the original certificate being lost, a copy can be issued by the General Register Office in Belfast.[19]

---

18 Irish passport holders who wish to marry abroad and who need further information should contact the Department of Foreign Affairs, St. Stephen's Green, Dublin. 19 British passport holders who wish to marry abroad should approach the General Register Office, Belfast if they need further information. The address is: Oxford House, 49-55 Chicester St., Belfast BT1 4HL (tel. 01232 252000; fax: 01232 252044).

APPENDIX 4: MIXED MARRIAGES IN IRELAND

Historical background

666   Even before the Reformation civil authorities in Ireland had a political interest in the area of marriage. The Dublin administration, out of concern for the security and the cultural identity of the colonial settlement, attempted to restrict intermarriage between members of that settlement and those hostile to it. An ordinance of 1351 forbade marriage between the colonists and any enemies of the king, whether Gaelic or Anglo-Irish. In 1366 the Statute of Kilkenny imposed a ban solely on ethnic grounds, prohibiting any "alliance by marriage ... concubinage, or by caif ('coibhche') between the Anglo-Irish and the Gaelic Irish".[20]

667   Early in the seventeenth century the Catholic Church in Ireland began the organisation of a diocesan and parish system. Synodal legislation accepted that in Irish conditions the *Tametsi* decree could not be introduced but it insisted that all catholic marriages take place before a catholic priest and at least two witnesses. Corish outlines the situation of "propertied catholics":

> Propertied catholics ... reached a working compromise with the authorities of the established church. Since the fourteenth century there had been a practice of parties to a marriage receiving a licence to be married without banns in return for the payment of a fee. The catholics of Ireland paid their fee for such a licence to the authorities of the established church, after which it was tacitly agreed that they were free to seek the religious service of their own church. That this practice continued after the restoration is clear from the correspondence of Archbishop John Brenan ...[21]

668   An act of Parliament in 1697 (9 Wm III, c. 3) laid down that if a protestant woman with an estate valued £500 or more married a person without having obtained a legal certificate that he was a protestant, the officiating minister, whether he were a popish priest, protestant minister or any other person, should be fined £20 and imprisoned for a year. Ten years later – in 1707 – an act to safeguard the marriages of propertied minors (6 Anne, c.16) laid down a special penalty for a popish priest celebrating such a marriage (he was to lose his benefit under the Registration Act of 1704); in 1709 (8 Anne, c.3) it was enacted that a popish priest indicted under the act of 1707 was to be deemed guilty unless he could prove his innocence by producing certificates from the ministers of the parties showing that they were not Protestants. Corish comments on this legislation:

---

20 Stat. Ire. John-Hen.V, 386-87, 432-33 (cf. A. Cosgrove, "Marriage in Medieval Ireland" in *Marriage in Ireland* (ed. A. Cosgrove), 49, footnote 30. **21** "Catholic marriage under the penal Code" in *Marriage in Ireland* (ed. A. Cosgrove), 69.

Legislation in 1709 ruled out any possibility that catholics might acquire land illegally. It did this by introducing the "Protestant discoverer" who, if he could prove in court that property had been illegally acquired, received that property as his reward. This provision made the laws against catholic acquisition of property self-enforcing.[22]

An act of 1725 laid down that if "a popish priest, degraded clergyman, or layman pretending to be a clergyman" officiated at a marriage where one or both of the parties was protestant, he was to be guilty of felony, and in consequence liable to the death-penalty.[23]   **669**

In 1745 (19 Geo. II, c. 13) it was enacted that a marriage between two parties one or both of whom was protestant, if celebrated by a popish clergyman, was to be absolutely null and void "without any process, judgement or sentence of law whatever".[24] Although these penal laws might appear to be motivated by bigotry, a study of the relevant texts shows "that the motive was the safeguarding of property".[25] The strict enforcement of these laws coincided with periods of political and civil unrest, as during the Jacobite scares, but by the 1730s the worst of the restrictiveness was over.   **670**

The penalty of death for treason, hanging over a priest who celebrated a mixed marriage, was removed in 1833 (3&4 Wm IV, c. 103), by "an act to repeal certain penal enactments made in the parliament of Ireland against Roman Catholic clergymen for celebrating marriages contrary to certain acts made in the parliament of Ireland". This act was confined to the abolition of penalties; mixed marriages celebrated by a catholic priest were still void in civil law. This provision was repealed in 1870 (33&34 Vict., c. 110).[26]   **671**

The *Tametsi* decree was not promulgated in some parts of Ireland, including Dublin. Following the 1745 act, the clergy of the archdiocese of Dublin were strongly opposed to its promulgation as implementing it would put them in a perilous position. In the 1780s Archbishop Troy of Dublin supported them; later they were supported by the Bishops of the Province of Munster. In 1785 the Holy Office extended to Ireland a concession granted to the Netherlands, that "mixed marriages not celebrated in the presence of a catholic priest were to be regarded as valid".[27]   **672**

By 1827 *Tametsi* had been promulgated in all the dioceses of Ireland.[28] However even after that "the principle acted on was that mixed marriages were exempt from the *Tametsi* decree".[29] When the legality of this development was questioned towards the end of the nineteenth century, the Archbishop of Dublin obtained a declaration from the Pope (in 1887) that mixed   **673**

22 Corish, *The catholic community in the seventeenth and eighteenth centuries* (Helicon History of Ireland), Dublin, 1981, 74. **23** Ibid., 71-2. Corish adds that "a few priests would appear to have been put to death under this act".   **24** Ibid., 72.   **25** Ibid., 71. **26** Ibid., 75. **27** Ibid., 72. This remained the position until *Ne temere*. **28** T. P. Cunningham, "Mixed marriages in Ireland before *Ne temere* decree" in *Irish Ecclesiastical Record* 101 (1964), 54. **29** Ibid., 54-5.

marriages in Ireland were valid irrespective of whether or not the *Tametsi* decree had been published there".[30] Thus a mixed marriage contracted before a non-catholic minister, or before a civil registrar, or without any witness, official or otherwise, was canonically valid.[31]

674 There is abundant evidence in Irish provincial and diocesan statutes and in letters and statements of Irish Bishops that mixed marriages were discouraged or forbidden before and during the nineteenth century; they were allowed only if certain conditions respecting the Catholic faith of the Catholic partner and of the children were fulfilled.[32] Cunningham observes that "a principle is one thing and usage another, and that, particularly before the repeal of the statute of George II in 1871, it was not always feasible to insist on the carrying out of the conditions under which the Church allowed mixed marriages. There was, for example, a custom that the male children would follow the religion of the father and the female children would follow the religion of the mother.[33]

675 Prior to the Synod of Thurles (1850) a dispensation or permission for a mixed marriage could be obtained in Ireland from the Bishop or vicar General without reference to the Holy See; after the Synod of Thurles dispensations were granted only "by apostolic authority".[34]

676 The *Ne temere* decree came into effect at Easter 1908.[35] Its provisions were subsequently incorporated into the Code of Canon Law (1917).

Contemporary context

677 *N. Ireland* The particular circumstances of Irish history outlined above and their effects in the political, social and religious composition of Irish society give the issue of mixed marriages a special sensitivity. This is illustrated by the impact which the promulgation of the *Ne temere* decree had in Ireland generally and particularly in N. Ireland. Dunlop writes:

> The *Ne temere* decree ... which required that written undertakings be given that the children of mixed marriages be raised as Catholics, was the final push that tipped the waverers [in the Protestant community] over to the Unionist side. That decree persuaded them that Catholic ecclesiastical imperialism would predominate in a Home Rule Ireland.[36]

678 *Ne temere* had a profound influence on Protestant thinking in Ireland. The sensitivity of mixed marriages was highlighted in the report of a working party that was submitted to the Irish Inter-Church Meeting in 1993. The report *Sectarianism: a discussion document* defined sectarianism as "a com-

---

30 Cf. *Acta et Decreta Synodi Provincialis Dublinensis*, 1908, 197. **31** Cunningham, 55. **32** Ibid. **33** Ibid., 56, footnote 2. **34** Ibid., 56. **35** *ASS* 40 (1907), 525-30. **36** *A precarious belonging: Presbyterians and the conflict in Ireland*, Blackstaff Press, Belfast, 1995, 49-50.

plex of attitudes, beliefs, behaviours and structures in which religion is a significant component, and which (i) directly, or indirectly, infringes the rights of individuals or groups, and/or (ii) influences or causes situations of destructive conflict".[37] It maintains that although religious differences in themselves need not lead to conflict, "acts and attitudes with no sectarian intent can have sectarian consequences, and we are responsible for these unintended consequences as well as for our intentions".[38] Those responsible for the pastoral care of couples in mixed marriages – helping them to prepare for marriage, celebrating their marriages, and supporting them in living out their relationships – have a particular responsibility to act with sensitivity for the feelings of the persons involved, their families and the communities from which they come. In a survey of couples in mixed marriages, it was reported that at the time of preparation for the marriage, "many people were made to feel embarrassed by their Church".[39]

This report stated that "it is in the area of mixed marriage that the unresolved differences between the Churches are most acutely and personally felt".[40] These problems were described:

679

> For some the problem had settled into an uneasy peace where encounters with the wider family were superficially cordial but there was often a leitmotif of reluctant or unhappy acceptance. For others failure to truly accept the fact of intermarriage had eventually caused family relationships, with parents, brothers, sisters, etc. to become estranged and distant. Few couples felt they were absolutely accepted by both families, though in some cases one side was perceived to be more accepting than the other. Problems had also arisen as children raised in inter-church marriages reached the age of making decisions for themselves and chose one side or the other, or neither. Many of the children and the partners seemed to be conscious of an ongoing, albeit muted, battle for their hearts and minds directed from the wider family circle and not within the immediate family itself. The 'battle' took many forms, from direct challenge, to backbiting, to proselytising, to praying for conversion, to the simple feeling of being not quite acceptable. For some families the inter-church marriage was seen as a betrayal of the struggle of their forefathers to hold their place in the scheme of things. It was not enough to see their offspring in happy relationships. It was important that those relationships furthered a cause, or protected a species or an identity. It was evident that many inter-church partners carry a burden of guilt and loneliness, or have it imposed on them.[41]

---

37 *Sectarianism* (the report of the working party on sectarianism), published by the Department of Social Issues of the Irish Inter-Church Meeting, Inter-Church Centre, 48 Elmwood Avenue, Belfast, 1993, p. 8. **38** Ibid., 9. **39** *Irish Times*, 19 May 1992. **40** *Sectarianism*, 103. **41** Ibid., 72.

680   The report recommended a number of courses of action to the Churches:

> Understand the fears of the other tradition and seek to act in such a way as to remove, or at least mitigate, those fears. Even though we may feel these fears to be unreal or exaggerated, they are part of the problem for everyone and will continue to be part of the problem until they are acknowledged and allayed. For instance, there is a significant fear of the Roman Catholic Church. How is this to be dealt with by Roman Catholics?...
>
> Seek as far as possible to remove, or at least mitigate, some of the adverse social consequences of theological or doctrinal differences (e.g. over mixed marriages or attitudes to the Roman Catholic Church).[42]

681   In a divided society the issue of mixed marriages is particularly sensitive. It is all the more important that clergy handle these marriages with special care. They should show respect for the couple and their decision to marry and also keep in mind the implications of their actions on wider inter-church relations and indeed peace within society. They should remember that for many members of other Churches, this will be their first contact with a priest and with the liturgy and procedures of the catholic Church.

682   *Republic of Ireland*   The Catholic Church's regulations on mixed marriages have caused much bitterness over the years in the Protestant community in the Republic of Ireland and many have regarded them as one of the reasons for its reduction in size. J.H. Whyte wrote:

> Many Protestants would argue that in the particular circumstances of [the Republic of] Ireland, where Protestants are a small and scattered minority, it is not so easy for them to find marriage partners of their own faith and that the regulation [*Ne Temere* and subsequent legislation] therefore acts as an instrument for the erosion of the Protestant community.[43]

683   A paper submitted to the Forum for Peace and Reconciliation (1995-6) claimed that the situation was as follows: in 1981 86% of children in mixed marriages were catholics; in 1991 78% were catholic; in 1991 nearly one quarter of all persons from the minority religious communities were in mixed marriages. The authors conclude: "Mixed marriages are therefore very relevant to the numerical loss in so far as the minority religious communities are concerned as the children of these marriages are disproportionately brought

---

42 Ibid., 100-1. **43** *Church & State in modern Ireland 1923-1979*, Gill & Macmillan, Dublin, second ed. 1981, 170.

up as Catholics. These losses assume even greater significance if cumulative or generational effects are taken into account".[44]

At the New Ireland Forum (1984) the delegation representing the catholic Church was asked whether, for the sake of community reconciliation, the general law of the Church could not be tailored to Irish conditions in a way that "would leave Protestant partners in mixed marriages feeling in a condition of absolute equality with the Catholic partners so far as making decisions about children's upbringing is concerned".[45] Archbishop Cassidy replied that the Irish Bishops' Conference had considered petitioning the Holy See for a derogation from the requirement in *Matrimonia mixta* that the catholic party make a promise prior to entering a mixed marriage. He continued: "There is no question of violating the conscience of another person. We ask them [catholics] to give a personal promise to do their best. A decision comes later within the unity and the context of the marriage. That is a joint decision by the couple. They, the parents, decide with due regard for each other's rights and conscientious convictions".[46]

684

APPENDIX 5: MARRIAGE TRIBUNALS IN IRELAND

By a decree dated 24 March 1975, the Irish Bishops' Conference decided to establish four Regional Marriage Tribunals of first instance to be located at Armagh, Dublin, Cork and Galway. This decree was formally approved by the Supreme Tribunal of the Apostolic Signatura on 6 May 1975. In accordance with the terms of the Roman rescript, the Bishops' Conference, in a decision of 30 September 1975, determined that the Regional Tribunals would come into effect on 1 January 1976. From that date they alone have jurisdiction for marriage nullity cases. In the same decree, the Bishops' Conference sct up a sole Appeal Tribunal, located in Dublin, to hear second instance cases from the four Regional Tribunals. It also came into effect on 1 January 1976. Its personnel and administration are wholly distinct from all the regional tribunals. Each tribunal is subject to the diocesan Bishop in whose diocese the Regional Tribunal office lies.

685

Although the tribunals follow the same general lines of procedure as outlined in the Code of Canon Law, they have developed their own detailed procedures to deal with annulment applications. These procedures are the result of practical, pastoral considerations; they have also been influenced

686

---

44 J. J. Sexton and R. O' Leary, "Factors affecting population decline in minority religious communities in the Republic of Ireland" in *Building trust in Ireland*, Blackstaff Press, Belfast, 1996, 293. 45 *New Ireland Forum: public session*, Thursday, 9 February 1984, Dublin Castle; *Report of proceedings: Irish Episcopal Conference Delegation* (hereafter *New Ireland Forum*), published by the Stationery Office, Molesworth St., Dublin, 48. 46 *New Ireland Forum*, 49.

by the unique geography of each region. The Armagh tribunal has also been influenced in its development by the civil unrest which has continued throughout N.Ireland since it was set up.

Armagh Regional Marriage Tribunal

687 In 1976 the Armagh Regional Marriage Tribunal was set up and acquired premises in Armagh.[47] On 1 January 1986, with the agreement of the Bishops of the region, offices were set up in each diocese. Applications for annulment are made to each diocesan office. In each diocese, except Down and Connor, the applicant presents a written account of his or her marriage under three headings: courtship, marriage and breakdown. If necessary, further details may be sought using a supplementary questionnaire. In the event of an application being rejected, the applicant will first be interviewed by an Instructor-judge in the diocesan office. In Down and Connor applications are received via a local priest who interviews the applicant using a detailed questionnaire. The Armagh Regional Tribunal does not reject applications without a judgement; a petition is rejected only by a collegial decision of the Tribunal and the parties are advised of their right to appeal.

688 Cases are instructed in the diocesan office where the application was received. Much of the interviewing of witnesses is now carried out by lay auditors.

689 At the discussion stage, each case is sent to the central office of the Tribunal and is submitted to an advocate and a defender of the bond drawn from the region. A number of lay people now act as advocates.

Dublin Regional Marriage Tribunal

690 The Dublin Regional Marriage Tribunal has its office in Dublin.[48] Its procedure is as follows: when a nullity application is made, a Fact Form is sent to the petitioner; on receipt of this Fact Form, an initial interview takes place in the diocese where the person lives. One party or both may be psychologically assessed, depending on the nature of the case. This assessment may be done before the acceptance of a case or afterwards.

691 On acceptance of a case, it is assigned to a Judge-instructor whose task it is to oversee the instruction of the case. He generally re-interviews the parties, draws up questions for the witnesses and decides on any other steps that are to be taken. Witnesses are interviewed in the diocese where they live.

---

47 15 College St., Armagh BT61 9BT. The Armagh Regional Marriage Tribunal is competent for the dioceses of Armagh, Clogher, Derry, Down and Connor, Dromore, Kilmore and Raphoe. **48** Diocesan Offices, Archbishop's House, Dublin 9. The Dublin Regional Marriage Tribunal is competent for the dioceses of Dublin, Ferns, Ossory, Meath, and Kildare and Leighlin.

When the evidence is assembled the instruction of the case is assessed to ensure that all the proper steps have been taken. After the pleadings of the advocate and the comments of the Defender of the Bond have been completed, the case is assigned to three judges who return the first instance decision.

Cases coming from the other dioceses of the region – Meath, Ossory, Ferns, Kildare and Leighlin – are given a certain preferential priority. This is done because otherwise their progress would be delayed by the large number of cases originating in the archdiocese of Dublin. Each of the smaller dioceses has its own office and a priest-representative, along with a number of lay auditors who help with the interviewing of witnesses. While the procedure in each diocese is not identical, as much work as possible is carried out at local level; however major decisions – acceptance or rejection of petition, first instance decisions – are made at the tribunal offices. **692**

Cork Regional Marriage Tribunal

The Cork Regional Marriage Tribunal has its office in Cork.[49] Applications come in the form of a letter from the person who is seeking the annulment of the marriage, often on the recommendation of parish clergy. On receipt of the initial letter, the applicant is asked to fill out a Fact Sheet/Particulars Form and witness nomination forms. In about 10% of cases the petitioner is directed to one of the tribunal advocates who will assist in the preparation and presentation of the case. In all cases, when the tribunal is satisfied that it enjoys competence in the case, the petitioner is invited for interview. **693**

Galway Regional Marriage Tribunal

The Galway Regional Marriage Tribunal has its office in Galway.[50] Most people who seek an annulment are referred to the Tribunal by their local clergy, others by a friend, and others apply directly to the Tribunal. When an application is received, a Fact Sheet is sent to the Petitioner. The facts contained in this Form normally enable the question of competence to be determined. On receipt of the completed Fact Sheet, an appointment for an initial interview is arranged. Most initial interviews take place in the Tribunal Office. Sometimes, due to long distances and scarce financial resources, they are conducted nearer to the residence of the petitioner. Normally it possible **694**

---

49 Tribunal Offices, The Lough, Cork. The Cork Regional Marriage Tribunal is competent for the dioceses of Cashel, Cork and Ross, Cloyne, Kerry, Limerick and Waterford.
50 7 Waterside, Woodquay, Galway. The Galway Regional Marriage Tribunal is competent for the dioceses of Tuam, Galway, Achonry, Killala, Killaloe, Clonfert, Elphin, Ardagh and Clonmacnoise.

to make a *prima facie* judgement as to whether some grounds of nullity may be present. If that is not possible, the full sworn evidence of the petitioner, the respondent and perhaps a key witness is obtained. Occasionally, in order to determine whether a *prima facie* case exists, a psychological assessment of the parties is sought. When a decision is made that a *prima facie* case exists, the *contestatio litis* is decided. At this stage, the case is handed over to a Judge-instructor who begins collecting evidence in the case. When all the necessary and available evidence is obtained, a copy of the Book of Evidence is given to an advocate who pleads the case for nullity. When the advocate's pleadings are prepared, the Book of Evidence and the advocate's pleadings are sent to the defender of the bond. When the submission of the latter is completed, the case is sent to three judges and a date is set for a hearing.

National Marriage Appeal Tribunal of Ireland

695   The National Marriage Appeal Tribunal (NATI) is the only Tribunal of second instance in Ireland. Its office is in Dublin.[51] The personnel of the Appeal Tribunal consists of two full-time officials, the Judicial Vicar and the Administrator, and a number of part-time judges. The tribunal is accountable to the Irish Bishops' Conference. Responsibility for the tribunal is exercised by the Archbishop of Dublin.

696   Sessions of the tribunal take place both in Dublin and throughout Ireland, depending on the location of the judges. In advance of each session, the judges are given copies of the Acts, the sentence of the First Instance tribunal and any further documentation or information that is available.

697   On occasion the Appeal Tribunal will disagree with the decision of a First Instance tribunal. In this case it must cite the parties, explaining to them the composition of the Court, the grounds on which the case is being heard. The parties are asked if they wish to submit further evidence. They may also be asked to clarify certain points on which the decision to be given depends.

698   If a case submitted to the appeal tribunal received a negative decision at First Instance, the appeal tribunal is required to admit the case to ordinary examination at Second Instance. This second examination is an important protection for parties who feel aggrieved by the First Instance decision. It ensures that the case has the benefit of an independent assessment.

699   When the decisions at First Instance and at appeal are both in favour of the annulment of a marriage, a decree of nullity is issued. Those whose marriage has been declared invalid may contract a new marriage as soon as the second judgement has been notified to them unless there is a prohibition (*vetitum*) attached to the judgement or decree itself, or imposed by the local Ordinary (Can. 1684 §1).

---

51 The Diocesan Offices, Archbishop's House, Dublin 9.

Length of time

The length of time taken on cases is determined in practice by the volume of **700**
cases pending before each tribunal. On average cases are heard at First Instance within four years. The time taken at appeal also depends on circumstances. Some cases are clear from the start; others are more complicated.
Some are readily ratified; when cases are admitted to the ordinary examination at Second Instance the time taken is inevitably longer. The time taken
varies from six to twelve months.

Costs

The expenses involved in nullity cases are determined by the Bishops' Con- **701**
ference. At the present time the amount established by the Irish Bishops'
Conference is £500IR. Petitioners contribute in accordance with their means.

APPENDIX 6: A STUDY AND AN EVALUATION OF PRE-MARRIAGE COURSES (RAPHOE)[52]

Pre-marriage courses

While it would appear that the general title for each session need not be **702**
radically altered, it is very clear that the manner and method of presentation
and the emphasis placed on aspects and details of content do not impact on
the participants. It is also clear that if the couples were accepted as equal
partners in the educational process and thereby were allowed and encouraged to participate in the selection of topics, manner of presentation and
orientation/style of the session, the couples' needs and aspirations could be
more appropriately met.

In particular, the data suggests that more attention should be given to **703**
aspects of relationship that promote growth and positive development. At
the same time, there is a counterbalancing need to deal with crisis manage-
ment and crisis coping skills with special reference to unemployment, death,
alcoholism, gambling, emigration, abuses, illnesses and the effects that derive from contradictory attitudes to these and other aspects of living that
impinge on the marriage bond. It is felt that the terms of reference be confined to the first five years of marriage rather than try to deal with a full
married life in a comprehensive way.

It is also recommended that the marriage preparation course be identified **704**
and accepted for what it is, namely, an adult education experience through a
programme that must be planned and prepared in accordance with well-es-
tablished adult education principles and methodologies. Consequently, it must

52 The report from which this extract is taken was prepared by the Adult and Community
Education Centre, St Patrick's College, Maynooth (Director: Rev Liam Carey) in 1993.

be learner (couple) centred in all its aspects. It is important to integrate into the course and its presentation, and indeed its publicity system that:

- adults can learn;
- adults have resources and experiences on which they can draw and, indeed, want to bring into learning situations;
- adults want to and can own their own learning, especially when that learning is self-directed and relevant to their needs, interests and concerns;
- not all adults in groups learn in the same way or at the same pace nor are they at the same level of readiness to participate in some of the learning processes;
- some adults have had very negative experience of school/learning which tends to demotivate rather than promote and support participative learning;
- adults have a personal style of learning, and knowing how one learns and providing a variety of approaches to learning are more likely to facilitate adult learning.

705 It is also clear, and backed up by empirical research, that the most efficient forum for adult learners is the small group which tends to be self-directed and seeks personal transformation...

706 The future of the marriage preparation course lies in the development of small learning groups of adult couples. These groups should have access to specially trained adult education facilitators whose background in Christian values, spirituality and principles enrich their interpretation of any content. These facilitators may be supported by the presence of, or in consultation with, experts in relevant areas when the specific needs of the couples emerge and also when the couples themselves feel the need for expertise and support.

APPENDIX 7: DOCUMENTS ISSUED BY THE IRISH BISHOPS' CONFERENCE

707 Pastoral letter *Handing on the faith in the home* (1980)
Directory on mixed marriages (1983)
Pastoral letter *Love is for life* (1985)
Pre-nuptial enquiry: pastoral guidelines (1991)

708 Two further significant documents have been issued in the area of catholic education: *Life to the Full* was issued in 1996 by the Council for Catholic Maintained Schools (N Ireland) with the approval of the Bishops of the region. *Developing a policy for RSE (Relationships and Sex Education) in Catholic Schools* was issued in 1997 by the Catholic Primary Schools Managers Association (Republic of Ireland) with the approval of the Bishops.

Index

References are to paragraph numbers, not page numbers

references are to paragraph nos.

references are to paragraph nos.

references are to paragraph nos.

references are to paragraph nos.

references are to paragraph nos.

references are to paragraph nos.